Advances in Contemporary Educatic

Jonas F. Soltis, Editor

The Cultural Dimensions of Educational Computing:
Understanding the Non-Neutrality of Technology
C. A. Bowers

Power and Criticism:
Poststructural Investigations in Education
Cleo H. Cherryholmes

The Civic Imperative:
Examining the Need for Civic Education
Richard Pratte

Responsive Teaching:
An Ecological Approach to Classroom Patterns
of Language, Culture, and Thought
C. A. Bowers and David J. Flinders

A Critical Theory of Education:
Habermas and Our Children's Future
R. E. Young

Education as a Human Right:
A Theory of Curriculum and Pedagogy
Donald Vandenberg

Education and the Good Life:
Autonomy, Altruism, and the National Curriculum
John White

The Challenge to Care in Schools:
An Alternative Approach to Education
Nel Noddings

A Post-Modern Perspective on Curriculum
William E. Doll, Jr.

Dialogue in Teaching: Theory and Practice
Nicholas C. Burbules

DIALOGUE
IN
TEACHING

Theory and Practice

NICHOLAS C. BURBULES

Teachers College, Columbia University
New York and London

Published by Teachers College Press, 1234 Amsterdam Avenue
New York, New York

Library of Congress Cataloging-in-Publication Data

Burbules, Nicholas C.
    Dialogue in teaching : theory and practice / Nicholas C. Burbules.
        p.   cm. — (Advances in contemporary educational thought ; 10)
    Includes bibliographical references (p.   ) and index.
    ISBN 0-8077-3242-7 (alk. paper). — ISBN 0-8077-3241-9 (pbk. :
alk. paper)
    1. Questioning. 2. Teaching. 3. Interpersonal communication.
I. Title. II. Series: Advances in contemporary educational thought
series ; v. 10.
LB1027.44.B87   1993
371.1′02—dc20   92-44879

Printed on acid-free paper
Manufactured in the United States of America
99 98 97 96 95 94 93 7 6 5 4 3 2 1

Contents

Foreword

There is something fundamental and perennial about the idea of teaching as dialogue in the history of education. Socrates and the slave boy, Mark Hopkins and his student at the other end of a log, Freire and the oppressed peasants of Brazil—these and other such examples highlight a historically persistent ideal of teaching as a special dialogical engagement of minds.

In this book, Nicholas Burbules takes us through a sophisticated and sensitive exploration of various forms that dialogue can take and the pedagogical moves that players of the dialogue game can make. This is not a book of recipes and techniques, however, nor is it a treatment of dialogue as a mere pedagogical game. It is a serious and philosophically astute recognition of the complexity, spontaneity, and pragmatically context-dependent dimensions of dialogue as a form of human pedagogical communication.

Burbules treats dialogue as a symbiotic, communicative relationship between equals that requires emotional as well as cognitive involvement. Genuine dialogue, if it is to have a chance at success, rides on the participants' mutual feelings of concern, trust, respect, appreciation, affection and hope as well as on cognitive understanding. As a human practice with a long tradition, it also embodies and requires a set of virtues that include tolerance, patience, openness, restraint, and the willingness to listen, thereby empowering the other to speak.

The theoretical perspectives of Bakhtin, Freire, Gadamer, Habermas, Vygotsky, and Wittgenstein are masterfully drawn upon to illuminate the multiple dimensions of the dialogical process in a way quite accessible to non-philosophers, but it is Dewey's concept of democracy as the free exchange of ideas across diversity that underwrites Burbules' claim that dialogue is essential to the spirit of a genuinely pluralistic democratic society. Unfortunately, our present educational system, Burbules notes, could not have been better designed to be antidialogical if we had consciously set out with that purpose in mind. Our pedagogical and social ideals are clearly at

odds with reality. Thus, while Burbules deftly enhances our understanding of dialogue, he leaves us with challenges and questions
rather than prescriptions and easy answers.

To sing the praises of pedagogy as dialogue without recognizing
the forces that thwart it in today's schools and society would be to
act irresponsibly. To engage the minds of others in a responsible dialogue about dialogue as it might be encouraged and practiced in a
hostile environment is the main purpose of this first-rate philosophical work. It succeeds admirably and indeed provides the groundwork
for an advance in contemporary educational thought and practice.

Jonas F. Soltis
Series Editor

Introduction

Precisely this is what characterizes a dialogue, in contrast with the rigid form of the statement that demands to be set down in writing: that here language, in the process of question and answer, giving and taking, talking at cross purposes and seeing each other's point, performs that communication of meaning which . . . is the task of hermeneutics. . . . Thus it is characteristic of every true conversation that each opens himself to the other person, truly accepts his point of view as worthy of consideration and gets inside the other.

Hans-Georg Gadamer, Truth and Method

We use the Socratic method here. I call on you, ask you a question, and you answer it. Why don't I just give you a lecture? Because through my questions, you'll learn to teach yourselves. Through this method of questioning, answering, questioning, answering, we seek to develop in you the ability to analyze that vast complex of facts that constitute the relationships of members within a given society. Questioning and answering. At times, you may feel that you have found the correct answer. You will never find the correct, absolute, and final answer. In my classroom, there is always another question, another question to follow your answer.

Professor Charles W. Kingsfield, Jr., in The Paper Chase

In this process, arguments based on "authority" are no longer valid; in order to function, authority must be on the side of freedom, not against it. Here no one teaches another, nor is anyone self-taught. Men [sic] teach each other, mediated by the world. . . . At the point of encounter there are neither utter ignoramuses nor perfect sages; there are simply men [sic] who are attempting, together, to learn more than they now know.

Paulo Freire, Pedagogy of the Oppressed

*What kind of man am I? One of those who would gladly be refuted
if anything I say is not true, and would gladly refute another who
says what is not true, but would be no less happy to be refuted myself than to refute, for I consider that a greater benefit, inasmuch
as it is a greater boon to be delivered from the worst of evils oneself
than to deliver another. And I believe there is no worse evil than a
false opinion. . . . If you have any interest in what has been said
and wish to set it right, then . . . retract whatever you please,
question and answer in turn, . . . and refute me and be refuted.*

Plato, Gorgias

This book is an examination of dialogue and the many forms it takes
in teaching. Although it is possible to consider any sort of conversation as a dialogue, here I want to limit the term to refer to a particular
kind of pedagogical communicative relation: a conversational interaction directed intentionally toward teaching and learning. Not all of
our conversations are pedagogically directed; conversely, not all pedagogical communicative relations are forms of conversation (there are
lectures, for example). While many hybrid and borderline forms of
communication span these sharp distinctions, I will argue in this
book that there is a more or less discrete set of engagements that we
can usefully think of as "dialogical"; that within this set there are
distinct genres or approaches to dialogue, suitable to different teaching styles, different students, and different subject matters; and that
there are typical moves that characterize effective dialogical teaching,
which we can identify, study, and improve through practice. This
book, therefore, is not just an extended philosophical analysis of a
particular conception of teaching; it is also, I hope, a useful guide for
learning to teach in this manner. Exhorting teachers to engage in
various liberatory practices, as many progressive educational theorists do, without also providing a realistic means to acquire, reflect
on, and improve those practices has often had the effect of discouraging teachers more than inspiring them.

The examples quoted at the beginning of this Introduction represent four quite different views of dialogue. They illustrate one of
the central themes of this book: that while many have characterized
dialogue in terms of something called the "Socratic method," the
Socratic method can refer to several quite different things, and is
therefore not truly a "method" at all but a repertoire of dialogical
approaches that the skillful teacher knows how to select and adapt to

varied pedagogical circumstances. All four of the teachers quoted (Gadamer, Kingsfield, Freire, and Plato) credit Socrates as the common source of their approaches, different as they are. Admittedly, Socrates himself often spoke as if all dialogue was based on a singular intellectual process, the dialectic.

> Is not dialectic the only process of inquiry that advances in this manner, doing away with hypotheses, up to the first principle itself in order to find confirmation there? And it is literally true that when the eye of the soul is sunk in the barbaric slough . . . dialectic gently draws it forth and leads it up. (Plato, 1961c, p. 765)

However, writers such as Gadamer (1980) and Sophie Haroutunian-Gordon (1987, 1988, 1990) have demonstrated that in the many Socratic dialogues we actually see a broad range of dialogical styles—and that Socrates's true genius as a teacher was in his eclecticism and willingness to break even his own rules (Burbules, 1991b). As David Hansen (1988) has put it, Socrates himself was not always a "Socratic" teacher!

An approach to teaching that requires such flexibility, adaptability, and judgment is difficult to label a "method." Dialogue is, I will argue, more an expression of *praxis* than of *techne* (Hostetler, 1991). Engaging in dialogue successfully is something we need to learn to do, through practice, not by following any sort of recipe or algorithm. This book will be organized around the metaphor of *playing a game*, in order to illuminate the creative, spontaneous, and enjoyable aspects of dialogue at its best—an emphasis intended to offset current tendencies to consider teaching as a technique. Of course, there is a technical aspect even to many games; I will claim that, as in any game, there are some general rules and moves that broadly enable us to distinguish skillful from less skillful playing. By knowing these and practicing them we can improve at teaching and learning through dialogue. Hence, if I am successful I will be explaining both the spontaneity *and* the structure of dialogical practice.

My account here is strongly indebted to the ideas of Paulo Freire, and to a related body of work in critical pedagogy that has elevated dialogue to a central place in our approach to teaching. Yet if there is one abiding shortcoming in the literature inspired by Freire, it is its frequently rhetorical and abstract level of generalization about what dialogue is and what it is good for. One reads these writings with a growing sense of inspiration and moral purpose, but only the broadest sort of idea about how to teach in this manner (a notable exception is the work of Ira Shor, 1980, 1987). The understandable desire to avoid technicism has often meant a lack of analytical clarity and specificity, as well as an almost total disregard for a substantial body of empirical literature in linguistics and psychology on our actual patterns of conversational interaction. In this book I hope to remedy this imbalance without compromising the fundamental values of social equality and personal freedom that motivate our interest in dialogue in the first place.

The sequence of my argument and division of topics by chapter are as follows. First, I will examine further the definition of dialogue as a kind of *pedagogical communicative relation* (Chapter 1). One of the mistakes often made in understanding dialogue is thinking that it is essentially like any other kind of conversation and that, since we all know how to have conversations, we must already know the basics of dialogue. People often use "dialogue" synonymously with "discussion," "chat," and related terms. But good, effective dialogue is much more difficult than ordinary conversation, although obviously it has some elements in common with conversation.

Next, I will focus on one aspect of this definition, that dialogue is best thought of as a type of communicative *relation* (Chapter 2). Lately, it has become fashionable to use dialogue as a verb, as in "Let's dialogue about this some time." This cheapens the term in two ways: First, as noted above, it makes it merely a pretentious word for "talk"; but more than this, it conceptually distorts the nature of dialogue, in my view. Dialogue is not something we *do* or *use;* it is a relation that we *enter into*—we can be caught up in it and sometimes carried away by it. Considering dialogue as a kind of relation (with one or more other people) emphasizes the aspects of dialogue that are beyond us, that we discover, that we are changed by. Thinking of dialogue as a verb, on the other hand, reinforces a one-dimensional and instrumental view of it, one wholly inappropriate to the complexities and subtleties of pedagogy. The creation and maintenance of a dialogical relation with others involve forming emotional bonds, such as respect, trust, and concern; as well as the expression of character traits or virtues, such as patience, the ability to listen, a tolerance for disagreement, and so on. Such factors are rarely addressed in the literature on dialogue.

Next, I will extend this relational analysis by exploring various aspects of the metaphor of dialogue as a *game* (Chapter 3). Games are things that we play. They are engaging. They are fun. They involve appropriate rules and moves. Certain games are oriented toward "winning" in some sense; others are pursued for more intrinsic rea-

sons of pleasure and companionship. Some games are more competitive than others; sometimes a game can become too competitive to be
fun. Most games are played with others; some games we can play
ourselves, but always against some type of resistance (an imaginary
opponent, a physical barrier, the laws of chance, and so forth). There
are other things that we play, too, such as music. Gadamer (1982)
attributes the essence of playing in all of its forms to a "to and fro"
movement—a deep insight, I believe, full of implications for the "dialogue game."

The purpose of this game metaphor, as I will develop it here,
is to emphasize the *process*, rather than the *outcome*, of a dialogical
encounter. While we certainly have intentions and goals when entering into a dialogue, one of the reasons for engaging in dialogue rather
than more direct modes of assertion or questioning is precisely because we are willing to be carried away from, or beyond, our initial
purposes. A game can be engrossing; it can take on a life of its own,
beyond our control—and the same can be said for dialogue. Many
have noted that Socrates himself never wrote; we know his dialogues
only through the writings of Plato and others. What this suggests is
that there is something about a living dialogue (at least in Socrates's
view) that is never finished, that can never be recorded or repeated
without losing something of its initial vitality. Dialogue is continually
created in the act of engaging in it, and every time we create it, it is
different. In this, also, it is like a game.

The following two chapters (Chapters 4 and 5) examine in detail
what the *rules* and *moves* of this dialogue game might be. "Rules"
may be a bit too rigid—perhaps "standards" is better: constitutive
principles that help define and govern an activity, without which it
would not be that activity, but something else. Because not everything communicative counts as dialogue (for example, booing a politi-
cian passing in a motorcade), there must be some criteria, albeit fairly
broad and flexible ones, that help us in identifying generally when
something is dialogue, and when it is not. People implicitly agree to
play by these in order for the game to go forward at all.

"Moves," on the other hand, are not constitutive of an activity.
They are particular actions, choices, or gestures within it that have
no rule behind them, yet are prototypical in that repeated experience
has shown them to be useful within the rules. Moves are practical
artifacts of convention and tradition. For example, you can shoot a
free throw in basketball underhanded, backward over your head, or
with your eyes closed—the rules don't regulate this—but it turns out
that most players shoot free throws more or less the same way.

Moves, too, are an expression of the relational character of games: Skillful players have experience at recognizing, and developing, patterns of interaction that help yield successful results. The same is true in dialogue. Here I will draw from some perceptive empirical work that helps identify some of these effective dialogical approaches. Skillful players are also adept at exercising judgment, of knowing when and how to draw from a repertoire of moves to fit novel situations, and in recognizing when an unexpected circumstance arises in which formalized responses are not useful and something more original and creative is called for.

These two chapters suggest some rules and moves that characterize the dialogue game; and the point of trying to make them explicit is to enable us to reflect on them, practice them, and improve in using them.

Carrying this metaphor one step further, repeated playings of games often reveal certain patterns of practice that result in particular genres or styles of game (Chapter 6). I will argue that there are at least four distinct types of dialogue (corresponding to the four examples cited at the beginning of this Introduction), each of which can be characterized in terms of certain prototypical patterns of moves—for example, the use of certain kinds of questions. These four genres may not be exhaustive of all types of dialogue, but I believe they comprise most of the major examples. Nor are they entirely distinct from one another. There are numerous hybrid versions, and a dialogue that begins in one style might change into a quite different style—indeed, it may change into something else besides dialogue. These four types are what I will call *dialogue as conversation* (in a specific and narrow sense), *dialogue as inquiry*, *dialogue as debate*, and *dialogue as instruction*. These differ from one another in a number of ways, including their assumptions about knowledge, their degree of tolerance for alternative points of view, their degree of cooperativeness or competitiveness, and the kind and degree of authority they generate. Yet each in its own way can be useful for teaching and learning.

Between the final two chapters is an Interlude, a sample dialogue co-authored with my friend and colleague, Ladd Holt. In this imaginary discussion, a university professor and public school teacher discuss their respective views of teaching, conversation, and collegial relations. Beginning with some conflicts and misunderstandings, they work together through the various kinds of dialogical interactions toward some conclusions about themselves, their relation to one another, and the nature of dialogue itself. If this exercise is successful, it will entertain as well as inform, illustrating in the process the four types of dialogue, how they can succeed, and why they sometimes fail. It is not meant in any way as an "ideal" dialogue, and as readers will discover there are many missteps made by the two participants as they struggle to come to some mutual understandings about the issues at hand.

Finally, having laid out an extended account of what dialogical teaching *can* be, I will conclude by considering the features of schools, as we have created them, that make the formation of dialogical relations between teachers and students problematic (Chapter 7). Philosophers of education and other scholars are notorious for proposing visions of education that are completely unattainable in the world where we live. Such utopias have their purpose: They can inspire, expand awareness of alternatives, and promote critical reflection on the status quo. But they are rarely themselves catalysts of change. I hope that teachers reading this book will see numerous ways in which we can change our teaching to make it more dialogical. But this outcome is possible, I believe, only if we also develop a heightened critical awareness of the circumstances that inhibit us. Despite widespread agreement that the so-called "Socratic method" is the paragon of good teaching (see, for example, Bruner, 1971), we have somehow managed to create institutions of learning that make it difficult, if not impossible, to practice in most classrooms.

This book is an invitation, in two senses. First, it is an invitation for each of us, individually, to reflect on and improve our teaching, and to consider where and how dialogue can play an increased role in our repertoire of teaching practices. But it is also an invitation to join into a dialogue, directly or indirectly, with me, with the authors discussed here, and with each other about the nature of dialogue and its possibilities. An important question for us as teachers is how to model a range of dialogical approaches, and the flexibility to change approaches, with our own students; how to engage them in the dialogical process in such a way that they become independently able to carry it forward. Skillful dialogue is learned, I will suggest, primarily by being "caught up" in good dialogues with others; and the legacy of Socrates's life as a teacher demonstrates this point (Haroutunian-Gordon, 1989). Because Socrates chose never to write, we know him only through his teaching, and his influence comes to us through the unbroken chain of dialogical relations that join him, through his students, to us, and through us in turn to our students.

Acknowledgments

As I think back on the many conversations with friends and colleagues that contributed to this project, and as I count up the books and articles (those I remember) from which I have borrowed ideas that appear in these pages, it occurs to me that very little of my writing actually counts as "original," and that perhaps originality is an overvalued commodity in our intellectual work generally. It may be that most of what I have done is to select, interpret, and recombine ideas that came from others. I hope that my reference list does some justice to that obligation.

Much of this book springs directly from discussions and written interchange with Andrew Gitlin, Sophie Haroutunian-Gordon, Ladd Holt, Frank Margonis, Ralph Page, Mike Parsons, Bert Powers, Ralph Reynolds, and Suzanne Rice. Suzanne worked with me on this project as a graduate assistant and has had a significant influence on my thinking about dialogue, as indicated by our several publications together. Ladd is coauthor of the dialogue included here as an Interlude. He died while this book was in production, and I am terribly sad that he did not live to see it in print.

Parts of this book have been presented at annual meetings of the American Educational Research Association and the Philosophy of Education Society; in Friday seminars at the University of Illinois, Urbana-Champaign, the Institute of Education, University of London, and the University of Utah; at meetings of the Philosophy of Education Discussion Group, in the Department of Educational Policy Studies at UIUC; and in some of my own classes and seminars. Participants in those conversations offered a number of excellent criticisms and suggestions, many of which have shaped what is written here. More concretely, the following colleagues read all or part of this manuscript, and provided extremely helpful advice and encouragement along the way: Kal Alston, Donna Alvermann, Mike Apple, Bonnie Armbruster, Chip Bruce, Walter Feinberg, Sophie Haroutunian-Gordon, Ladd Holt, Frank Margonis, Nel Noddings, Ralph

Page, Bert Powers, Suzanne Rice, Harvey Siegel, Suzanne Wade, and Philip Zodhiates.

The late Ron Galbraith, and particularly Susan Liddicoat and Peter Sieger of Teachers College Press have been a pleasure to work with editorially in the development of this book. I appreciate especially the sensitivity (and patience) with which they shepherded this first-time author through the travails of completing a difficult manuscript. Most of all, I want to thank Jonas Soltis, who first encouraged me to undertake a book on dialogue, and whose experience, wisdom, and understanding have been essential in guiding me through this process.

This book is dedicated to my students and teachers.

Dialogue in Teaching

Theory and Practice

CHAPTER 1

Why Dialogue? Why Theory and Practice?

A good beginning point may be to discuss this book's title. Dialogue has long been a central concern of both Western philosophy and educational theory. In fact, it rests at the borderline between philosophy and education in a way that makes their fundamental connection clear (McKeon, 1990). Dewey (1916) said of the link between philosophy and education:

> At this point, the intimate connection between philosophy and education appears. In fact, education offers a vantage point from which to penetrate to the human, as distinct from the technical, significance of philosophic discussions. . . . If we are willing to conceive education as the process of forming fundamental dispositions, intellectual and emotional, toward nature and fellow men [sic], philosophy may even be defined *as the general theory of education.* Unless a philosophy is to remain symbolic—or verbal—or a sentimental indulgence for a few, or else mere arbitrary dogma, its auditing of past experience and its program of values must take effect in conduct. . . . Education is the laboratory in which philosophic distinctions become concrete and are tested. (pp. 383–384)

More recently, James Giarelli (1991) has argued that once we abandon the assumptions of a foundational, transcendental philosophy, we see that education—broadly construed—is the means by which epistemological, ethical, political, or aesthetic "truths" are established and justified.

> Philosophy . . . is rooted neither in some privileged access to reality nor in some neutral procedure, but rather in an analysis of the practices by which human communities maintain, extend, and renew their continued existence. In short, philosophy is rooted in an analysis of educational practices. . . . The future of philosophy depends upon its ability to become an educative element in the life of the community. . . . I call this emerging view philosophy *as* education. (pp. 36–37)

In other words, the significance of philosophical questions about what is true, or good, or right, or beautiful needs to be assessed in terms of their relation to, and effect on, social life. We are justified in making claims about such matters only when we have the means to bring others along with us to such a conclusion. While from one vantage point it might make sense to say that something is the case regardless of whether others recognize it, as a matter of practice this assertion comes to nothing unless we can back it up with an educational—argumentative, persuasive, demonstrative—effort. This effort frequently relies on a dialogical engagement.

Dialogue, therefore, provides a unique perspective on the interplay of philosophy and education. For a variety of contemporary authors the status of dialogue as a source of knowledge and understanding, as a medium for interpersonal discourse, and as a pedagogical relation has been a central topic of interest and dispute. Specifically, among various writers on education and society, especially those writing from contemporary "postmodern" perspectives, dialogue has been a focal point for debating broader conceptions of language, epistemology, ethics, and politics. I will refer to some of these debates in this chapter and throughout this book.

THE POSTMODERN CRITIQUE

Postmodernism is a notoriously vague term, difficult to define as a unified intellectual or cultural movement (Harvey, 1989). But three general issues have been stressed in most postmodern writing, which merit consideration as serious challenges to the major traditions and institutions of our time.

First is the centrality of an analysis of power and hierarchy as the basic dynamics of social and political organization. Certainly postmodernism did not discover the reality of power relations as a determining factor in society; but no tradition has emphasized so strongly the infusion of power relations into culture, language, sexuality, and other aspects of human life that are not usually seen as arenas of domination and oppression (Foucault, 1980, 1988; for a range of postmodern and nonpostmodern views in the educational literature, see Apple, 1982; Burbules, 1986; Cherryholmes, 1988). This power analysis has extended the critical gaze of Left politics beyond the traditional stakes of redistributing wealth, gaining political self-determination for the disenfranchised, or challenging institutionalized status and privilege, toward a much broader "cultural politics" that emphasizes the institutional and ideological nature of various forms of cultural marginalization and oppression (Giroux, 1988; Giroux & McLaren, 1989; Giroux & Simon, 1989).

In the academy this cultural politics has translated into a wholesale challenge to the intellectual traditions of Western culture as the embodiment of centuries of domination by particular class, gender, racial, and national groups. Postmodernists hope to reveal the political character of institutions and discourses whose credibility has traditionally been based on claims to objectivity, impartiality, and universality. Philosophy, of course, has not been spared this assault, and the values of rationality, knowledge, beauty, ethics, or political ideals that have grounded modern thought are now being criticized as the relics of a legitimating superstructure that has excluded, disadvantaged, and silenced subordinate groups. Traditional ways of talking about and adjudicating questions of truth or rightness have been "deconstructed," often with little remaining to take their place.

This leads to the second major theme of postmodernism, which is an emphasis on the irreducible plurality of cultural world views. Partly as a political strategy and partly as an intellectual claim, marginalized groups who are gaining a voice in these matters now insist on the uniqueness and worth of their ways of thinking, valuing, or speaking, in contrast to traditional standards. To avoid being judged by criteria they had no voice in shaping, these groups often insist on the impossibility of comparison or judgment across such differences, and rely on relativistic philosophical positions such as "paradigm difference" or "incommensurability" to buttress their claims. In stronger versions of this position, even the possibility of communication across such differences is questioned, and its advocates correspondingly do not feel the need to bother trying to explain or justify themselves in others' terms.

This position is, in turn, closely related to a third theme, the assault on what is often termed "the logic of identity"—the philosophical view that our intellectual aim is to find common underlying principles, generalizable rules, universal definitions as the sign of theoretical coherence and credibility (I. Young, 1990a). Postmodernists deny that there can be any one system of thought or value that will comprise the variety of human beliefs, feelings, and experiences; and, denying this, they argue that any attempt to systematize thought inevitably ignores legitimate alternatives and forces disparate groups to account for themselves in terms of monolithic categories that are alien to them—which further estranges them by confronting them with the unacceptable bind of trying to succeed on someone else's terms while becoming more and more alienated from their own deeper character and the cultural forms that unite them with similar others. In the face of this tendency, postmodernists insist on the plurality of differences, seeking to create and preserve cultural spaces in which it is safe to act, feel, and speak differently.

These assaults on hierarchy, tradition, and uniformity come together in a characteristic intellectual style that underlies most postmodern writing: one insisting on context, historicity, variety, and the constructed nature of all systems of belief and value. In its forms of speech and writing, as well as in explicit content, postmodernism challenges traditional Enlightenment categories (reason, freedom, human nature, community, even education itself) as hypostasized, exclusionary, excessively formalized, and based on false assumptions about the universalizability of certain values. In response, many postmodernists seek to redefine and broaden these categories to acknowledge the diversity of human cultures and the temporality of human institutions. In a more radical version of postmodernism, which Suzanne Rice and I have elsewhere called "antimodernism" (Burbules & Rice, 1991), the very *possibility* of such categories, or any such standards, is denied, leading to a posture that allows for no objectivity, no judgments of better or worse, and—of special concern here— no hope of dialogue and understanding across differences.

TELEOLOGICAL AND NONTELEOLOGICAL VIEWS OF DIALOGUE

Given the absolutist character of many traditional views of dialogue, the postmodern critique is understandable. Plato (1961b) believed that dialogue is both the rational path to knowledge *and* the highest form of teaching, and for him these two claims were inseparable, since he argued both that one teaches by leading another through the steps by which truths can be deduced and that one discovers truths by undergoing a dialectical give-and-take between provisional hypotheses and skeptical questioning. These claims were based on his particular view of Truth, Goodness, and Beauty as unchanging intrinsic ideals, the certainty of which would be apparent to anyone who was exposed to them; and on his assumptions about learning as recollection, namely, that having been exposed to these eternal verities in a prior existence, persons can be led to recall them by a universal process of instruction, the dialectic. I call this a "teleological" view of dialogue, since it assumes that dialogue can, and should, have a definite, predetermined end point.

Juxtaposed to this view of dialogue and knowledge is the "anti-epistemology" of one postmodern writer, who argues that dialogue should disclose

> negative knowledge as opposed to positive, in which certain categories precede the process of discussion and are held as necessary foundations if the debate is to unfold. Whereas in positive knowledge underscored by epistemology conceptual categories are relatively inexpungeable, in dialogue they are exposed to questioning and to criticism. These operations tend to replace the categories as cornerstones in the edifice of knowledge. . . . Opposed to the epistemological focus on positive knowledge, whether ideal or practical, dialogue remains as the hope of overcoming the dogmatic dominance of certain meanings over others, a dominance spawned by rigid conceptions of dwelling, subject, language, and meaning. (Maranhão, 1990, pp. 1–2, 20)

If I might reframe this assertion in other terms, I would say that it challenges the ways in which Platonic assumptions about knowledge, reason, language, and universal method actually *impede* the possibilities of dialogue as a method of open communication and investigation. Instead, Tullio Maranhão suggests, we should follow a more critical and constructivist spirit of dialogue—as indeed Socrates and Plato often meant it—without the assumption that in practice it will always lead its participants to common and indubitable conclusions; its benefits are more in edification than in finding the Truth. I call this a "nonteleological" conception of dialogue.

This tension between teleological and nonteleological conceptions of dialogue can be understood further by considering the ideas of Paulo Freire, a Brazilian educator whose work with illiterate peasants is aimed at improving both their literacy skills and their political awareness. Freire (1970, 1985a) makes dialogue the centerpiece of his "pedagogy of the oppressed." He seeks to supplant theories of knowledge as a reified and static possession, which he says lead to a "banking view" of education, in which a valuable commodity—Truth—is "deposited" into learners. For Freire, "dialogue is the sealing together of the teacher and students in the joint act of knowing and re-knowing the object of study. . . . Instead of transferring the knowledge *statically*, as a *fixed* possession of the teacher, dialogue demands a dynamic approximation towards the object" (Shor & Freire, 1987b, p. 14). Three important aspects of Freire's theory, which have strongly influenced my own thinking on dialogue, are illustrated by this quote: the relational character of dialogue, a constructivist view of knowledge, and a nonauthoritarian conception of teaching. For Freire, the goal of dialogical teaching and learning is the mutual development of understanding through a process of shared inquiry, not the transmission of truths from a knowledgeable expert to a passive recipient.

Moreover, what is learned in dialogue is always given meaning in terms of the developing personal and political awareness of its participants. By regarding all static conventions and truisms as open to reflection, Freirean pedagogy seeks to emancipate the "oppressed" from the shackles of ideology, learned helplessness, and dependency. Freire (1985b) is primarily concerned with teaching adults the skills of literacy, but for him "literacy" is also a metaphor for a much broader sense of enablement: "Reading the word" means not only decoding text, but an inclusive capacity for cultural and political criticism ("reading the world"). The teacher, the text, and the state no longer stand over the subject as something imposing and authoritative, but rather as objects for scrutiny and questioning with one's own liberatory purposes in mind.

Freire's work has had a tremendous influence on postmodern educational theorists in the United States and elsewhere, most notably in the *critical pedagogy* of Henry Giroux (1985), Peter McLaren (1986), and Ira Shor (Shor & Freire, 1987a). Freire's work has also had a significant influence on feminist pedagogy, in which nonauthoritarian relations and "dialectical partnerships" for learning are strongly emphasized (Maher, 1985; Schniedewind, 1987; Weiler, 1991). In turn, feminist pedagogy has reciprocally contributed insights of theory and practice to the critical pedagogy tradition (Giroux, 1991; Weiler, 1988). Overall, the very term *pedagogy* has come to connote a politically charged, Left approach to education.

Clearly, Freire's account is in tune with much of the postmodern spirit: his explicit commitment to a liberatory pedagogy for the "oppressed," his rejection of monological approaches to teaching and reified conceptions of knowledge, and his questioning of teacher authority. Yet it is unclear whether his conception of dialogue is nonteleological or teleological; whether it represents a decentered process by which marginalized groups generate their own understandings of the world and their own visions and strategies of political change, or whether it is simply a more humane instrument—but an instrument nonetheless—for bringing groups to a particular analysis of their situation and what to do about it. Partly for this reason, his work and that of other critical pedagogues has come under sharp criticism, particularly by some feminist authors (for example, Ellsworth, 1989).

The central question of this book, therefore, is whether a theory and practice of dialogue that respond to the postmodern critique are possible. I hope to suggest an approach to dialogue that challenges hierarchies and traditional conceptions of teacher authority; that is tolerant and supportive of diversity; that does not rely on teleological presumptions of right answers and final truths; that does not rest on isolated individual efforts, but on mutual and reciprocal communicative relations; and that keeps the conversation open, both in the sense of open-endedness and in the sense of inviting a range of voices and styles of communication within it.

TOWARD A REVISED CONCEPTION OF DIALOGUE

To draw on a familiar distinction, dialogue is a phenomenon of discourse (*parole*), not of formal language (*langue*); it is a human practice, responsive to context and changing purposes (Crowell, 1990; Swearingen, 1990). What this suggests is that there will be a limit in the degree to which one can establish a purely formal characterization of what counts as dialogue and what does not. Dialogue is continuous with conversation generally, and in many particular cases it will be difficult to demarcate some section of speech and say, "Here, now it has become (or ceased to be) dialogue." Further along in this book, I will argue that it is an important feature of dialogue that it *can* phase in and out of any singular pattern, as the participants shift their approaches in response to one another. Yet at the same time it does seem useful to be able to characterize broadly certain kinds of verbal interaction as dialogue, and others not. It is possible to imagine clear paradigms, at the extreme, of conversation generally and of dialogical interaction per se: "The essence of 'conversation' is informality and structurelessness, total openness; whereas dialogue is far from amiable rambling" (Swearingen, 1990, p. 63). The challenge is to develop what Wittgenstein (1958) called "family resemblance" criteria, which allow us to cluster related kinds of verbal interaction together without expecting a clear, sharp demarcation under some universal, formal definition.

Generally speaking, we can say that dialogue involves two or more interlocutors. It is marked by a climate of open participation by any of its partners, who put forth a series of alternating statements of variable duration (including questions, responses, redirections, and building statements, which I will define in Chapter 4), constituting a sequence that is continuous and developmental. Dialogue is guided by a spirit of discovery, so that the typical tone of a dialogue is exploratory and interrogative. It involves a commitment to the process of communicative interchange itself, a willingness to "see things through" to some meaningful understandings or agreements among the participants. Furthermore, it manifests an attitude of reciprocity among the participants: an interest, respect, and concern that they share for one another, even in the face of disagreements.

I hope that this characterization of dialogue does not strike readers as arbitrary or inaccurate; I will try to flesh it out as this book goes along. It is important to note that specific dialogues might be imagined that lack one or more of these characteristics; but most things that we call "dialogues" do seem to possess several of them—which is what a family resemblance means. Nor should we assume that these conditions can be taken for granted in most contexts; indeed, the more one thinks about dialogue, and the societal barriers to it that we have created, the more remarkable it appears that dialogue ever happens at all (I will return to this issue in Chapter 7). This broad definition of dialogue can be summarized, I believe, by calling dialogue a *pedagogical communicative relation*, and next I will examine each part of this claim separately. My purpose is to suggest the scope of issues that are raised by an examination of dialogue and to show why dialogue is a fundamental issue, not only for education per se, but for a range of broader human concerns.

Dialogue as Pedagogical

Dialogue is not like other forms of communication (chatting, arguing, negotiating, and so on). Dialogue is an activity directed toward discovery and new understanding, which stands to improve the knowledge, insight, or sensitivity of its participants. This is true even when the roles of the participants do not break out neatly as "teacher" and "student" (or even when the dialogue is internal and imaginary, within thought). Dialogue represents a continuous, developmental communicative interchange through which we stand to gain a fuller apprehension of the world, ourselves, and one another. In some cases, a dialogue might have an intended goal, such as answering a specific question or communicating an already-formulated insight. In other cases, however, none of the participants knows exactly where the dialogue is headed, or whether it will be successful; if one takes a process-oriented view of dialogue and its benefits, this uncertainty can be seen as educationally worthwhile. And even when dialogue begins with a particular purpose, the dynamic of communicative interaction can lead the participants to alter or abandon that purpose. For these reasons, narrow categories of "teaching" and "learning" do not fit many instances of dialogue well; they dichotomize the roles of teacher and student, and they connote the pursuit of particular learning outcomes, as opposed to a broader (and more mutual) process of edification (Rorty, 1979).

(There are, of course, other kinds of worthwhile pedagogical communication besides dialogue: lecturing, explaining, and so on. But they are not my topics here.)

Although dialogue is idealized as a relation between two participants, it can also be used to characterize some forms of group discussion. David Bridges (1988a) has made some extremely helpful observations about this link, noting that through dialogical classroom discussion participants can learn not only about the subject matter at hand, but also about expressing themselves clearly to others; learning to regulate their discussions through such conventions as taking turns, listening, and so on; and learning about other people. Bridges wants to organize classrooms so that students not only learn about history, math, or whatever, but also become socialized into the "moral culture of group discussion," a virtue he identifies not only with good education, but with the very survival and vitality of democratic society (p. 32).

Finally, dialogue tends toward a decentered and nonauthoritarian view of learning, even when there are discrete teacher and student roles (Haroutunian-Gordon, 1991). This view can be supported empirically by reference to contemporary cognitive psychology. Many current studies of learning emphasize that knowledge is structured in memory by "schema," cognitive structures that comprise complex relations of words or concepts (Anderson, 1977; Bransford & McCarrell, 1974; Spiro, 1977). In this view, understanding, or "comprehension," involves incorporating new information into existing schemata and/or altering schemata in light of new information. An important corollary of this model, from the standpoint of learning, is that merely presenting students with new information without adequate attention to their current structures of understanding virtually guarantees that the new material will be forgotten (because a student has no clear associations for it) or misunderstood (altered to fit existing preconceptions).

For this reason, schematic models of comprehension, along with constructivist theories of knowledge, have given rise to the idea of teaching as "scaffolding," working with students to build up levels of understanding appropriate to their state of readiness, and helping to draw their attention to the explicit processes by which ideas are related to one another as new information is provided. For example, we might walk a student step-by-step through the process of reading and interpreting a poem ("Why did the author choose this word over that one? Look, this line ends in mid-sentence. Why do you think she did that?"). Such scaffolds "make it possible for the novice to participate in the mature task from the very beginning; and they do this by providing support that is both adjustable and temporary" (Cazden, 1988, p. 107). Dialogue, or, as it is sometimes called, "reciprocal teaching," is described in this work as one form of such instruction; it is concerned not simply with providing new information but with fostering an explicit understanding of how knowledge is made (Collins & Stevens, 1982, 1983; Palincsar, 1986; Palincsar & Brown, 1984). In this, it seeks to develop an independent and autonomous learner.

Since I know that it will puzzle and disturb some readers to see a critical theorist citing cognitive psychology as an empirical source, let me also give this thesis a more explicitly political interpretation. In pedagogical encounters, we do not change other people. They change themselves: They construct their own understandings, they change their minds, they decide on alternative courses of action, they redefine their priorities, and so on (Fay, 1977). This process may be only partly conscious, and it may come as the result of so many microchanges that even the person who changes may see the culmination only after the fact. But beginning from this vantage point leads to a fundamentally different teaching stance, one defined less by "giving" students certain things, "shaping" students in particular ways, or "leading" them to particular conclusions, and more by creating opportunities and occasions in which students will, given their own questions, needs, and purposes, gradually construct a more mature understanding of themselves, the world, and others—an understanding that, *by definition*, must be their own. The scaffolding model of teaching shows that there is no necessary incompatibility between a significant role for the teacher in dialogue and an active and respectful conception of the learner.

Dialogue as Communicative

Humans live by communication, and many of the practices that we think define us as human are a direct outgrowth of the ways in which we communicate: our language, our reasoning, our morality, and our social organization. In this section, I want to examine how dialogue is central to each of these four interrelated areas of human practice.

LANGUAGE. According to Mikhail Bakhtin (1981), language is fundamentally dialogical. Obviously, we use and create language by speaking with others, but Bakhtin has a deeper point to make. Our language is a fabric of new and old, in which each new use is entwined with previous uses. Our clichés, our slogans, our proverbs, and the web of connotations associated with each utterance contain within them a history of agreements and disagreements in prior conversations. Thus, a human statement is less like a precise laser beam of reference, and more like a knitted catchall in which we try to contain meaning, with mismatched yarns and numerous dangling threads that we cannot get rid of without unraveling the rest. Bakhtin calls this "the internal dialogism of the word."

> The word is born in a dialogue as a living rejoinder within it; the word is shaped in dialogic interaction with an alien word that is already in the object. A word forms a concept of its own object in a dialogic way. . . . Every word is directed toward an *answer* and cannot escape the profound influence of the answering word that it anticipates. . . . The word encounters an alien word, cannot help encountering it in a living tension-filled interaction. . . . The dialogic orientation of discourse is a phenomenon that is, of course, a property of *any* discourse. It is the natural orientation of any living discourse. (pp. 279–280)

In other words, we find our language already used, and through language we are joined to previous as well as present speakers. In this sense, language is both the means to dialogue and the product of it, and in finding our voice we inevitably hear the echoes of others. Bakhtin (1981) calls this "heteroglossia," a topic I will return to later (see also Daelemans & Maranhão, 1990; Holquist, 1981; Quantz & O'Connor, 1988; Wertsch, 1991). Gadamer (1982) made a similar point when he said: "The literary form of the dialogue places language and concept back within the original movement of the conversation" (p. 332). For these authors, therefore, we find in dialogue "a hermeneutics of all discourse" (Swearingen, 1990, p. 48).

REASON. Dialogue is also related to our capacity for thought, especially our ability to solve problems, to think sensibly toward conclusions, to weigh competing considerations, and to choose reasonable courses of action. If Lev Vygotsky (1962, 1978; see also Wertsch, 1991) is correct, language precedes thought. Our ratiocinative capacities are formed by the internalization of communicative interactions we have with others from a very early age. We start by having them guide, explain, question, or argue with us, and end by representing this dialogue within ourselves (Kuhn, 1992). So, for example, we often will see young children speaking aloud to themselves, as if from another person, directing themselves through the steps of a complex and difficult process.

But in addition to this, once formed our capacities to be reasonable are also affected by the social circumstances in which we find ourselves: with whom we talk, how others around us are thinking and acting, and how they respond to us. Even if, in the short run, we can keep a level head while others around us are losing theirs (as the saying goes), in the long run our own capacities will be diminished, or atrophy, if they are not sustained by a reasonable community within which the limited and imperfect capacities in each of us are supported and supplemented by regular interactions with others (Burbules, 1991a, 1992). Dialogue is the form that many of these interactions take. This relational and communicative conception of reasonableness is close to what Nel Noddings (1991) calls "interpersonal reasoning."

> In contrast to logico-mathematical reasoning that proceeds step by step according to a priori rules, interpersonal reasoning is open, flexible, and responsive. It is guided by an attitude that values the relationship of the reasoners over any particular outcome, and it is marked by attachment and connection rather than separation and abstraction. (p. 158)

MORALITY. Our capacity for dialogical communication also has a fundamental link with our self-conception as moral creatures, and within this conception dialogue is frequently invested with an ethical imperative of its own: "The quintessence of our being is to *be dialogical.* . . . [It is] a real potential of every person—a potential that ought to be realized" (R. Bernstein, 1986, pp. 65, 113). The concept of dialogue as a process of communication is closely tied with the values of involvement, respect, and concern for one's partner(s) in discussion. It connotes an egalitarian spirit and an open-mindedness about considering other points of view that are fundamentally admirable. For authors as different as Nel Noddings (1984) and Paulo Freire (1970) dialogue is associated with a caring sentiment and with love.

At a more abstract level, a dialogical model of communication has been posited as the basis for ethical theory generally: Morally defensible norms are those that will be consensually agreed to by partners in a "dialogue free of coercion" (Mecke, 1990, p. 207). In the recent work of Jurgen Habermas (1990a) and Seyla Benhabib (1986, 1987, 1989, 1990; Benhabib & Dallmayr, 1990) this model has been labeled a "communicative ethics."

> The discourse model of legitimacy is an aspect of a communicative theory of ethics. The discourse model develops the basic idea of this theory in its application to institutional life. Communicative ethics is first and foremost a theory of moral justification. The question from which it proceeds is how to defend the cognitive or rational kernel of moral judgements without assimilating these either into statements about the world (naturalism) or into statements about my preferences (emotivism). Briefly, the answer is that we should view moral judgements and other statements defending the validity of norms as assertions whose justifiability we establish via moral argumentations named "discourses." Moral justification amounts to a form of moral argumentation. This is the fundamental principle governing a discourse ethic. . . . "Only these norms can be called valid, which all concerned agree to (or would agree to) as participants in a practical discourse." (Benhabib, 1989, p. 150)

I will have more to say later about this model; here I mean only to suggest that viewing dialogue as a process of openly negotiated meaning and value has a close kinship with a metatheory about how generalizable moral values can be identified and justified.

SOCIAL ORGANIZATION. Then there is the close link between communication and politics, particularly democracy. Dewey (1916) is famous for arguing that what sustains democracy is not primarily its political forms (such as voting), but its social organization, grounded in equality, respect, and public discourse. Dewey argues strongly in favor of the need for open communication within social groups in a democracy, and across those groups over issues of common concern. The fabric of society, he believes, is more sturdy the greater the variety of concerns that can be discussed within the public sphere. From a societal standpoint, it should be clear, such discussions make possible the establishment of relations of negotiation, cooperation, mutual tolerance, the pursuit of common interests (where they exist), and the nonviolent resolution of conflicts. Such an ideal speaks particularly to the present context, where a wider and wider range of diverse cultural groups live in closer and closer proximity to one another, and in which certain traditional categories of unification (such as national identity) have begun to break down.

Admittedly, such communicative efforts across different groups will often fail. They may in fact heighten tensions; dialogue across differences does not necessarily entail agreement, and greater communication will, in some cases, make the conflicts between groups all the more apparent. But there is no reason to *prejudge* this outcome, and weighed against that possibility are the many instances in which, to one's surprise perhaps, and to everyone's benefit, understanding and commonalities of interest can be, at least provisionally, established. There are benefits in this sort of discussion for the individual as well: To the extent that group identification is an element in the formation of personal identity, one's identity will be more flexible, and more autonomous, to the degree that one can see oneself as a member of various different subcommunities simultaneously. Such simultaneous identification can, at its extremes, produce internal conflict and a feeling of cultural schizophrenia, but more commonly it has a beneficial effect in fostering a broader and more inclusive sense of oneself and one's relations to others.

In general, then, democracy in a full sense can exist only when different individuals and groups are able to learn about and understand competing positions on issues and, while not necessarily always coming to agreement or consensus about them, grasp sufficiently the points of view of others so that the outcomes reached by democratic processes are acceptable, if not the most favorable, to every group. In this sense, dialogue is essential to democracy (Barber, 1984).

In this section, I have tried to elaborate several themes concerning the *communicative* aspect of dialogue as a pedagogical communicative relation, and specifically to show how dialogue relates to, and underlies, four important features of human life: the nature of language itself, our forms of reason, our ethics, and our possibilities as a democratic society. I hope to have suggested not only that dialogue is a significant topic in narrowly educational contexts, but that it is essential to much larger questions of social existence—because these larger questions should be seen as fundamentally educational ones.

Dialogue as Relational

One of the central themes of this book is that we should consider dialogue as a relation that comprises the parties to it and catches them up in a spirit of interaction that they do not entirely control or direct as individuals (see Chapter 2). As a beginning to that argument, it is useful to examine the etymology of the term *dialogue* itself. It is easy enough to see that "dia-logue" has something to do with two people speaking together, but some of the connotations of the Greek expressions tell us a bit more than this. *"Dia"* means more than simply "two": It is a preposition meaning "between," "across," or "through," and hence can apply to more than two persons as well (Crapanzano, 1990; Swearingen, 1990). The key idea expressed is of spanning or connecting.

"Logos" is a term used not only for "word" or "speech," but also for "thought," "reason," and "judgment" (Crapanzano, 1990; Swearingen, 1990). Even more specifically, if Heidegger (1977) is correct, it connotes the particular way in which credibility is established in concrete speech situations.

> If we say that the basic meaning of *logos* is speech, this literal translation becomes valid only when we define what speech itself means. . . . *Logos* as speech really means to make manifest "what is talked about." . . . *Logos* lets something be seen . . . for the speaker (who serves as the medium) or for those who speak with each other. . . . *Logos* acquires the meaning of *relation* and *relationship*. (pp. 79–82)

This conception of *logos*, then, connotes the negotiated, relational status of validity claims. It situates meaning and truth not in transcendent criteria, but in the practical attainment of understanding and agreement between persons—an endeavor that can, of course, fail. As Vincent Crapanzano (1990) puts it, "etymologically, a dialogue is a speech across, between, through two people. It is a passing through and a going apart. . . . It is a relationship of considerable tension" (p. 276).

This insight suggests that effective dialogue depends on the establishment and maintenance of a particular kind of relation among its participants. Dialogue, even though it does have some generally characteristic formal properties, is not bounded by these. What underlies and shapes the patterns of interaction in a dialogue are the attitudes, emotions, and expectations that participants have regarding each other and the value of dialogue itself; these are formed partly out of the dynamic of interaction as the discussion moves along. What sustains a dialogue over time is not only lively interchange about the topic at hand, but a certain commitment to one's partner; a commitment that might not precede the dialogue, but arises only gradually in the spirit of the engagement. Further, as I will discuss later (in Chapter 4), where dialogue does follow certain rules or principles, one of their important functions is to establish a degree of reliability and consistency in the discussion that allows the participants to engage confidently in open interchange. Frequently, though, such features of the dialogical relation will not be sufficient to draw participants into the interchange or for them to feel safe within it. We also need to attend to the institutional and ideological contexts that constitute the speech situation; needless to say, these factors often impede the dialogical possibilities for specific participants in particular situations, and they are not always remediable, even given persistence and good intentions among the participants. Nevertheless, such possibilities should not be entirely foreclosed.

THEORY AND PRACTICE

What does "theory and practice" mean in the context of dialogue? I have laid out a basic picture of dialogue as a pedagogical communicative relation and sketched in general terms how dialogue works educationally: as a way of expressing and creating new understandings; as a way of reflecting upon and adjudicating ethical or political norms; and as a way of drawing participants into a particular type of communicative relation with one another. Dialogue, I have suggested, underlies our practices of language, reasoning, ethics, and politics, not as a medium for the apprehension of Truth or Justice (as it was for Plato), but as the best available means we have for identifying among ourselves acceptable answers, workable solutions, and reasonable accommodations. A pragmatic outlook guides this investigation; and the only justification I would claim for my account is that it can be helpful in thinking through the complex questions of how dialogue works in educational contexts.

Discussions of theory and practice frequently make two errors. One is to separate these dichotomously as two realms of activity, when what they actually indicate is the gulf that exists between two groups of people engaged in different (potentially related) endeavors. "The relation between theory and practice" becomes an issue when the relation between theoreticians and practitioners is an issue, and this is certainly the case in education today. Many practicing teachers (especially in public schools) regard theoretical work, much of it generated by relatively privileged academic scholars in universities (such as myself), as out of touch with and irrelevant to their concerns. Theoreticians regard many practicing teachers, on the other hand, as insufficiently reflective about their practice and encumbered by ill-formed understandings about the purpose and value of their endeavor.

This is, I believe, at heart a sociological problem, grounded in conflicting organizational contexts, competing value systems, and frequently incompatible discourses about education. Hence the resolution of this problem is not itself an intellectual/academic endeavor, such as articulating a new conceptual synthesis or formulating better arguments for "praxis" or "grounded theory." The resolution of this problem lies fundamentally in working to establish more and better communication between theoreticians and practitioners, and addressing the serious institutional and prejudicial barriers (on both sides) that impede it.

The second problem of many discussions of theory and practice constitutes one of these barriers, namely, the tendency, theory and practice having been dichotomized, to grant priority to one over the other. Errors are made on both sides: among those who underestimate the theoretical import and complexity of effective practice, and among those who denigrate the value of the "ivory tower" and assume that experience and a make-it-up-as-you-go attitude can substitute for "academic learning."

This book is about avoiding such dichotomies of thought: about identifying general formal properties of dialogue, while seeing these as always needing to be interpreted and applied in context; about avoiding the tendency to prejudge the limits and possibilities of an educational situation either positively (utopianism) or negatively (cynicism); and about drawing insights from various available sources of understanding and trying to integrate them coherently, without being trapped by presuppositions about the incompatibility of "qualitative" and "quantitative" scholarship (Howe, 1985, 1988), or the priority of philosophical over experiential or narrative understandings.

Finally, while this book is concerned with describing and defending a particular educational ideal—dialogue—it is a *process* ideal. I have tried to suggest here the benefits of a nonteleological conception of dialogue, in which participants commit themselves to an intersubjective relation of exploratory and negotiated understanding without necessarily having a definite outcome in mind. To be sure, the communicative activities outlined here are not entirely neutral as to potential outcomes. Some outcomes will be clearly incompatible with the establishment and maintenance of dialogical relations—or with the conditions for the continuation of further dialogue. This incompatibility provides a reason, in my view, to challenge such outcomes;

not just anything goes. Hence, dialogue as a process ideal provides the sort of standard that is compatible with a postmodern understanding—flexible and inclusive within a broad range of possible values and perspectives, but with sufficient substance to exclude at least some possibilities (otherwise it could not serve as a *standard* at all).

Education is an inherently political undertaking, and no account of education can legitimately claim to be entirely separate from political assumptions and commitments. We must be able to identify and criticize the power relations and ideological barriers that undermine dialogical possibilities, in schools and in society generally. Hence, the pragmatism I argue for here is a *critical pragmatism* (Cherryholmes, 1988). But one of the most troubling characteristics of Left scholarship, in my view, has been its tendency to conflate such critical investigations with the advocacy of a *specific* social vision; this has often led authors to the unfortunate error of distorting their own writing for the sake of promoting a particular outcome. This has had the effect of taking decisions about the best solutions to problems, or the most just and workable social arrangements, out of the hands of people who need to be involved in those determinations—and who, generally speaking, are given the fewest opportunities to do so. The ironies of this position are obvious. The account of dialogue here is explicitly dedicated to the proposition that we must do better in involving and enabling people as participants in the ongoing dialogue that is a democratic society; and that educational institutions, seriously flawed as they are, still constitute one potential starting point for fostering and reinvigorating that dialogue.

CHAPTER 2

The Dialogical Relation

There are many useful things that one can say generally about dialogue: the typical patterns that it follows, the communicative rules or standards that help guide it, and the varied purposes it can be useful for. But deeper than any of these is the nature of the commitment that joins interlocutors in an ongoing communicative relation. This is the most characteristic thing about dialogue, the element that sustains it over time, and the chief quality that attracts us to it as an educational ideal: the bond that joins two (or more) persons in the cooperative pursuit of knowledge, agreement, or interpersonal understanding. Because the actual success of dialogue in achieving any of these outcomes is uncertain, something more substantial than the promise of a guaranteed outcome must be involved in attracting participants to the discussion and keeping them in it even when it becomes frustrating, confusing, or conflicted—as any dialogue may as it follows its course. David Bohm and F. David Peat (1991) put this point well.

> In dialogue . . . a person may prefer a certain position but does not hold to it non-negotiably. He or she is ready to listen to others with sufficient sympathy and interest to understand the meaning of the other's position properly and is also ready to change his or her own point of view if there is good reason to do so. Clearly a spirit of good will or friendship is necessary for this to take place. . . . The *spirit* of dialogue is, in short, the ability to hold many points of view in suspension, along with a primary interest in the creation of common meaning. (p. 82)

What this "spirit of dialogue" entails is my central topic in this chapter. I will argue that dialogue is not fundamentally a specific communicative form of question and response, but at heart a kind of *social relation* that engages its participants. A successful dialogue involves a willing partnership and cooperation in the face of likely disagreements, confusions, failures, and misunderstandings. Persisting in this process requires a relation of mutual respect, trust, and concern—and part of the dialogical interchange often must relate to the establishment and maintenance of these bonds. The substance of this interpersonal relation is deeper, and more consistent, than any particular communicative form it might take.

Freire (Shor & Freire, 1987b) calls dialogue an "epistemological relation . . . sealing together . . . the teacher and the students in the joint act of knowing and reknowing the object of study" (p. 14). But in addition to this cognitive interest, and inseparable from it, participants in a dialogue also share particular characteristic ways of *feeling* toward one another, even if the verbal interaction itself may be somewhat contentious. This point is put well by Nel Noddings (1984).

> What I am advocating is a form of dialectic between feeling and thinking that will lead in a continuing spiral to the basic feeling of genuine caring and the generous thinking that develops in its service. Through such a dialectic, we are led beyond the intense and particular feelings accompanying our own deeply held values, and beyond the particular beliefs to which these feelings are attached, to a realization that the other—who feels intensely about that which I do not believe—is still one to be received. . . . [Such] dialogue . . . is vital in every aspect of education. (p. 186)

Moreover, it is the nature of this dialogical relation to be able to "carry away" its participants, to "catch them up" in an interaction that takes on a force and direction of its own, often leading them beyond any intended goal to new and unexpected insights. This kind of dynamic involves more than simply combining the perspectives and knowledge of two separate individuals: Maurice Merleau-Ponty (1962) points out how "the objection that my interlocutor raises to what I say draws from me thoughts I had no idea I possessed, so that at the same time that I lend him thoughts, he reciprocates by making me think too" (p. 354). Hans-Georg Gadamer (1976) puts this point even more strongly.

> When one enters into a dialogue with another person and then is carried further by the dialogue, it is no longer the will of the individual person, holding itself back or exposing itself, that is determinative. Rather, the law of the subject matter is at issue in the dialogue and elicits statement and counterstatement and in the end plays them into each other. . . . We say that we "conduct" a conversation, but the more fundamental a conversation is, the less its conduct lies within the will of either partner. . . . Rather, it is generally more correct to say that we fall into conversation, or even that we become involved in it. (p. 66)

This perspective involves a different way of thinking about the self in relation to others: Dialogue is not a matter of two isolated persons who simply decide to start talking with one another (although this may be how it seems at first). Once constituted as a relation, the dialogical encounter engages the participants in a process at once symbiotic and synergistic; beyond a particular point, no one may be consciously guiding or directing it, and the order and flow of the communicative exchange itself take over. The participants are *caught up*; they are *absorbed*. Certainly, the persons in the relation are to some degree acting autonomously within it—thinking, making choices, expressing their personality and outlook—but they are *relational selves*, not discrete individuals (Benhabib, 1987; Whitbeck, 1989).

These interrelated factors—the cognitive interest in pursuing understanding, knowledge, or agreement; the affective qualities of concern and commitment that draw us into the dialogue and hold us within it; and the capacity of dialogue to involve us and carry us beyond our intentions—all are aspects of the *dialogical relation*. In this chapter I will examine these three areas of concern in detail, showing how a pragmatic and relational conception of dialogue helps us to rethink certain problems that are recurrent in the educational literature. Then I will turn to the question of how our capacities for communicative interchange are fostered and motivated in the dialogical relation.

To avoid a potential misunderstanding, I want to mention briefly that Mikhail Bakhtin (1981, 1986) develops the idea of a "dialogic relation," and while I draw from some of Bakhtin's views, I mean something quite different by this phrase than he does. For Bakhtin, the dialogic relation is a relation between *utterances* within a dialogical encounter (indeed between present utterances and all human utterances that have come before).

> *Dialogic relations* have a specific nature: they can be reduced neither to the purely logical (even if dialectical) nor to the purely linguistic (compositional-syntactic). They are possible only between complete utterances of various speaking subjects. . . . Where there is no word and no language, there can be no dialogic relations; they cannot exist among objects of logical quantities (concepts, judgments, and so forth). Dialogic relations presuppose a language, but they do not reside within the system of language. (1986, p. 117)

What Bakhtin describes as a dialogic relation is a relation between the things people have actually said; his main concern, as discussed in Chapter 1, is with the ways in which multiple layers of meaning are constituted by the ways we use language and, in a sense, are used by it. So, for example, it is impossible to utter a term such as *freedom* without invoking, at some subtle level, its range of meanings and connotations arising from previous uses; the term is laden with the significance that others have attached to it, which becomes part of one's own intended or inadvertent meaning. Without debating that picture of language here, I simply want to make clear that what I mean by the dialogical relation is something else: a relation between and among *persons*, when they are drawn into a particular dynamic of speaking with and listening to one another.

IDEAS AND UNDERSTANDINGS

Recent Criticisms of Freire and Critical Pedagogy

A useful starting point of any relational analysis "unfolds from the notions of Self and Other as mutually constituting" (Maranhão, 1990, p. 4). This perspective leads to a breaking down of certain conventional dichotomies of social thought—especially, in the present context, the dyad of teacher and student. Freire, Dewey, and many others have made the point that when teaching and learning come to be seen as interactive processes, the roles corresponding to these positions can no longer be easily assigned to discrete individuals. What remains unclear is how this view can be reconciled with a recognition that there often *are* real differences in knowledge, insight, or expertise that attract persons, for different reasons, into teaching/ learning encounters. While a broadly egalitarian commitment and mutual respect ought to frame our pedagogical outlook, these should not obscure the ways in which some participants clearly do stand to benefit from an opportunity to learn from (not only *with*) others who know, understand, or can do things that they themselves cannot. Within the context of a dialogical relation, attitudes of trust and respect can acknowledge differences in knowledge, insight, or expertise without reifying them into inflexible and authoritarian status or role identities.

The possibility of establishing this sort of dialogical relation, as it has been presented by Freire and other critical pedagogues, has been challenged by Elizabeth Ellsworth (1989).

The concept of critical pedagogy assumes a commitment on the part of the professor/teacher toward ending the students' oppression. Yet the literature offers no sustained attempt to problematize this stance and confront the likelihood that the professor brings to social movements (including critical pedagogy) interests of her or his own race, class, ethnicity, gender, and other positions. (p. 306)

Similarly, on the subject of teacher knowledge and teacher authority, she writes:

"Emancipatory authority" . . . implies . . . a teacher who knows the object of study "better" than do the students. . . . [Such authority emphasizes] the student's less adequate understanding, [and allows] the teacher to devise more effective strategies for bringing the student "up" to the teacher's level of understanding. (pp. 308, 306)

Ellsworth argues that in cases where the topic of discussion is the oppression that students experience, and the goal is to create educational and political avenues toward transforming that state of affairs, teachers who are different from the groups involved cannot claim any special expertise or authority on the subject. Indeed, Ellsworth seems to say that the barest attempt to assert special authority, even with the best of motives in mind, inevitably sets the teacher against those with whom he or she wishes to be engaged.

I believe Ellsworth is correct in perceiving in parts of Freire's work (and in the work of those influenced most strongly by him) a latent assumption that the teacher should lead students to particular conclusions of belief and action, which *is* in conflict with the basic conception of an "empowering" pedagogy. However, one can also find many passages in Freire where he rejects the attitude of "generosity" (as in, "Let *me* bring *you* up to my level of understanding"), and where he explicitly warns that a teacher must be humble in the presence of those who are experts in the conditions of their own oppression—in other words, that the teacher must be a learner (for example, see Freire, 1970, pp. 39, 46–47, 53–56, 78–79, 84, 121–124).

Ellsworth's (1989) concerns about the dangers of teacher authority, and her postmodern skepticism about the possibility of reasoned discourse across disparate groups, lead her to an extremely negative view of what she calls "the repressive fictions of classroom dialogue" (p. 315).

By prescribing moral deliberation, engagement in the full range of views present, and critical reflection, the literature on critical pedagogy implies that students and teachers can and should engage each other in the classroom as fully rational subjects. . . . Dialogue . . . consists of ground rules for classroom interaction using language. These rules include the assumptions that all members have equal opportunity to speak, all members respect other members' right to speak and feel safe to speak, and all ideas are tolerated and subjected to rational critical assessment against fundamental judgement and moral principles. . . . Dialogue in its conventional sense is impossible in the culture at large because at this historical moment, power relations between raced, classed, and gendered students and teachers are unjust. The injustice of these relations and the way in which those injustices distort communication cannot be overcome in the classroom, no matter how committed the teacher and students are. (pp. 301, 314, 316)

It seems to me that any prescriptive account of how and what we should teach must acknowledge the dangers Ellsworth rightly points to: the risks of excessive reliance on teacher knowledge and expertise, the false confidence that sensible and fair rules of participation alone can make the classroom feel "safe" to many students, the dangers of assuming that goodwill and reasonableness will settle all political injustices, and the many ways in which our own cultural positions impede our capacity to understand and empathize with the experiences and problems of others.

Yet at the same time Ellsworth's account also exhibits assumptions that, if she truly means them at a literal level, abrogate the very possibility of educational intervention. Is it useful to say that teachers do not have *any* special knowledge and experience that justify their role as something more than an equal partner in a conversation? Is it plausible to assert that dialogue is *impossible*? Is it helpful to assume that attempts at undistorted communication must fail "no matter how committed the teachers and students are"? Without wanting to overlook Ellsworth's valid critical insights, I must say that these claims seem greatly exaggerated. Specifically, I believe that they make a fundamental intellectual (and political) error: They *prejudge* the question of whether undominated communication and undistorted understanding are possible, and they *preempt* the possibility that in specific contexts, and in an uncoerced fashion, participants in a discussion may choose to cede a certain degree of authority to particular individuals, an authority they all agree to because of a common interest in advancing the discussion.

It is one thing to point out the danger that when it appears that rules are neutral and that all participants have a "right to speak and feel safe to speak," the situation may not be experienced as such by all participants. But it is much less plausible—indeed, it is counter-educational—to assume that such is necessarily the case. Even Ellsworth herself exhibits some ambivalence about this conclusion, for later in the same essay she does seem to hold out the possibility of dialogical encounter.

> If you can talk to me in ways that show you understand that your knowledge of me, the world, and the "Right thing to do" will always be partial, interested, and potentially oppressive to others, and if I can do the same, then we can work together on shaping and reshaping alliances for constructing circumstances in which students of difference can thrive (1989, p. 324; see also Ellsworth, 1990).

Which begins to sound very much like the "dialogical relation" described here.

Dialogue in Contexts of Difference

A question that repeatedly arises in the literature on critical pedagogy is whether *difference* (cultural, racial, gender, or class) creates potential barriers to dialogue; or whether it should be viewed as a positive opportunity for creating relations of understanding and cooperation across such difference. My answer in this book will be, both.

The dialogical relation does not require identity among its participants; nor does it seek to create this. Dialogue does not assume up front that people are the same, speak the same way, or are interested in the same issues. It only assumes that people are committed to a process of communication directed toward interpersonal understanding and that they hold, or are willing to develop, some degree of concern for, interest in, and respect toward one another. Within this relation, there is a great deal that people, however different they might be, can do to pursue ways of speaking with and understanding one another (Burbules & Rice, 1991, 1992). A variety of ethnographies and more informal travelogues provide evidence that even across broad gulfs of cultural and linguistic difference a surprising amount of successful communication and understanding can occur. One cannot presume that such a process of translation will be easy or always successful (indeed, no translation is ever perfect, although this does not prevent its being useful). Such understanding is inhibited at times by deep cultural or paradigmatic incongruities, by real or perceived relations of power, and by personal shortcomings such as impatience or intolerance. At this stage in my argument, I only want to point out that it is possible, despite such barriers, for persons to allow themselves to be drawn into a relation in which they acknowl-

edge and respect their differences, regarding them as positive opportunities to gain new perspectives *precisely because* they come "from
the outside"—from a world view and set of experiences that are quite
different from one's own (Feinberg, 1990).

Nor does dialogue need to be aimed at the reconciliation or re-
moval of such differences where it does find them. There are obvious
dangers in seeking to impose one's view on others, or to eliminate
or reduce diversity under the false umbrella of "consensus." This
frequently happens, unfortunately, in many educational contexts,
where one person's (or group's) motives for embarking on "teaching" others may be to press on them, "for their own good," the
particular beliefs and values that the person assumes will benefit the
others. No particular political, religious, or cultural orientation has a
monopoly on this failing. But once we recognize this danger, there
are ways of conceiving pedagogical communication that help us to
avoid it; and dialogue, in particular, can be framed in such a way
that it seeks to preserve and sustain differences. Indeed, if we were
not substantially different from one another in experiences, outlook,
and substantive knowledge, why would we be drawn into educational situations at all?

The pursuit of mutual understanding or agreement on some matter of common concern, therefore, does not necessarily threaten, and
is not threatened by, difference. The key criterion to be applied here
is whether understanding or agreement is achieved in ways that
allow participants a full range of opportunities to question, challenge,
or demur from each other's views. If, after an extended process of
such interchange, persons arrive from their various different starting
points at some common conclusion—or if, failing this, they at least
have an enhanced degree of understanding and appreciation for each
other's positions, then there is no reason to assume that this must
be an imposed or monolithic outcome. Whether the achievement of
understanding moves toward agreement cannot and should not be
prejudged—the participants will determine that, in the process of
their interaction. It is a mistake to assume that understanding or
agreement must follow from such an endeavor, and it is a mistake to
assume that it must fail. Neither stance helps in coping with the
concrete contextual problems of pursuing the goals of understanding
and *possible* agreement, without prejudging the outcome one way or
the other. In education especially, this pragmatic attitude is indispensable, acknowledging differences without seeking to submerge or
override them, since without differences to play against, learning
itself is impossible.

Dialogue, Equality, and Community

While many are drawn to dialogue as a pedagogical approach because of egalitarian sentiments, equality per se is not necessary for dialogue to exist. Were this not true, dialogue could not exist, for example, between adults and children. The fact that participants are unequal in knowledge, experience, or intelligence is not a detriment to the possibilities of dialogue—on the contrary, it often helps explain why partners are drawn into the relation with one another. Two other characteristics are more important than equality for this dialogical relation to succeed. There must be some level of reciprocity that binds the partners together in a mutual relation of concern and respect (a relation that is fully cognizant of their differences); and there must be a real chance for everyone concerned to participate in, contribute to, or withdraw from the discussion. While in specific dialogical situations the nature and degree of actual participation by each member will not be exactly equal to that of every other, this cannot in itself be read as a failure of dialogue. Frequently, given differences in knowledge, experience, or insight, some participants will judge it in their own interests to allow others special latitude in, for example, posing questions to them; or they may choose to listen more than to speak. It goes without saying that in contexts of power and institutional privilege, the background against which these choices are made might make them problematic even when they appear voluntary. Certainly it is in the spirit of dialogue to work toward a stage in which participants trade off various roles, fluctuating from active to more passive involvement, questioning authorities as well as attending to them. But it is necessary to work *within* an ongoing dialogical relation to bring participants to this point, and every step along this developmental path may not follow a pattern of equal participation (even if in principle it is a prerogative of all participants).

The dialogical relation, then, has in itself a strongly pedagogical element, in which participants seek to teach and learn from one another; and the voluntary aspect of this participation is crucial, since a reluctant partner in dialogue is not likely to gain, or contribute, anything at all. But within this set of mutual choices, the actual patterns of participation may vary. Deeper than equal participation per se is a spirit Seyla Benhabib (1989) calls "egalitarian reciprocity."

All communicative action entails symmetry and reciprocity of normative expectations among group members. . . . "Respect" is an attitude and a moral feeling first acquired through such processes of communicative socialization. This implies that the basis for respect can be disturbed if the conditions for developing a sense of self-worth and appreciation from others are lacking. Respect may cease to be an aspect of our life experience under conditions of extreme war and hostility leading to the breakdown of mutuality, or it may shrivel in a culture given to extreme indifference and extreme forms of atomized individualism. (p. 152)

Yet, the possibility of such reciprocal and respectful communication is thrown into doubt by criticisms such as those raised by Ellsworth, cited earlier. If in fact the history of relations of domination among social groups, and among individuals representing them, set inevitable limits on the possibilities of communication and understanding, and if the divergence of experiences among categories of "difference" leads to insurmountable gulfs of mutual incomprehensibility, then dialogue in the sense described here is a fond illusion—or worse, an idealized conceit that overlooks the myriad ways in which marginalized groups are silenced, or feel silenced, by communicative situations they did not create and have no way of altering.

This criticism has been elaborated further by a contemporary postmodern feminist theorist, Iris Young (1990b). Young rejects the very ideal of community, which she argues "privileges unity over difference, immediacy over mediation, sympathy over recognition of the limits of one's understanding of others from their point of view" (p. 300). She also rejects the goal of intersubjective understanding, in which "persons will cease to be opaque, other, not understood, and instead become fused, mutually sympathetic, understanding one another as they understand themselves. . . . Political theorists and activists should distrust this desire for reciprocal recognition and identification with others" (pp. 309, 311). Instead she calls for a "politics of difference," based on what she sees as the positive experiences of "modern urban life." Having criticized previous models of community as "wildly utopian and undesirable," she then posits "a vision of the good society. Our political ideal is the unoppressive city" (pp. 316–317):

City life is the "being together" of strangers. Strangers encounter one another, either face to face or through media, often remaining strangers and yet acknowledging their contiguity in living and the contributions each makes to the others. In such encounters people are not "internally" related, as the community theorists would have it, and do not understand one another from within their own perspective. They are externally related, they experience each other as other, different, from different groups, histories, professions, cultures, which they do not understand. (p. 318)

It is impossible to disagree with Young's call for "celebrating the distinctive cultures and characteristics of different groups" (p. 319). But it is essential to recognize that the very reason for celebrating such differences is based on the ability of different groups to coexist nonviolently and to interact in a way that enriches and invigorates each other's lives. These values *assume* some ability to communicate and coordinate actions across differences. Dale Bauer (1988), presenting a critique similar to Young's, argues that no community of dialogue can "exist without the tension between the marginal and the central" (p. xiii). Such a tension certainly does exist. But there is no reason to assume that dialogue across differences necessarily involves either eliminating those differences or imposing one group's views on others; dialogue that leads to understanding, cooperation, and accommodation can *sustain* differences within a broader compact of toleration and respect. Thus what we need is not a denial of community, but a grounding of community on more flexible and less homogeneous assumptions (Burbules & Rice, 1991).

Here again we see the problems when postmodernism shifts from *problematizing* the conventional assumptions of modern society to *foreclosing* the possibility of achieving certain kinds of understanding or consensus. Interestingly, this willingness to abandon the possibility of pursuing certain kinds of public dialogue is shared by some political theorists coming out of the liberal tradition as well. Bruce Ackerman (1989) has argued, for example, that in cases of deep disagreement or misunderstanding over issues of public concern (for example, contentious moral issues such as abortion), the only alternative is to set such disputes aside and focus instead on points where common agreement is possible, relegating such serious moral debate to the private sphere.

> When you and I learn that we disagree about one or another dimension of the moral truth, we should not search for some common value that will trump the disagreement; nor should we try to translate it into some putatively neutral framework; nor should we seek to transcend it by talking about how some unearthly creature might resolve it. We should simply say *nothing at all* about this disagreement and put the moral ideas that divide us off the conversational agenda of the liberal state. (p. 16)

Admittedly, Ackerman is limiting his argument for "conversational restraint" only to areas where public disagreement has been persistent and where resolution of differences has been shown to be unlikely. He does believe, in general, that public dialogue as a way of understanding and adjudicating competing positions is important to democracy. But his pessimism about reconciling differences in certain cases, and his strong bifurcation of public and private discourse, arguing that different norms and expectations should be applied to each, gives away too much. In response to Ackerman, Benhabib (1989) argues that this model of conversational restraint "imposes arbitrary as opposed to reasonable limits on the content and scope of public dialogue." Instead, she suggests that where there are deep political or power issues that impede the progress of public discourse on closely contended issues, it is precisely a normative theory of discourse, as in the model of communicative ethics described earlier, that allows us the *possibility* (not guarantee) of publicly identifying the ideological and institutional barriers that inhibit mutual understanding and consensus. "The discourse model of legitimacy is reflexive, that is, it allows radical self-questioning; it is critical, which is to say that it allows us to challenge existing forms of power relations that hinder the conversation from being fair, just, or genuinely open" (pp. 145–146).

I will return to this Habermasian model of communication in Chapter 4, but for now two points are worth stressing. The first is that Benhabib's response to Ackerman works equally well as a response to Young's rejection of the possibility or desirability of community. The second is that the superiority of this account of dialogue as a form of political communication is in its ability and willingness to disclose its own premises and standards for critical examination *within* the communicative situation itself. This is preferable to views that relegate such reflexive analysis only to a pristine meta-level discourse, or to a separate domain of activity (for example, only within certain relatively homogeneous subgroups, or only within a discrete sphere of personal and private relations). In the model of discursive ethics

> we can do two things. First, we can allow the conditions of the procedure to be thematized within the dialogue situation itself. The dialogue must be so open that we can even discuss how the rules of dialogue are set up, while seeing, however, that we are in Neurath's boat, that we can throw overboard only some of the planks at certain points in time, but that we cannot remove all the planks of the boat and continue to remain afloat. In other words, even while challenging the rules of dialogue we have to respect some rules to keep the conversation going. Second, we must seek to justify the presuppositions of dialogue in the context of our most explicit assumptions about human nature, history,

and society. . . . I see no way of justifying a dialogic or discursive model of legitimacy . . . without making some strong assumptions about morality and about rationality. (Benhabib, 1989, pp. 147–148)

Hence, it is possible to develop an account of pedagogical communication that responds sympathetically to the issues raised by postmodern critics, without abrogating the possibility and worth of the educational encounter. First, such an account must acknowledge the reality of conflicts and relations of domination that exist in our world and distort the conditions under which communication takes place. Second, it must avoid the twin errors of a fond utopianism or a bitter cynicism; of prejudging the question, either positively or negatively, of whether and how pedagogical communication can succeed (Burbules, 1990). Third, it must focus on the nature and value of the educational *process*, without reifying or constraining the range of possibilities that this process might actually yield in real contexts of practice. Fourth, it must be especially sensitive to the diversity of experience and modes of expression that participants bring to a communicative situation; it cannot assume that people will speak the same way, mean the same things, or share the same concerns when they speak (or, for that matter, that they will feel safe speaking at all). But also, and finally, if it claims to be educational, it cannot give up the aspiration to communicate and understand across differences. While it is often difficult to communicate and understand one another across differences, this very situation stands to teach us the most, since it can bring to our understanding the perspective, values, and experiences of a contrasting point of view. The fundamental tension underlying the dialogical relation is this: We need to be similar enough for communication to happen, but different enough to make it worthwhile (Burbules & Rice, 1991).

Dialogue and Authority

These arguments about power, privilege, and authority also have direct implications for the fundamental question of authority in education. Many feminist authors, for example, have questioned whether there is any conception of legitimate authority that is compatible with the spirit of egalitarian teaching and learning (Friedman, 1985). Ellsworth (1989), as we have seen, reserves some of her sharpest criticisms for attempts to identify an "emancipatory authority" that legitimates the special role and status a teacher may have within critical pedagogy. Ellsworth also identifies another issue: that personal authority in a teaching situation cannot be abstracted from an institutional history and social context that arrogate to the teacher privileges and status to which he or she may not be entitled. The teacher may not desire these, but they are not avoided simply by saying one does not choose or intend them. Ellsworth argues, correctly, I believe, that a more honest stance is to own up to this situation and encourage students to question it, rather than pretending that because one has good intentions one is somehow exempt from criticism. Certainly, the *presumption* of authority, and the privileges and status that go with it, should be avoided even when that authority might be justified on grounds of special knowledge, experience, or expertise.

Yet I do not see how we can avoid some sort of authority in every educational endeavor, no matter how earnestly we strive for egalitarian communicative relations; nor is authority necessarily a threat to such egalitarian relations. We often seek out information from a better-informed source, advice from an experienced mentor, insight from a friend who knows us well, direction from a group facilitator, and so on. These are all instances of authority. While it is essential that credible authority not be taken for granted but be periodically scrutinized and re-established, this scrutiny cannot take place continuously, and at particular moments such authority will be an unstated element in an ongoing dialogical relation. The question ought to be framed: What *types* of educational authority are justified?

The justification of authority in terms of institutional role reifies what are in many cases problematic positions of status and privilege; and justifications of authority in terms of "expertise" are often simply thinly veiled pleas back to institutional status. Here I want to suggest how thinking of dialogue relationally helps to provide more useful criteria for evaluating authority.

At a basic level, a relational attitude toward dialogue involves asking seriously the questions "Who am I?" and "Whom am I speaking with?" On the one hand, it is not enough to frame our position in terms of a particular role ("I'm a teacher") or to justify our authority simply by reference to that role. In many ways, this role arrogates to us privileges and status we do not deserve. At the same time, we must be honest with ourselves about the knowledge, insights, or talents we do possess, and that led us to the educational situation in the first place. It is also important to be honest about the satisfactions we derive from playing a role in others' learning—after all, is that not a primary reason we became teachers?

On the other hand, it is important to understand the perspective of our partners in dialogue: what motivates them to enter into the process; what they stand to learn and what they stand to teach us; what tendencies they might have to defer to us whether we desire it or not; what experiences or contextual factors might interfere with their ability or willingness to enter into a fully mutual communicative partnership with us; and so on.

Beyond the level of individual introspection and reflection, these topics may need to be raised openly within the conversation and discussed as aspects of the relation at hand. In many educational contexts, the critical examination of authority can further the aim of re-examining educational aims and methods. Yet it seems clear that a consensual authority, a respectful deferral to the experience or expertise of our partner, might well emerge from such discussions. I see no reason to *assume* that it cannot, or should not.

Moreover, the nature of any dialogical relation over time is that it is fluid: Roles shift back and forth; patterns of interaction change; various reversals might take place. In dialogue particularly, clear demarcations of teaching moments and learning moments are impossible; so that even if one person is doing all the questioning and the other all the answering (to pick an extreme case), both parties stand to learn. Furthermore, topics within the dialogue change, and this change might mean that a partner more knowledgeable in one area may stand to learn from the other in a different area. This sort of shifting pattern does not mean that there is no authority, but simply that authority cannot be singularly attached to one participant.

Listening is an important aspect of legitimate authority, not only as a way in which one stands to learn something new, but as a concrete relational activity that alters the status of one's authority. Listening exhibits respect, interest, and concern for one's partner. It is a specific way of enabling another's voice to be heard. When it is an active effort, and not just a passive receptivity, it can encourage others to develop and express their own points of view. The dialogical relation also requires sensitivity to the environmental circumstances, institutional contexts, personal histories, or interpersonal dynamics that might impede dialogical participation. It often will not be enough just to listen; one might have to work to create an environment in which a silenced voice feels the confidence or security to speak.

Finally, authority within a dialogical relation must be to some degree self-undermining over time. There may be cases in which a particular claim to authority must be taken at face value, because to demand a complete justification would distract necessary time and attention from a problem at hand. But the aim of dialogue should be to make such cases less frequent over time; to create a situation in which authority as a basis for certain communicative privileges is no longer appropriate—in which, conceivably, one's partners are brought to the point where they reject one's authority or find it no longer necessary for their development. To my way of thinking, an authority that is not in some sense working toward this end runs the risk of taking its own status too seriously. Yet at the same time I would say that a teacher who *can* offer perspectives and insights that would foster the development and autonomy of a partner, but refuses to do so because of a misguided or disingenuous rejection of authority in any form, does the other no good service. Even such choices as encouraging the questioning of one's own authority, or provisionally setting it aside, are decisions that only a person in authority has the latitude to make. Indeed, such choices have the effect they do, in many cases, precisely because it is clear in all parties' minds that they occur within a broader framework in which authority is agreed to.

It seems unquestionable that the very notion of being a teacher entails the claim to some degree of legitimate authority; all the interesting questions arise in examining what justifies that authority, how it can best be exercised for educational purposes, and what limits it should be bounded by. Of course, some problematic assertions of authority will still exist, and the danger is that we will slip back into institutionally reinforced patterns from time to time. There are, for many of us, attractions to being held as an authority, and there are attractions in deferring to others as such. But even where such mistakes are made, students of all ages can be quite resilient and creative in finding ways to deflect unwarranted authority. To assume a devastating and oppressive impact in every problematic assertion of authority is (ironically) to exaggerate the power teachers have in many situations. While we should certainly criticize problematic assertions of authority in others and avoid them ourselves to the degree that we can, at the same time we should not underestimate students by assuming that what we claim is necessarily what they grant us.

Thus, authority in the context of a dialogical relation can have legitimacy, based neither in institutionalized roles and privileges nor in unexamined assumptions about expertise. Nor need it be seen as a static possession of one partner, brought to the dialogical encounter as an a priori condition. Rather, authority should be viewed as growing out of an ongoing communicative interchange that acknowledges differences in knowledge, experience, or ability without reifying them; that allows for changing authority relations over time or from topic to topic; that manifests reciprocity and respect by allowing either party to speak as well as to listen; and that is directed toward an end in which authority no longer needs to be a necessary or appropriate status for *either* participant. Admittedly, our fulfillment of these intentions will be imperfect; as mentioned, an important barrier to this end will be institutional and historical definitions of an authority role that persist even when participants resist them.

In conclusion, a dialogical relation should be aimed toward making authority superfluous; but authority, properly conceived and sensitively exercised, can be a helpful element in attaining that end. Specifically, dialogue as a pedagogical communicative relation constitutes in form and process a practical *repudiation* of hierarchical conceptions of authority: As Michael Oakeshott (1962) says, "Voices that speak in connection do not compose a hierarchy" (p. 198). Instead, authority should be seen as constituted within an ongoing relation, neither preceding nor transcending it. The authority anyone deserves to have is one that can be credibly established and maintained in terms that others grant credence to; an authority that cannot withstand such scrutiny is an authority not worth having.

EMOTIONS AND VIRTUES

In discussing cognitive interests in dialogue, such as gaining knowledge, learning about others or about oneself, or reaching agreements, I have already invoked affective terms such as *concern* and *respect*. In fact, it is impossible in the context of the dialogical relation to treat cognitive and affective topics separately. Part of what draws us into a communicative engagement with others, and what encourages us to persist in this involvement even when it becomes difficult, frustrating, or contentious, is our feeling toward others. Our interests in dialogue are not solely cognitive, and the pleasures we derive from successful dialogue with others are not purely intellectual; yet many accounts of dialogue neglect such emotional factors. Here I would like to examine some of the emotional elements involved in creating and sustaining a successful dialogical relation, in order to clarify the ways in which the participants in a dialogue may need to attend to the feelings of one another, and not only to their ideas.

This problem can be framed, to use John Gumperz's phrase, as one of maintaining "conversational involvement" among the participants in a dialogue (discussed in Tannen, 1989, pp. 9–12). One or more of the partners to a discussion may need to reflect upon, and be aware of, the communicative process itself, and might occasionally need to intervene in order to maintain the quality of the relation, including its emotional style or tone, or in order to keep partners involved in the process. Deborah Tannen (1989) describes the "internal, even emotional connection individuals feel which binds them to other people as well as to places, things, activities, ideas, memories, and words. . . . I see it not as a given but an achievement in conversational interaction" (p. 10). These considerations begin to make the fabric of the relation that joins partners in a dialogue more visible. Many of the comments partners make in a dialogue—encouragements, praise, expressions of gratitude, explicit statements of agreement, and so on—cannot be understood merely as comments on the substance of the discussion, but should be viewed as direct attempts to create and maintain the bonds of mutual concern, trust, respect, appreciation, and affection that are crucial to a successful ongoing dialogical relation.

Emotional Factors in Dialogue

CONCERN. We are involved with our partners in dialogue, interested in them as well as in what they have to say, to a degree that goes beyond the casual level of commitment we have in conversation generally. Because of the intensity with which we regard *this* person, in *this* situation, as someone important to us, this is a bond that has been compared with Martin Buber's I–Thou connection (Buber, 1958; Crowell, 1990; Kean, 1967; Noddings, 1984). We follow what our partners in dialogue are trying to say, we think along with them, we try to imagine matters from their point of view, to a degree that we do not bother with in ordinary speech encounters. We could not, in fact, be this involved in every conversation; it would exhaust us and dissipate our best efforts. Besides, the topics of many casual conversations do not merit such involvement. But in dialogue we endeavor to be fully *with* our partner, and to engage him or her with us, because we recognize that something more is at stake than simply the topic at hand. We are being drawn into a social bond of broader significance to us, namely, the opportunity to be connected to others through ties of mutual empathy and commitment. One of the primary reasons why such concern is important in dialogue is that the unfolding of ideas and understandings takes time; dialogue can be a very "inefficient" way of pursuing information. In order for us to persist with a partner in pursuit of some topic, we need to feel something for the person as well as for the matter at hand.

TRUST. Trust is another emotional factor that partly constitutes the dialogical relation (Freire, 1970). Patricia White (1990) has offered some extremely helpful observations on the role of trust in education. Trust has a belief component (as many emotions do): the belief that you can rely on someone or something where there is an element of risk. But trust also involves a feeling, a commitment, that underlies and strengthens the belief that one can depend on another's goodwill. Two aspects of White's account are especially pertinent here. The first is that trust is at its strongest when no one notices it, when it is an unstated assumption that the parties take for granted. The more attention that needs to be given to establishing and maintaining trust, the more problematic and uncertain the relation is. This is certainly true in the dialogical relation.

A degree of effort usually needs to be made early on, particularly when we are engaged with someone new, to create a context of feeling and commitment in which both participants feel safe to offer up their beliefs, and the experiences or feelings that accompany them, even when they know that they might be disagreed with. Explicit assurances, and implicit (perhaps nonverbal) gestures of sympathetic interest will be part of this process. Another aspect of developing trust is initiating certain sensitive or personal disclosures ourselves, demonstrating trust before we ask others to trust us. Eventually, White says, these sorts of conscious efforts should no longer be necessary; it is a sign of something uncertain and untrusting when they are. The significance of the dialogical relation, once it is established and catches us up in the spirit of exchange, is that trust can become an unquestioned background condition, something that might need occasional reinforcement, but that most of the time literally goes without saying (see also Thomas, 1989).

The second aspect of White's account that is especially pertinent to dialogue is the context of risk in which trust is necessary. We are generally concerned with trust as an emotional bond where the reliability of another person is something we need to depend on. As Steven Crowell (1990) explains, for Gadamer this risk is entailed as soon as we disclose our prejudices to one another.

Dialogical inquiry [involves] an essential "selflessness" of the partners, that is, a freedom from purely rhetorical intentions of persuasion, a mutual readiness to place at risk the fundamental prejudices for taken-for-granted (truths) that are nevertheless held fast as enabling initial approach to "the issue." The expression for such selflessness, this putting oneself into play at risk, is the dialectic of question and answer.

. . . [Dialogue consists] in the symmetrical movement toward a fusion
of horizons between reciprocally self-effacing participants who "risk"
inherited prejudices within a common interrogative orientation toward
the truth. (pp. 344, 347)

There are other risks at stake in dialogue, as well. We trust our partners to keep certain things that we say in confidence; we trust our
partners to withhold judgment upon some of our comments, at least
initially; yet we also trust them to tell us honestly what they think
and feel about a topic, even if it disagrees with us. In many ways
the fundamental risk in dialogue, especially perhaps in educational
contexts, is the risk of extending ourselves outward conversationally,
endeavoring to express as well as we can a point of view, belief,
feeling, or experience in the expectation that our partner will respond
thoughtfully and sympathetically, but not knowing if they will. The
dialogical relation needs to be developed over time so that we can
establish and sustain this confidence in the reliability of our partners,
and they in us.

RESPECT. As mentioned earlier, Benhabib (1989) discusses the
importance of respect in the dialogical relation, which is more important than equality, or sameness, in maintaining an "egalitarian
reciprocity" among participants. This point cannot be stressed too
strongly: People will not know the same things, or the same amount;
they will not always agree with one another, or always understand
one another. If exact similarity or compatibility were necessary for
dialogue, it would rarely happen. But in place of these, respect for
one another can sustain the relation even in the face of sharp differences in knowledge, value, or belief. Freire (1970) discusses repeatedly the importance of maintaining this attitude of respect toward
one's partners in dialogue; that even when there are substantial differences, say, in formal educational attainment, we recognize that we
stand to learn from and with one another. Respecting one's partner
and, for that matter, respecting oneself are conditions that make us
believe in the worth of carrying on dialogue in the first place. Since
the essential nature of the dialogical relation is one of give and take,
of questioning and being questioned, we will submit to this only if
we believe, and feel, that we have both something to offer and something to gain.

Respect is also a factor in why we often grant to our partners an
initial benefit of the doubt, in considering what they say, even when
we disagree with them. If we did not do this, certain points of view

would never even make it into the conversational arena. However, it is not simply respect for the other that we seek to cultivate: It is also their respect for us, and our respect for ourselves. Dialogue can be destroyed by assertions of authority that force respect into a one-way mode and diminish the self-respect of partners over time. Such assertions lessen the ability and willingness of others to continue in a fully dialogical interaction, and hence are self-defeating from an educational standpoint.

APPRECIATION. An emotion closely related to respect is appreciation: valuing the unique qualities that others bring to a dialogical encounter and feeling an esteem for them. Like concern and trust, respect and appreciation may to some extent precede the dialogue, but they also stand to be enhanced over time as the dialogue develops. Appreciation is a factor that seems especially important in contexts of difference, culturally or otherwise. If we are to go beyond mere "tolerance" for such differences, to actually valuing them on their own terms, and being interested in learning from them, a feeling of appreciation must play some role.

AFFECTION. A sentiment that does not receive as much attention in educational writings as it should is affection, a feeling with and for our partners (Alston, 1991). For those of us who are educators, there is a strongly ingrained commitment to offer every student a common level of effort, regardless of our personal feelings. Yet honest reflection tells us that there are cases where we are willing to exert an exceptional degree of effort because of an affection that we feel for some students but not for others. Nowhere is this clearer than in dialogue. The dialogical relation involves a drawing together of two or more persons, and there is no reason to pretend that this does not involve elements of liking one another, or even more. Freire (1970) stresses that love is an element in all true dialogue, and while that may be overstating the point somewhat, it does acknowledge the general point that some feeling of affection is a condition of dialogue, one that can grow and develop over time. Certainly this is true of dialogue in the context of friendships, family ties, and other personal relations.

Mary Field Belenky and her coauthors (1986) make a similar point when they emphasize the feeling of connectedness that underlies certain conversational encounters. They stress the ways in which this connectedness affects the substance and form of the conversational process; specifically, where participants make a special effort to listen

sympathetically to what their partners have to say, suspending judgment at least until they feel they have grasped the point being made
from the other's point of view—in Peter Elbow's (1986) phrase, playing the "believing game." While this effort to grant a respectful plausibility to others' beliefs and values, and to cultivate a degree of
empathy in our regard for others, is a general virtue, we must admit
that we exercise this more carefully and conscientiously when we
are dealing with those for whom we have some real affection. Such
affection may run only in one direction, although obviously the relation will be more enduring when it is mutual.

As I will detail later, Belenky and coauthors (1986), as well as
Tannen (1990), make the point that creating this feeling of connectedness and intimacy often involves conversational content that might
seem trivial or marginal to the matter at hand, but that is valuable
from the perspective of establishing the quality of relation that makes
the exploration of that matter possible. One example, they say, is
gossip.

These emotional bonds of concern, trust, respect, appreciation,
and affection influence why we are drawn to and remain in a dialogical relation, as well as shaping the particular ways we choose to act
within it. Most of all, they are a substantial part of the benefit we
derive from dialogue, since these are pleasing emotions to feel toward
others, and to have others feel toward us.

HOPE. Finally, an attitude that is not purely emotional, but is
also pertinent to successful dialogue, is hope. We enter into, and
persist in, an ongoing dialogical relation because we see in it the
possibility of new insights and understandings, as well as a connection between us and others. Yet we should be wary of the teleological
view of dialogue discussed earlier, in which the guarantee of a "pay-
off" is the justification for engaging in dialogue in the first place.
Hope helps to reconcile this apparent paradox: Feeling hopefulness,
we work toward possible outcomes of understanding, and persist
even when the path becomes difficult or uncertain, without the promise of success. As Gadamer (1982) and Freire (1970) both note, hope
is an essential component of dialogue, because the process of discussion so often does *not* have a clear terminus, and because there is so
often much to discourage us from embarking on the journey at all
(lack of time, initial barriers of misunderstanding, difficult conflicts,
uncertain prospects for success, and so on). Because the dialogical
relation typically changes and takes shape only over time, participants must adopt a willing forward-looking attitude in their assess-

ment of whether the discussion is worth their while. In the short run, dialogue may prove unsuccessful; hope, as well as a general goodwill toward one another, motivates partners to give the interaction time to succeed:

> [Dialogue] sees the relations between various discourses as those of strands in a possible conversation, a conversation which presupposes no disciplinary matrix which unites the speakers, but where the hope of agreement is never lost so long as the conversation lasts. This hope is not a hope for the discovery of antecedently existing common ground, but *simply* hope for agreement, or, at least, exciting and fruitful disagreement. (Rorty, 1979, p. 318)

These feelings—concern, trust, respect, appreciation, affection, and hope—are crucial to the bond that sustains a dialogical relation over time (of course, there may be others; I don't claim that this is an exhaustive list). While most of what has been written on dialogue stresses what we can teach or learn through it, this specifically cognitive interest is not all that attracts us to the dialogical encounter, or keeps us in it when it becomes difficult or contentious. Sometimes we speak and listen for other reasons, and educational gains come as a side benefit. To the extent that we view these as positive emotions to feel, or to have others feel toward us, we naturally seek out occasions to cultivate and express them. One of these is through dialogue.

Communicative Virtues and Dialogue

Tullio Maranhão (1990), drawing from the work of Bakhtin, Buber, and Maurice Levinas, identifies dialogue in an "ethics of answerability . . . of respect to otherness and of disclosure of identity. . . . From an ethical point of view the heart of dialogue lies in the relation between Self and Other, not in particular manifestations" (p. 16). These qualities of communicative openness and respect can be identified with an ideal of *reasonableness* (Burbules, 1991a, 1992). As Stephen Toulmin (1990) notes, for example, for sixteenth-century humanists this was an inclusive virtue of thought and conduct: "On the one hand, this meant developing modesty about one's capacities and self-awareness in one's self-presentation. . . . On the other hand, it required toleration of social, cultural, and intellectual diversity. It was unreasonable to condemn out of hand people with institutions, customs, or ideas different from ours" (pp. 199–200). Richard Rorty (1987) makes a similar point when he distinguishes rationality as a "method" from rationality as a set of "moral virtues": "toler-ance, respect for the opinions of those around one, willingness to listen, reliance on persuasion rather than force" (p. 40). These varied perspectives ground reason in aspects of character that we manifest when we conduct ourselves in communicative relations with others. What are these virtues?

The communicative virtues are general dispositions and practices that help support successful communicative relations with a variety of people over time. They include such qualities as tolerance, pa-tience, an openness to give and receive criticism, the inclination to admit that one may be mistaken, the desire to reinterpret or translate one's own concerns in a way that makes them comprehensible to others, the self-imposition of restraint in order that others may have a turn to speak, and—often neglected as a key element in dialogue—the willingness and ability to listen thoughtfully and attentively. As a process, dialogue requires a willingness to re-examine our own presuppositions and to compare them with those of others; to be-come less dogmatic about the belief that the way the world appears to us is necessarily the way the world is. These virtues shape one's capacities both to express one's own beliefs, values, and feelings accurately, and to listen to and hear those of others (Freire, 1985a). Yet these cannot be seen simply as properties of individual character. While it is persons who express these virtues (or fail to), through their actions, these virtues need to be seen as social properties, ex-pressed in the contexts of relations that connect persons; for example, I am a better listener when I am with some friends than with others.

These virtues are fostered and developed in the kinds of commu-nicative relations in which we are engaged, as children and into adult life. Learning rules and explicit injunctions (such as to "tell the truth") only partly help shape the same dispositions and patterns of conduct, as do more deep-lying virtues of character (such as "truth-fulness"). Virtues are attitudinal as well as behavioral. One acquires virtues not upon being told to do so, but through association with others who are similarly disposed. Virtues are acquired in relations and improved by practice; we develop virtues through coming to value and aspire to them, not by being trained in certain habits.

The communicative virtues, specifically, are developed in rela-tions with others who treat us and each other in certain ways (listen-ing carefully, explaining patiently, and so on), and who help to make explicit what they are doing and why. Hence, to develop the com-municative virtues is to be drawn into certain kinds of communica-tive relations. Because the development of these virtues is time-consuming, deeply personal, and intertwined with other emotional as well as intellectual factors, formal educational settings are not well equipped to develop these virtues when they are lacking. Typically, they are developed by family relations and friendships outside the school (which means that for many students they are barely developed at all). Yet if we are earnest in wanting to create dialogical relations with our students, and with others, there is little choice but to continue to model these practices ourselves, hoping to "catch up" prospective partners in the spirit of conversation.

Having emphasized the role of virtues as a condition of a successful dialogical relation, I do not want to reify these virtues or turn them into universal absolutes. The communicative virtues are to a degree context-sensitive. The conditions under which speech encounters take place foster or inhibit the development of the communicative virtues. Hence the failure to exercise certain virtues in certain contexts cannot automatically be attributed to personal shortcomings. In situations where histories of domination or alienation have harmed individuals from certain groups—situations that actively discouraged or punished the exercise of certain virtues—the burden of criticism ought to be on the context, more than on the flawed character it has produced. So, for example, while one would identify an openness to critical questions from others as generally a communicative virtue, this might be simply too much to ask from persons who have been psychologically demoralized to the point where any such criticism is regarded as a threat.

As Aristotle (1973) was famous for noting, the exercise of what might be a virtue in one context can be a vice when its exercise is exaggerated, or extended to inappropriate contexts. One can listen too much, without committing oneself to a position; one can bend over backward too far to avoid judging or disagreeing with others; one can stretch impartiality to the point that it becomes unfeeling. The point of these considerations is that the appropriateness of the communicative virtues to a specific dialogical situation is not a straightforward determination. A sensitivity to context and the effects of speech helps us to judge prudently when and how the communicative virtues are appropriate. It is the nature of virtues (as opposed to rule-following) to be selective, fitted to the circumstances and the particular persons at hand. Some people will exercise such judgments more wisely than others.

This observation turns us to the problem of which general conditions do and do not foster the development of the communicative virtues. The act of dialogical teaching, specifically, will often be concerned with finding ways to create these conditions, albeit within a limited sphere. David Bridges (1988a) discusses the importance of fostering a particular "moral culture" in the classroom, one that encourages and supports reasonableness, peaceableness, truthfulness, freedom of participation, equality, and mutual respect (pp. 21–24). Such a climate can, within specific arenas, be established within our educational system. While a teacher's efforts are not all-determining in this regard, making the pursuit of such a moral culture an open topic for discussion can often encourage participants to consider the ways in which they are or are not living up to these standards themselves. Reflection on communicative processes is one of the ways in which a group of disassociated individuals can begin to form itself as more of a dialogical community.

But communication alone does not create or sustain a sense of community; nor can it always override contexts where institutional or ideological factors inhibit participation (R. Bernstein, 1983). Various aspects of our social world have created contexts in which persons, as individuals or as representatives of certain groups, perceive (sometimes mistakenly, often rightly) that their interests are in fundamental conflict with those of others who confront them. These conflicting interests are one of the pathologies of a social system established on the basis of power and unquestioned privilege (Burbules, 1986). The genesis and nature of that social system is not my concern here. But given this reality it is fond naivete to believe that, if persons possess the communicative virtues, goodwill and persistent effort will allow them to cross all barriers of misunderstanding and prejudice.

In place of the conditions of conflicting interests that a power system engenders, it is possible to establish alternative communities (or subcommunities) based on communication and a sense of *solidarity*—by which I mean relations of mutual concern and consideration, cooperation in practical activities, and adjudication of conflicts by means of participatory democratic processes. Rorty (1989) describes this solidarity as an enlarging and encompassing conversation, in which disparate voices and points of view are respected; it is a community that unites "the 'we' of the people who have been brought up to distrust ethnocentrism" (p. 198). Solidarity in this sense, as my comments on Young suggest, is not threatened by contexts of diversity. This sort of political ideal merits extended treatment on its own; here I mention it only to refer to a broad social and political background condition for the pursuit of successful communication through dialogue.

> If solidarity consists of coordinating one's actions with actions of an-
> other . . . it also consists of a positive acknowledgment of the other,
> a due sign that one has taken cognizance of the actions of the other
> and has comprehended their "meaning." . . . Simultaneously . . . dia-
> logues suggest indexically that solidarity is present in the specific lin-
> guistic interaction in which it is employed; that is, they are also "models
> for" solidarity. (Urban, 1990, p. 109)

Hence the topic of virtues draws us into a much broader consideration of the kind of society we live in, and the kind of society
we desire. Emphasizing the primacy of the dialogical relation, and
situating that relation in the web of social relations within which we
feel, perceive, and act toward one another, forces us to reconsider
the pedagogical problem of fostering dialogue as a social and political
problem, challenging the institutional and ideological contexts that
impede dialogue, and changing them, or at least creating sustainable
alternatives to them.

> If we are really to appropriate this central idea to our historical situation,
> it will point us toward important practical and political tasks. It would
> be a gross distortion to imagine that we might conceive of the entire
> political realm organized on the principle of dialogue or conversation,
> considering the fragile conditions that are required for genuine dialogue
> and conversation. Nevertheless, if we think out what is required for
> such dialogue based on mutual understanding, respect, a willingness to
> listen and test one's opinions and prejudices, a mutual seeking of the
> correctness of what is said, we will have defined a powerful regulative
> ideal that can orient our practical and political lives. If the quintessence
> of what we are is to be dialogical—and this is not just the privilege of
> the *few*—then whatever the limitations of the practical realization of this
> ideal, it nevertheless can and should give practical orientation to our
> lives. We must ask, what is it that blocks and prevents such dialogue,
> and what is to be done . . . to make such genuine dialogue a concrete
> reality. (R. Bernstein, 1983, pp. 162–163)

Fostering successful dialogical relations is an essential aspect of this
process of social change, but is not all of it (Barber, 1984).

The development of the communicative virtues is a process involving nothing less than the transformation of our ways of relating
to one another, our traditions, and our educational priorities. Making
such personal qualities as tolerance, patience, or the willingness and
ability to listen into *primary* educational objectives has enormous implications for the organization of classrooms, our assumptions about

curriculum and instruction, and the relation between school and home (where many of these virtues are actually developed). The most basic aspect of this educational task, I believe, is to become clearer and more explicit about the norms of honesty, clarity, empathy, and respect that are inherent in our very attempt to communicate with one another. These sorts of communicative standards are exemplified in their purest form in the activity of dialogue, and specifically in the formation and maintenance of the dialogical relation. We acquire an appreciation for these values, and learn to express them conscientiously in our own speech acts, through the relations in which we are raised as children, through our friendships, and through a few public communicative activities that begin with our families and gradually extend outward to our neighborhoods, communities, and beyond. Needless to say, there are more negative examples of these relations than there are positive ones. Yet it is the peculiarly self-reflexive character of fostering the communicative virtues that we can develop them only by seeking out and sustaining better alternatives, and drawing participants into them, thereby enhancing their capacities and our own in the endeavor of carrying dialogue further.

Thus, the most complex problem in the formation and maintenance of a dialogical relation concerns aspects of character among the participants themselves. For all that can be said about explicit patterns of verbal interaction, the fundamental success of a dialogical encounter springs from the personalities, values, and habits of the participants themselves, with all their strengths and flaws. Much more needs to be said about these virtues than is possible in this book; aside from the fact that they strongly shape the conduct of participants in dialogue, they constitute significant educational aims in their own right (see Burbules & Rice, 1992; Rice & Burbules, 1993).

CREATING AND SUSTAINING
THE DIALOGICAL RELATION

Maintaining what Gumperz, cited earlier, called "conversational involvement" is particularly important in teaching, where a mutual concern and involvement are needed to counterbalance the potentially critical or conflictual tone of questions, challenges, or counterarguments. Dialogue without challenges or disagreements is impoverished, but challenges or disagreements without an underlying relation of personal commitment will break down the communicative process very quickly. I have already discussed the role of emotional bonds in maintaining this commitment, but as the dialogical relation develops over time it becomes a bond of association in itself. The participants come to feel independent and compatible (but not necessarily identical) motivations for coming to the dialogical encounter and remaining in it.

> What, then, is talk viewed interactionally? It is an example of that arrangement by which individuals come together and sustain matters having a ratified, joint, current, and running claim upon attention, a claim which lodges them together in some sort of intersubjective, mental world. (Goffman, 1983, pp. 70–71)

> Dialogue provides the particulars by which listeners and speakers collaborate in imagining and participating in similar worlds. (Tannen, 1989, p. 173)

In this context, the very dichotomy of cognitive and emotional interests begins to break down.

Dialogue, viewed in this strong relational sense, rather than as a fixed pattern of speech acts, reveals a *developmental, diachronic* nature. Dialogues change over time; they move through different phases or stages; they take shape gradually as the participants discover more about the communicative process, about each other, and about the topic at hand. Often a conversation starts off with one pattern of interaction, but shifts to another: A discussion can *become* dialogical, or it can start off as a dialogue but turn into something else (an argument, for example). Reflecting on the range of factors that help support a successful dialogical relation, as well as those that inhibit it, helps us in recognizing where our conversations might fall short of that ideal and what we can try to do about it. Of course, such knowledge, and the efforts that grow out of it, carry no guarantee of success in creating or sustaining a dialogical relation, even where all parties concerned are motivated by goodwill.

Considering further the activities by which we establish the dialogical relation, we might pursue what Tannen (1989) calls "involvement strategies": various communicative acts intended to shape the substance of what one has to say with one's partner in mind, and meant to strengthen the sense of connection between interlocutors. In other words, acts such as restating what one's partner has just said, using analogies that will resonate with the other's experience, internal cross-referencing within the conversation (for example, "This is similar to what you were discussing earlier"), using vivid imagery, using humor, volunteering significant new information, and other activities all provide examples of how certain speech acts within a dialogue have effects at both cognitive and affective levels—they communicate messages about meaning, but they also establish a feeling of intimacy and connectedness. In such activities (some of which may be nonverbal as well), the interdependence of understanding and empathy becomes clear.

There are also extra-communicative experiences that underlie and can help sustain an ongoing dialogical relation, and I can only sketch them here. The activities that we share in, the aesthetic and cultural formations we have experienced in common, coincidences of proximity or parallelism (having the same middle name, as Kurt Vonnegut once pointed out), a network of indirect social relations that connect us to others—all can have an impact on whether we see a value in entering a communicative situation with someone else, or remaining in it when the conversation becomes difficult. In many contexts, creating some commonality of *extra*-communicative associations (for example, working on something together, undergoing a particular experience at the same time, noting common friends, and so on) may be a condition of establishing and maintaining the right atmosphere. In teaching contexts, such commonalities of practice, experience, or association may be indispensable as facilitators to dialogue, and teachers may need to find ways to invoke them as part of fostering a dialogical relation with, or among, students.

Considering dialogue diachronically and developmentally also implies that certain accommodations may be necessary in the short term for the sake of creating a relation that can evolve differently over time—accommodations that in themselves might not conform to ideal patterns of communication (such as withholding certain points of view or avoiding some relevant but intimidating topics). Developmental considerations, judged in context, might override strict application of identical rules of participation to each participant at every step along the way. Nevertheless it is also important to recognize that such short-term concessions do not characterize the dialogical relation we eventually want to have. If such an aim is not kept in mind, short-term compromises could simply create new imbalances or encourage participants not to come to grips with challenges that they eventually need to confront and consider.

For this reason, it is important in an ongoing dialogical relation to articulate and defend the aim of creating a more fully participatory and egalitarian dialogue. The connotations of the term *dialogue* itself have a particular normative influence that helps strengthen the association people feel between one another, even when there is relatively little else to draw them together (as when political leaders of nations in conflict insist on the need for "dialogue" to resolve disputes).

> *Dialogue* is a culturally and historically specific way of conceiving of certain verbal transactions and as such has considerable rhetorical force. . . . It suggests friendship, mutuality, authenticity—an egalitarian relationship. So understood, dialogue not only describes such relations but *can* create the illusion of such relations where they do not exist. (Crapanzano, 1990, p. 270)

What Vincent Crapanzano calls "the ideology of dialogue" is accurate, I believe, in all but one respect: The rhetorical force that the concept of dialogue carries does not simply create the *illusion* of such relations (although like any normative term it can be used ideologically). To the extent that it helps draw participants into such relations, and the communicative interactions they support, it can promote the *actual* development of these relations, to the point where they do become self-sustaining.

Here again we see the reflexive character of the dialogical relation: that we develop our capacities for creating and maintaining such a relation only by being in it, and so must work with, and within, at least some of the relations we have available to us. Waiting for ideal conditions in which to pursue or express these values means that we will be waiting a terribly long time. This bootstrapped process is the essential problematic of learning in and through dialogue. We teach our partners, they teach us, and we each teach ourselves in the context of sustaining and developing the dialogical relations we actually have. We improve by imitating, practicing, and experimenting in the midst of real-time activities. In this way, I would suggest, learning to engage in dialogue successfully is like learning a game.

CHAPTER 3

Playing the Dialogue Game

Play can be serious, as well as fun. As Hans-Georg Gadamer (1982) has discussed, play (*spiel*) arises in a variety of contexts: We play musical instruments, we play games, and we play roles. We can play with a purpose in mind—to win, to impress, to make a point—or we can play frivolously, "just for fun." Gadamer also notes more unusual uses: the play of a door on its hinges, or the play of light on the surface of water. What makes these all instances of playing? Gadamer identifies the essence of all play in a "to-and-fro" motion.

> If we examine how the word "play" is used and concentrate on its so-called transferred meanings we find talk of the play of light, the play of waves, the play of a component in a bearing-case, the inter-play of limbs, the play of forces, the play of gnats, even a play on words. In each case what is intended is the to-and-fro movement which is not tied to any goal which would bring it to an end. . . . The movement backwards and forwards is obviously so central for the definition of a game that it is not important who or what performs this movement. . . . The play is the performance of the movement as such. (p. 93)

In this chapter I will explore the metaphor of playing at dialogue and describe dialogue as a kind of game. As with other things that we play, dialogue constitutes a relation in which spontaneity and creativity are possible. In the to-and-fro of exchanged comments and responses, dialogue builds upon itself to reach new and unexpected results—and this can give us pleasure and delight. We appreciate dialogue even when we are challenged, puzzled, or disturbed by it. As in other kinds of play, we enjoy dialogue most when we are fully engrossed in the activity, and because we enjoy it, we seek ways to keep it going. In its purest forms dialogue becomes intrinsic; we are carried forward in the dynamic of the to-and-fro movement without regard for any particular goal or end point.

Both Gadamer and Johan Huizinga (1950) have argued that in the phenomenon of play we discover something deep, enduring, and universal about human experience: for Gadamer (1982), the basis of "aesthetic consciousness" (pp. 91–99, 446, 453); for Huizinga (1950), a sense of the sacred (pp. 14–27). I would like to begin by contrasting the similarities and differences of their accounts, then play out some larger implications of their analyses for understanding dialogue.

THE SIGNIFICANCE OF PLAY

For Gadamer (1982), the most striking fact about play as a human phenomenon is that when we are drawn fully into it, it ceases to be a simple matter that we are playing—in his conception, *play happens*, and when we are *at play*, we are caught up in the appreciation of the play as both actor and acted-upon.

> We say that something is "playing" somewhere or at some time, that something is going on. . . . This linguistic observation seems to be an indirect indicator that play is not to be understood as a kind of activity. As far as language is concerned, the actual subject of play is obviously not the subjectivity of the individual who among other activities also plays, but instead the play itself. . . . This suggests a general characteristic of the way in which the nature of play is reflected in an attitude of play: all playing is a being-played. The attraction of a game, the fascination it exerts, consists precisely in the fact that the game tends to master its players. (pp. 93–95)

Consider situations in which we play. In theatre, an actor plays a role or character, and invests it with his or her unique personality and style. But the character to some extent exerts its own independence over the interpretive discretion of the actor; it will not be played in just any way. The actor must interact with the script, the direction, and the influence of other characters, if he or she is to inhabit fully the role being played.

In music, there is usually a script as well (the musical score), and this very structure makes interpretation or improvisation possible; the musician plays an instrument, or sings, but can be taken over by the music. In ensemble playing, there is the active interplay of different voices or instruments, each responding to and influencing the other, with a net result beyond what any single musician alone could achieve. One can even have a sense of discovery and surprise in hearing music that one plays oneself.

Similarly, in a game we can very quickly lose track of time and place; we forget the score, forget winning or losing, forget the last game or the next game, and simply *play*. Whatever the game, this is the moment we play for. While many games are organized around winning and losing (unlike some other things that we play), it is not the goal of winning or losing that gives us pleasure *at the moment that we play*. Indeed, we are all familiar with the experience of becoming so competitive, so concerned with winning or losing, that a game ceases to be enjoyable. We have stopped playing, really, and started judging the pleasure of what we are doing against an external standard, which undermines the sense of play.

These examples illustrate the principles that, for Gadamer, underlie our appreciation for and involvement in art: that when we create, perceive, or participate in an artistic endeavor we are caught up in something beyond us, something that plays us. Our delight in art derives from the simultaneous perception that what we behold also represents us back to ourselves, because we see in it not only what is before us but also the process by which we see something in it. Aesthetic consciousness is fundamentally playful, for Gadamer, in this to-and-fro between perceiver, creator, or participant, and the artistic object or process. *Art happens.* In our epiphanic moments, says Gadamer, appreciation and involvement pass over into *absorption,* and we lose a separate sense of ourselves at the precise instant when we feel most fully pleasured and alive.

Huizinga (1950) has quite different ideas about the significance of play in human culture. While Gadamer identifies in play some of our most basic and enduring human qualities, Huizinga stresses the *discontinuity* between play and other human activities: Play "resists all analysis, all logical interpretation" and resists "any attempt to reduce it to other terms" (pp. 3, 6). Huizinga mystifies play, investing it with a quasi-religious aura, tying it to related concepts such as ritual: "In the form and function of play itself, an independent entity which is senseless and irrational, man's [sic] consciousness that he is embedded in a sacred order of things finds its first, highest, and holiest expression" (p. 17). Unfortunately, this way of thinking about play, setting it apart into a realm all its own and investing it with mystical significance, does not help to illuminate the continuity between play activities and other aspects of human life, or to explain its appeal for us in terms of more ordinary concepts, such as interest, pleasure, and engrossment; in this regard Gadamer's account is, I believe, more fruitful.

Nevertheless, Huizinga's account of play is rich in perception. He stresses the voluntary aspect of play; that we must choose to play, if it is to be truly enjoyable (see King, 1987). He mentions, as Gadamer does, the capacity of play to "run away with the players" (pp. 7–8). He notes how play can create an aesthetic sense of orderliness and beauty: "Play has a tendency to be beautiful. . . . Play casts a spell over us; it is 'enchanting,' 'captivating.' It is invested with the noblest qualities we are capable of perceiving in things: rhythm and harmony" (p. 10). Huizinga also notes the essential aspects of tension, uncertainty, chanciness, and risk that are part of play, and discusses examples such as puzzles, gambling, or target shooting, which are goal-oriented. Yet one might note that some of these are traditionally masculine forms of playing, and that other qualities might be stressed when we think of more traditionally feminine forms, such as "playing house" or "playing dress-up," in which the performative quality, the sense of cooperatively participating in the representation of something sophisticated and "grown-up," overrides more goal-oriented purposes. Gadamer's account, I think, gives us a better grasp on these performative and representational aspects of play. Yet Huizinga is quite correct in pointing out the way in which play often involves "playing off of," or responding to, a resistant form, pattern, or counter-activity, an attempt to transform it or master it (as in climbing). We often take delight in the solution of something complex, strange, or difficult. (How else do we explain the peculiar appeal of jigsaw puzzles and why, for example, once we have put a puzzle together, we lay it aside and put together another one, even though it is substantially similar to the first?)

Finally, Huizinga revealingly analyzes the formation of a "play community," the constitution of a deep relation to the others who play with us (even if we are competing against them). Because our mutual goal is to make play happen, each for our own pleasure, if also for the other's, we implicitly agree to conduct ourselves in certain ways so that the activity can go forward. From examples as simple as children on a playground to actors in a theatre, it is easy to see the many ways in which players must coordinate their efforts with each other, responding to each other, in order for play to be successful and pleasurable for all. Hence, as Huizinga stresses, we can then understand the peculiar threat that the "cheat" and the "spoilsport" pose to the maintenance of this play community, and the unified will with which they are ostracized.

I suspect it is already becoming clear to the reader how much of this analysis of play is pertinent to the topic of dialogue. But before turning to that topic in detail, one manifestation of play merits a bit more examination: the notion of a game, and the rules that define and govern it.

PLAYING GAMES

As noted earlier, there are many things that we play, and playing is revealed in different ways in these varied contexts; games are only one such context, and even within this context there are different sorts of game. But the analogy of a game is particularly helpful for discussing issues of language and conversation, for several reasons. First, what Gadamer (1982) calls the interactive or to-and-fro movement of play is frequently expressed in games; this relational aspect is also revealed in verbal interactions such as dialogue. In fact, Gadamer goes so far as to say that "there is an ultimate sense in which you cannot have a game by yourself. In order for there to be a game, there always has to be, not necessarily literally another player, but something else with which the player plays and which automatically responds to his move with a counter-move" (p. 95). Games usually involve some degree of contention or resistance: against an opponent, against a physical obstacle, against time, or against the laws of probability. Hence the give-and-take of dialogue can be illuminated by reflecting upon the particular way in which playing a game involves anticipating and responding to a partner. Second, the nature of the relation that binds us to other players within a game, and the capacity of this relation to absorb us fully, to the point where "we are played" by the game, illustrates nicely the aspects of dialogue that are beyond us; the ways in which we lose a distinct and separate sense of self in the midst of an engaging, ongoing activity. Finally, a game is a play activity that is partly structured by rules and moves; ways of conducting oneself that move the game forward and contribute to playing it well. Communication also can be usefully described in these terms.

Probably the most famous analysis of this game analogy is Wittgenstein's discussion of *language games* and attendant issues, such as how we learn to play a game, what role rules play in this learning, and so on. Wittgenstein (1958) argues that there is no single definition that defines all games; rather, in a famous series of passages he discusses several different examples of games, and concludes:

> The result of this examination is: we see a complicated network of similarities, overlapping and criss-crossing: sometimes overall similarities, sometimes similarities of detail. I can think of no better expression to characterize these similarities than "family resemblances"; for the various resemblances between members of a family: build, features, color of eyes, gait, temperament, etc. etc. overlap and criss-cross in the same way.—And I shall say: "games" form a family. (pp. 3, 31–32)

Hence, Wittgenstein never offers a clear, specific description of what he means by a game. He asks, "What does it mean to know what a game is? What does it mean to know it and not be able to say it?" If one asks for a strict definition, Wittgenstein says:

> How should we explain to him what a game is? I imagine that we should describe different *games* to him, and we might add: "This *and similar things* are called 'games.'" . . . One might say that the concept "game" is a concept with blurred edges.—"But is a blurred concept a concept at all?"—Is an indistinct photograph a picture of a person at all? Is it even always an advantage to replace an indistinct picture with a sharp one? Isn't the indistinct one often exactly what we need? (pp. 35, 33–34)

To my mind, this is brilliant philosophy. Wittgenstein asks us to abandon the traditional philosophical assumptions that whatever we know we must know precisely and that imprecision in language is a mark of ignorance. Instead, he suggests that a degree of uncertainty and indefiniteness is inevitable, and often desirable, since the purpose of language is to suit *our* purposes, not vice versa. Effective communication does not always require strict reference to discrete objects in the world (the paradigm of positivistic philosophy)—indeed, for many things we need to communicate about, such as emotional states, strict accuracy is neither possible nor desirable.

Similarly, Gadamer (1982) says that different games have different objects, and certain games do not have a distinct object or goal at all. Sometimes we aim toward ending the game by winning, and sometimes we aim toward continuing the game because playing it is fun whether we win or not. Some games are contests; others are more cooperative in nature. There is a different *spirit* to each sort of game, Gadamer says, depending on the rules and structures that define it: "The characteristic lightness and sense of relief which we find in the attitude of play depends on the particular character of the task set by the game, and comes from solving it" (pp. 95–97).

For both Wittgenstein and Gadamer, the analysis of a game leads us back to the analysis of a *rule*. Rules are often thought to connote rigid injunctions that determine the boundaries of acceptable conduct in any field. But when these authors say that games have rules, they mean something quite different—and it will be in this sense that I will suggest, in Chapter 4, that the dialogue game has "rules." Wittgenstein (1958) typically wants to emphasize the many different roles that a rule can play in a game.

> The rule may be an aid in teaching the game. The learner is told it and given practice in applying it.—Or it is an instrument of the game itself.—

Or a rule is employed neither in the teaching nor in the game itself; nor is it set down in a list of rules. One learns the game by watching how others play. But we say that it is played according to such-and-such rules because an observer can read these rules off from the practice of the game. . . . One can also imagine someone's learning the game without ever learning or formulating the rules. (pp. 26–27, 15)

Notice that the significance of this analysis of rules for Wittgenstein is that it helps explain how one *learns* to play a game. But how can we reconcile his refusal to reify any particular set of rules as necessary or essential to the game with his view that "the game is supposed to be defined by the rules" (pp. 150–151)? Wittgenstein argues that a game does not require strictly codified rules; that it is impossible to formulate a finite set of rules that would anticipate every possible instance for their application. Yet a rule in the sense of an *ideal* or *hypothesis* is necessary for learning a game or conducting oneself within it. A rule for Wittgenstein is a "way of proceeding"; it is a guess or prediction about how activities are ordered within a larger process. We witness a sequence of events or actions, and when we think we see a pattern that accounts for them, we say, "Now I know how to go on." Such a hypothesis may not take the form of an explicitly formulated general rule. What matters for Wittgenstein is that we can conduct ourselves successfully within a given activity. Explicit knowledge of rules may or may not be a necessary factor in participation; even when other players tell us explicit rules, as we play they are quickly transformed into implicit knowledge. Hence, rules in this sense are pragmatic; their significance is subordinate to the practical activity to which they refer.

Furthermore, the usefulness of even explicitly formulated rules is bounded by several facts of experience. First, the application of a rule to any particular case still requires judgment (for example, we may know that murder is wrong, but still be uncertain of whether a particular act counts as murder). Wittgenstein says, "A rule stands there like a signpost," and goes on to explain the various ways in which one could follow it—it "leaves room for doubt" (pp. 39–40, 80). Second, he asks, "Is there not also the case where we play and— make up the rules as we go along? And there is even one where we alter them—as we go along" (p. 39). The repeated use of constructions like "as we go along" suggests that for Wittgenstein the activity is primary; the rules, simply an outgrowth and idealization of it. Formulating rules, he says, may be useful in some cases (teaching someone the game, adjudicating disagreements within it, etc.)—but the game cannot be seen as simply the playing out of the rules. For Wittgenstein, as for Gadamer, *play is primary*. Wittgenstein says, in fact, that attempting to formulate strict rules can interfere with the playing: "We lay down rules, a technique, for a game, and . . . then when we follow the rules, things do not turn out as we had assumed. . . . We are as it were entangled in our own rules" (p. 50).

For Wittgenstein, the concrete practice of any complex human activity is beyond the capacity of any rule or set of rules to capture; or, more accurately, it can be expressed by such a multiplicity of alternative sets of rules that no one subset could claim to *determine* it. Successfully following a rule is a matter of successfully conducting a practice, not vice versa. Yet at the same time, not everything will count as a successful interpretation or application of a rule. It must be possible to "break" a rule if it is to have any significance as a "rule" at all—if no one ever followed a rule, it could not, on this account, *be* a rule.

PLAYING AND COMMUNICATION

I have gone into Wittgenstein's account of games and rules in some detail, because I believe it is especially helpful in understanding the complex human practice of dialogue. First, by emphasizing the diversity of types of game, particularly in his analysis of different "language games," Wittgenstein illuminates the multiple purposes we have in human social practices such as communication. His outlook transforms the traditional philosophical search for a strict definition or determinative set of criteria across a diversity of cases into a search for broader and more flexible categories of inclusion and exclusion. Similarly, as I will argue in Chapter 6, dialogue does not take one single form, but instead comprises at least four different kinds of interchange, bound in spirit but potentially quite different in process.

Second, by considering language as a social activity, based on the game analogy, Wittgenstein situates traditional philosophical problems of meaning, truth, and explanation into a context of social purposes and fallible communicative processes. This too is in keeping with the account of dialogue I want to emphasize. Entering into dialogue is a commitment to an open-ended and uncertain interpersonal activity directed toward teaching and learning. While it is reasonable to hope that knowledge, understanding, or agreement will result from this interchange, there is something about the interchange that stands on its own; it is a relational activity, as a game is, that we pursue because of curiosity, interest in others, and a sense of enjoyment in the process itself.

Third, games have rules, but not in the sense of an algorithm that strictly shapes the conduct of activity within the game. It is possible to play a game without knowing all the rules; it is possible to interpret the rules differently in various incarnations of the game; and it is sometimes possible, even necessary, to ignore the rules in order for a game to move forward. In all of this, again, a game is understood as a human *practice*, which requires a degree of flexibility and indeterminacy in how any instance actually gets played out (otherwise, it would not be enjoyable to play); rules are subordinate to this practice. Yet at the same time, there is no game without *any* rules. When rules are repeatedly flouted a game can be jeopardized, and even when we need to "make up the rules as we go along," we are still making up *rules*. Similarly, the dialogue game has rules, although they are pragmatic rules that allow a wide range of discretion in their interpretation and application. I will return to this topic in Chapter 4.

Fourth, one of the central issues Wittgenstein raises concerning games is how we learn them; what role rules play, for example, in learning how we are supposed to act in order to participate successfully in the practice. Framing the goal of learning this way, we see that concepts of "initiation" or "involvement" are more appropriate in characterizing the process by which we are drawn into the activities of any complex human practice. A great deal of our learning is implicit, developed over time in the context of ongoing human relations and practices, not set out in the form of codified, explicit rules. Rules play a role in this inductive process, as ideals or hypotheses, Wittgenstein says, which we formulate in the attempt to grasp what is primary, namely, the self-adjudicating process of the game itself. Dialogue, too, is something we learn this way: through the communicative relations we are drawn into as we grow up, and that sustain us as we live. There is some value in formulating ideals of communicative conduct, but these have significance only as approximations or heuristics in fostering, supporting, and motivating our capacity for conversation itself.

One of the most important things that games teach us when we are young is the role of rules in helping to regulate human activities and the need for finding ways of adjudicating differences *within* a game, without jeopardizing the game itself. We say that children need to "learn how to play with others," and by this we do not mean learning to play any particular game, necessarily, but a general attitude of playfulness, a tolerance for disagreement, a willingness to compromise, an ability to cooperate, and so on. One of the most remarkable things about children in play is how effectively they can establish, alter, and adjudicate regulative agreements within play situations. The significance of "learning to play," seen through this lens, is that it shapes fundamental values and character traits—including, for example, many of the "communicative virtues" discussed in Chapter 2—that underlie the ability, later in adult life, to manage less apparently "playful" situations, such as work relations. From this standpoint, it is somewhat ominous to reflect on the increase of forms of play, such as video games, that are more asocial, involving direct interaction with a computer, not another person; that are relatively inflexible as to rules and procedures; and that are more purely teleological, marking success largely in terms of a cumulative numerical score. Such qualities are not unique to video games; but we should be concerned about their rising popularity and their tendency to drive other forms of playful interaction off the child's schedule.

PLAYING THE DIALOGUE GAME

I have been arguing for the general appropriateness of the "game" analogy in discussing dialogue; but what, exactly, does the idea of a "dialogue game" entail? (See Carlson, 1983, for a very different analysis of "dialogue games.") In this section I want to draw together the central aspects of Gadamer's, Huizinga's, and Wittgenstein's accounts in explicating dialogical interactions.

Gadamer emphasizes the centrality of a to-and-fro motion that relates the partners in play. Clearly, dialogue is based on this principle. It is not only that in dialogue talking and listening go on between two or more people, for there are many other contexts in which these things happen that we would not call dialogue. Dialogue is, as I argued in Chapter 2, an interactive, relational concept. It exists *in* the exchange back and forth between persons, and it has the particular nature that unlike other kinds of communication it is essentially committed to the interactive character of that relation. We enter into a dialogical relation the way players enter into a game relation, with the value of the interaction itself in mind, as much as or more than any particular result we may intend.

Related to this point, any game possesses a kind of continuity; a game may go through different phases, yet still be the same game. We know when we are playing a game, and so long as we are enjoying it we act in ways to keep it going. Often we become less interested in winning the game (if it is the sort of game that can be "won"), which would end it, than in keeping the game going. As I discussed before, we can become so engrossed in a game that it occupies the entire scope of our existential awareness. We lose our sense of being a certain person engaged in a particular pastime or diversion, and simply are at those moments a player in the game. In a sense, the game overwhelms us and takes us over as a player for its own purposes of moving forward. Dialogue, too, has this capacity to completely involve us as participants. The ongoing logic of a discussion, the enthusiasm of discovery, the excitement of vigorous disagreement, all can catch us up, to the point that we are unable to say whether we are steering or being steered by the course of the discussion.

This sense of engrossment has much to do with our enjoyment of the process of dialogue as an activity for its own sake; so much so that we choose to conduct ourselves within it so that the dialogue can continue, even as it passes through various phases. A dialogue cannot be assessed by a "snapshot" perspective at one point in time. For example, at any given moment one person will be talking, another listening; even for several minutes one person may do most of the talking. Within a short perspective we would say that this is a poor dialogue, that it lacks the reciprocity and egalitarian spirit we expect in dialogue. Or, in the short term a bitter disagreement may arise, in which there are hard feelings and sharp exchanges; again, this may be a poor indicator of the overall quality of the dialogical relation. Viewed as a game, dialogue can ebb and flow; it can have reversals, peaks and valleys of activity, shifting roles, varied paces, and so on. What maintains the dialogue over time is a *continuity* constituted by the relation and the process of interaction itself, and supported by the commitment of its participants to remain active in the game in order to keep it moving forward—were they to stop playing, the game by definition would end.

My comments earlier about how we learn a game are of central importance to the dialogue game. As Vygotsky (1962, 1978) argued, our general capacities for language develop through our social interactions with others. Even our capacity for "inner speech" is simply an extension of externalized conversations we have had: "A clear distinction between inner and outer speech is impossible, because the very act of introspection is modeled on external social discourse"

(Emerson, 1981). We learn how to engage in dialogue with others by having been engaged in dialogue previously. Even our capacity to carry on internal dialogues within our minds, or to imagine dialogues with people who are not present, derives from our experiences with dialogue in practice: these are "Dialogues conducted with imaginary addressees who may be more or less fully defined, but who are always drawn from voices one has already heard" (Morson, 1981b, p. 8). Hence, we often play the dialogue game when we are thinking to ourselves, responding to imagined counterclaims or points of view, and in this sense can even develop a kind of indirect dialogical relation with those who are dead (say, historical figures) or in other ways not actually present.

The dialogue game, like other games, can have both a sense of playfulness and a sense of contention that are not necessarily incompatible. We often characterize a dialogue as an open discussion that tolerates a "free play of ideas." David Bridges (1988a) lists various senses in which this sort of discussion can be "open."

- The subject matter is not circumscribed.
- The participants are open-minded.
- The participants are receptive to new points of view and to criticism.
- Anyone can participate.
- Time is not a serious constraint.
- The objectives of the discussion are open.
- The members' purposes and practices are overt and open to examination.

Such conditions, Bridges argues, create a climate in which participants feel secure in expressing their views and hearing those of others. Recalling Ellsworth's criticisms, mentioned earlier, we need to remember that success in creating such an atmosphere cannot simply be read from the surface features of the discussion; some participants may *feel* much less openness in a discussion than one might intend. Yet clearly Bridges's criteria for openness are the sorts of conditions we must aspire to if dialogue across a full range of positions is to have a chance. These conditions might also be justified in terms of broader social and political values, such as democracy, as they are for Bridges. But here I want to emphasize that they are fundamentally justified as the conditions under which we *must* play this sort of game, if we want to play it at all. We expect people to play by the rules, to play fairly, to play in the spirit of the game, and so on. As

Huizinga (1950) pointed out, when we are playing a game there is nothing worse than a cheat or a spoilsport, and while these are usually given juvenile connotations, the fact is that they can be conceived as quite accurate characterizations of the many ways in which participants of all ages fail to act within the spirit of dialogue.

Nevertheless, a degree of tension and contention are inherent in the dialogue game, just as the to-and-fro or back-and-forth interaction between an agent and some resistance, or between two or more agents, is part of games generally. Recall that Bakhtin's concept of heteroglossia incorporates the idea of different voices and meanings, not simply in the traditional pluralistic sense of many people with many points of view, but rather as an inherent condition of language. In one view, heteroglossia

> *prohibits* a unified individual or a consensual society. This is so because a dialogue requires more than one voice and each voice has its own identity. Since individuals' inward speech is dialogical and social, individuals must be understood to speak with many voices. . . . Language is impossible to perceive as something other than, in Bakhtin's words, "an authentic dialogue of unmerged consciousness." Society must be understood as in continuous dialogue and, therefore, multivoiced and nonconsensual. (Quantz & O'Connor, 1988, p. 99)

Richard Quantz and Terence O'Connor are correct, I believe, that the fact of heteroglossia limits the degree of consensus we can expect within a dialogical community. There is a sense in which one can characterize dialogue fundamentally as a "struggle" between different voices, rather than a smooth journey down the path toward agreement, or Truth. These sorts of ideas are adapted by authors such as Iris Young (1990a, 1990b) and Dale Bauer (1988) to suggest that although Bakhtin considered heteroglossia to be a "centripetal" force in language, opening up institutionalized meanings and clichés to a multiplicity of voices—in other words, as a source of freedom— in fact the multiple voices present in this broader conversation are not equal in status, respect, or power. Structural and institutional factors privilege some voices, and silence or discourage others. Hence for these authors, either community is not possible at all, or it is possible only conceived as an ongoing fight "between the marginal and the central" (Bauer, 1988, pp. xii–xiii, 5–7, 167–168).

I believe that there is a crucial insight revealed here. There is a danger in hoping fondly that discussion and goodwill can bridge all differences, especially in social contexts of power and domination; and it is also true that attempts to force agreement or consensus in such circumstances often simply result in submerging alternative views beneath a dominant one. In this sense, the struggle of divergent voices not to be silenced is admirable and progressive. But the search for theoretical articulation of this view has gotten lost in the thicket of its own rhetoric. Certainly, there are cases in which struggle, conflict, or competition over the "terrain" of language is the dominant form of interaction—*just as it is in certain other games*—but there are also cases in which a degree of tension can be reconciled with a more "playful" approach. It seems to me that there are different kinds and degrees of contention in the dialogue game, which can sometimes go too far, ruining the game in the process. But it is also true that the spirit of the game, and the quality of the relation that underlies it, can transform our perception of disagreement or difference, to see them less as threats and more as opportunities. The dialogue game can tolerate a degree of contention—indeed, thrive on it—without either turning struggle into a battle, on the one hand, or trying to eliminate the tension by eliminating all differences, on the other. If games are played against resistance, then we should appreciate the difference of our partners in the dialogue game as a condition of interest and variety; there is no paradox in partners to a dialogue also being contenders. I do not think there is any other sustainable approach to take in the midst of a complex, pluralistic democracy, such as our own.

The Bakhtinian concept that expresses this perspective on the dialogue game is the *carnival*: "a positive space, a community [Bakhtin] celebrates because of its activity, its engagement of others" (Bauer, 1988, p. xiv) and "a democratic, emancipatory, and transformative genre of social expression" (Quantz & O'Connor, 1988, pp. 99–104). Although somewhat romanticized in these quotes, carnival can provide a time and place of uninhibited self-expression, an explosion of voices, it represents well the idea of free play and open discussion.

> Because carnival potentially involves everyone, it sets the scene for dialogue, for communal heteroglossia. . . . Carnival suspends discipline—the terror, reverence, piety, and etiquette which contribute to the maintenance of the social order. The carnival participants overthrow the hierarchical conventions which exclude them and work out a new mode of relation, one dialogic in nature. (Bauer, 1988, p. 14)

But as Bauer goes on to note, the carnival is an extraordinary condition; because of its very energy and intensity, it cannot last in this form. To put it differently, a carnival in this sense does not—indeed cannot—have rules, and so is not sustainable as a human practice over time.

Here, then, is the dilemma: The dialogue game requires participants or contenders who are different enough to provide sufficient tension for the to-and-fro movement to have interest and pleasure; yet when this contention comes to be seen as a struggle or battle, the enjoyment is destroyed. To put this in less analogical terms, the development of new beliefs, new understandings, or new appreciations requires conflict (and a tolerance for conflict) between what we already "know" and some new information or perspectives that challenge us. Indeed, for these Bakhtinian authors such conflict is built into the very nature of language. Yet a cacophony or an excess of conflict is directly counterproductive to this goal, making us *less* able or willing to encounter other voices seriously. This dilemma, I believe, is inherent in communication, and we will occasionally find ourselves erring in one direction (encouraging the unreconciled plurality of contending voices and perspectives) or the other (assuming a greater degree of commonality and agreement than actually exists). The carnival cannot be sustained over time, but a battle over whose voice will "win" threatens to destroy the conversation. The idea of a dialogue game, I am suggesting, provides a way of keeping these alternatives in creative tension: retaining the element of spontaneity, pleasure, and freedom exemplified in the carnival, but within a framework that can be sustained over time, namely, a set of rules that we agree to play by in order for the game to move forward.

Enjoyment and pleasure play a central role in why people participate in, and remain in, the dialogue game. Because participants can derive satisfaction from the process of dialogical involvement and interchange itself, apart from any specific goal or purpose, there is a point at which the dialogue takes on a life of its own. Just as we often play for no other purpose than to keep a game moving forward, we often carry on with dialogue in order for further dialogue to occur. The understanding and empathy we have established so far help us in continuing the discussion even further: "Thus, it seems that dialogues inevitably give rise . . . to further dialogues" (M. Bernstein, 1981, p. 118). The maintenance and development of the *dialogical relation* becomes primary. Moreover, the dispositions and skills we develop in one dialogue also serve us in good stead for future dialogues. One important reason for persisting in a dialogical encounter, even when it becomes difficult, is because it can foster in us communicative virtues and skills that are fostered only through practice—sometimes difficult practice—but that will help us in future encounters (D. Bridges, 1987).

Yet all of these considerations, of what we stand to learn or teach through dialogue, of the social and political solidarity we can establish through it, and of the capacities we can develop by practicing it, valuable as they are, still revolve around a central matter: Playing the dialogue game can be fun and deeply satisfying. There is a sense of real joy in a successful dialogue, and an emotional bond that expresses something basic about our humanity. Gadamer (1976), again, captures this sense well.

> The common agreement that takes place in speaking with others is itself a game. Whenever two persons speak with each other they speak the same language. They themselves, however, in no way know that in speaking it they are playing this language further. But each person also speaks his own language. Common agreement takes place by virtue of the fact that speech confronts speech but does not remain immobile. In speaking with each other we constantly pass over into the thought world of the other person; we engage him, and he engages us. So we adapt ourselves to each other in a preliminary way until the game of giving and taking—the real dialogue—begins. It cannot be denied that in an actual dialogue of this kind something of the character of accident, favor, and surprise—and in the end, of buoyancy, indeed of elevation—that belongs to the nature of the game is present. And surely the elevation of the dialogue will not be experienced as a loss of self-possession, but rather as an *enrichment* of our self. . . .
>
> Now I contend that the basic constitution of the game, to be filled with its spirit—the spirit of buoyancy, freedom and the joy of success—and to fulfill him who is playing, is structurally related to the constitution of the dialogue in which language is a reality. (pp. 56–57, 66)

The enjoyment and satisfaction of playing a game, and playing it well, points to something at the heart of the human character—hence Huizinga's phrase: *Homo ludens*. I have tried to show how this sensibility underlies our experiences with dialogue as well, and how adopting a playful attitude toward dialogue helps us not only in understanding it, but also in conducting ourselves within it in the proper spirit—"the spirit of buoyancy, freedom and the joy of success," in Gadamer's phrase. Dialogue often deals with serious, even unhappy, subjects; yet even when this is so, we are drawn to the process of dialogue itself because it constitutes an arena in which we are bound to others in a relation of mutual appreciation, challenge, and stimulation.

CHAPTER 4

Rules in the Dialogue Game

In Chapter 3, I suggested that dialogue could be viewed as a kind of game: an ongoing interactive practice, guided by certain broad rules, and motivated by various intrinsic satisfactions as much as by any goal-oriented purpose. A game can be, and should be, playful, spontaneous, and creative. But in order for it to go forward it must involve various explicit or implicit agreements among the participants to coordinate their activities with one another in a more or less ordered and predictable way. When they all feel an interest in seeing the game go forward, they conduct themselves according to these underlying agreements. For a newcomer to understand what is going on in the game, and to learn to participate successfully in it, he or she must come to identify, at least hypothetically, the rules that describe and explain relevant patterns in the activity and thereby enable him or her to carry on similar patterns of practice. I have also tried to show how acquiring such rules is a *social* activity, learned through interactions with other participants.

All of these general considerations about the functions of rules in games apply to dialogue. In this chapter, I will examine in some detail the general functions of rules in language and communication, and then specifically their role in dialogue. Any general rules of communication apply to dialogue, of course; but dialogue has some additional rules, I believe, that set it apart as a more or less discrete domain of verbal interaction. However, it is also interesting to consider how dialogue "crystalizes" some of the basic elements of communication generally, and in this regard can be seen as exemplifying some of our highest standards of how we ought to conduct ourselves in talking with and listening to one another.

I must say something about the word *rule* at the outset. I use the term with some ambivalence, and will often use different terms instead, such as *standard, principle,* or *guideline.* Rules connote to many people a rigid set of injunctions that demarcate explicit patterns of mandatory conduct, and I do not think there are very many rules of language in this sense. Wittgenstein's insights, discussed in Chapter 3, are an especially helpful corrective in this regard. As I will argue, rules in communication are pragmatic, and following them in conversation entails interpretation, judgment, and the sensitive application of general guidelines to particular cases, including knowing when to "break" a rule for the sake of some more general communicative purpose (for example, using metaphors or other tropes that may be literally false statements, but that we do not condemn as lies). Yet to the extent that we can describe these guidelines in relatively clear and general form, I think the term *rule* is not inappropriate. Recalling the discussion in Chapter 3, rules help to define and govern a game, but at some point the game takes over and becomes the primary project; it does not exist to serve the rules, but vice versa. This is especially true of the dialogue game.

THE FUNCTIONS OF RULES

Rules provide a reliable form of organization to activities within a game, so that participants can anticipate and relate their actions to one another in order that the game can go forward. Rules, in this way, provide consistency, predictability, and continuity; but they do so in a manner that also allows for a wide range of spontaneity, creativity, and surprise. These two aspects of rules are not paradoxical, because it is often the very existence of rules—which participants "play off of"—that provides the occasion for surprise and delight within a game. What would be paradoxical is to imagine a situation where participants pursue spontaneity, creativity, and surprise in a context in which there are no common standards; one famous example of this is the pseudo-conversation between Alice and Humpty Dumpty in *Through the Looking Glass* (Carroll, 1916), where they are clearly operating by different linguistic standards much of the time, creating absurd misunderstandings as a result (Marcondes, 1985).

A classic discussion of the function of rules in this context is offered by John Searle (1962) in his book *Speech Acts*. The basic thesis of the book, Searle says, is that *"speaking a language* is engaging in a rule-governed form of behavior" (p. 41). Searle writes within the philosophical school of "speech act theory," a tradition tracing its origins to Wittgenstein, which seeks to explain our uses of language for the widely varying purposes it has in contexts of human practice (promising, requesting, questioning, joking, congratulating, and so on). In the expression of John Austin (1962), we "do things with words"—we perform acts by virtue of the words that we speak. The unique characteristic of speech act theories, such as Searle's, is that they seek to explain traditional philosophical problems of language, problems about meaning, reference, truth, and so forth, in terms of the speech acts in which those activities—*expressing* meaning, *making* reference, *asserting* the truth—take place. Hence, for Searle, the rules governing the successful use of language are the rules governing speech acts: how and when one is entitled to perform them, what are the necessary and sufficient conditions for their fulfillment, and so on. It is in this context that his discussion of rules arises.

Searle notes two general functions of rules. Some rules are *regulative*, he says; they provide order and structure to human activities that exist apart from the rules themselves. So, for example, we may have specific rules that govern proper conduct at the dining table, but people had already been eating for centuries, and could continue to, without them. Other rules are *constitutive*, he says; they define certain activities that could not exist without them—indeed, their purpose *is* to define the activity, as in, for example, the game of chess. Searle summarizes: "Regulative rules regulate a pre-existing activity, an activity whose existence is logically independent of the rules. Constitutive rules constitute (and also regulate) an activity the existence of which is logically dependent on the rules" (p. 34). The central thesis in Searle's book is that the problems of meaning, reference, and truth in language (which could be called "semantic" problems) can be explained fully by identifying them as instances of certain kinds of speech acts, speech acts defined and governed by certain constitutive rules, which he analyzes in detail in his book.

> There are a series of analytic connections between the notion of speech acts, what the speaker means, what the sentence (or other linguistic element) uttered means, what the speaker intends, what the hearer understands, and what the rules governing the linguistic elements are. . . . The semantic structure of language may be regarded as a conventional realization of a series of sets of underlying constitutive rules, and that speech acts are acts characteristically performed by uttering expressions in accordance with these sets of constitutive rules. (pp. 21, 37)

I have gone into Searle's account of speech acts in some detail, not because I think the particular rules he describes (pp. 66–67) are adequate for an account of dialogue (for one thing, they are a bit too formal and rigid for my purposes here), but because the issues he raises are important for any alternative account that tries to do so. Specifically, his analysis of the constitutive and regulative functions of rules frames the kind of project I am pursuing in this chapter: to identify principles that do not simply guide or direct dialogical conduct, but actually help in setting apart a more or less discrete set of activities that count as "dialogue," as opposed to something else. Furthermore, Searle's account has had a strong influence on others, notably Jürgen Habermas, whose work I will be drawing on more directly here.

Why do we need rules for dialogue at all? As noted above, rules help provide consistency, predictability, and continuity to any practice. Because dialogue is a communicative activity in which we take certain kinds of risks, and ask others to take them with us, we will be able to carry out this activity more confidently when we believe that we can rely on certain kinds of responses by our partners. Earlier, I alluded to a range of emotional bonds—mutual concern, trust, respect, appreciation, and affection—that help to establish an atmosphere in which dialogue "feels safe" and seems worthwhile. It is entirely consistent with that level of feeling to add that there are also implicit or explicit understandings that participants in dialogue share concerning what they can reasonably expect from one another in their communicative practice; just as the very closest of friends may still need to negotiate, in some circumstances, a formal compromise in the context of some fundamental disagreement—which does not necessarily make them any less friends and may perhaps preserve their friendship by establishing some agreements in a more explicit manner. Sometimes the existence of somewhat formal rules or agreements is part of what helps sustain a relation over time.

Another topic discussed earlier is the "communicative virtues" that we acquire over time as we learn how to talk and listen to others; and I suggested that these are deeply ingrained dispositions and aspects of character that have been fostered in the kinds of communicative relations we have been drawn into, as children and into adult life. Virtues, such as patience, a willingness to listen carefully, and a tolerance for alternative points of view, are not, I argued, simply the following of internalized "rules" or norms. Rather, they are fundamental characteristics of our way of being in relation to others; we act in these ways because this is the sort of person we have become, and choose to be. Virtues, generally, are part of who we *are*, and so it is inaccurate to say that we "exercise" them or "apply" them; we express them in our actions and personality at a much deeper, and frequently subconscious, level. There is much more to be said about the merits of this conception of moral conduct, and specifically communicative conduct; but my purpose in raising the topic in this con-

text is that "virtue talk" and "rule talk" come from different philosophical orientations. If we possess certain virtues, why do we need
rules? If we think in terms of formulating and applying rules, isn't
that antagonistic to an orientation that stresses the cultivation of character? These are crucial questions.

First, the Wittgensteinian conception of rules I have outlined
does not see rules as specific injunctions for how we must act. They
are pragmatic "guideposts" or "ideals" that still need to be interpreted and applied in context. In this sense, a set of guidelines for communicative practice, or specifically dialogical practice, only begins to
approximate the broad range of decisions and choices we need to
make in actual speech situations. What governs this process of interpretation and application will be characteristics of good judgment,
experience, sensitivity, patience, and so on—including some of the
communicative virtues I have been discussing. Some people will be
better, more careful, or more conscientious in seeing the relevance of
certain standards and applying them judiciously to particular contexts. For example, there is a general principle in certain kinds of
conversation to keep a partner's comments in confidence; but there
are numerous cases where that may not be the best thing to do, and
the principle or rule does not tell us what all these exceptions are.
Instead, we need to use the principle as a general rule of thumb,
without feeling absolutely bound by it when more fundamental moral
inclinations (such as concern for the person, or one's own sense of
personal integrity and responsibility) would be jeopardized by slavish
obedience to the rule. Moreover, some relations provide a more supportive context in which to exercise such judgment; the virtues are
not simply aspects of individual character, but patterns of conduct
that are partly encouraged and fostered by our relations with others.

Second, rules are important from a developmental learning
standpoint. We need some explicit rules to govern our conduct as
a stepping-stone toward the development of a more mature moral
sensibility that comes to see rules as approximations of good conduct,
but with exceptions in many cases. This is true for children, and it
may be true for many adults who lack a fully developed sense of
moral obligation. There is no benefit in being naive about the lack of
virtues, communicative or otherwise, in contemporary society, and it
is important to pursue some means of fostering these virtues, in
ourselves and in others. Learning certain rules can be a necessary
bridge to that fuller achievement. So, for example, early on in developing a dialogical discussion within a group we might have to set up

(and enforce) a formal agreement that we will let participants take turns; over time, of course, we hope that the participants' heightened sensitivity to listening as well as speaking, taking what others have to say seriously, and habits of patience and self-control will make the imposition of such a rule unnecessary. Participants will have learned to act within the spirit of the game, without direct reference to rules.

Third, the sorts of rules that we have in language are reflexive in a unique way; because stating and justifying rules are communicative acts, they do not stand outside the communicative process that they strive to regulate. One implication of this point of view is that they are *immanent* to communication, not *transcendent*.

> Dialogue no longer follows narrative scripts conforming to certain rules: rather, the [rules] . . . are incorporated into and made objects of conversation itself. Thus they emphasize one element of narration, the *event* that transforms the structure of dialogue itself, changing the rules of communication and allowing for the development of new codes. . . . In dialogue within the framework of grand narratives, the rules preceded communication: now they are included in it. This is exactly the case that Wittgenstein refers to: "And is there not also the case where we play and make up the rules as we go along? And there is even one where we alter them as we go along." (Mecke, 1990, pp. 211–212)

This perspective leads to a fundamental rethinking of the status of rules themselves. An appropriate communicative rule (and possibly other rules as well) is simply the kind of rule that can be established and maintained within an ongoing communicative process. The rules I will be discussing here are justified if they are those we implicitly agree to in our communicative practice, or would agree to were they to be made explicit and opened up for careful consideration. In other words, the credibility of communicative standards, such as those I will suggest here for dialogue, is grounded not in a purely philosophical argument (although I certainly hope that they are plausible at that level also), but in a prediction or guess about what communicative partners will agree to. If a sufficient number of people were to say, "But that isn't what *I* want in dialogue," and have reasons for their objections, then I would certainly have to modify or abandon these rules. I will first discuss some general rules of communication, and then specifically discuss three rules that I believe are helpful for understanding, and engaging in, that specific mode of communication we call "dialogue."

GENERAL RULES OF COMMUNICATION

As background to the specific topic of dialogue, it may be helpful to discuss briefly the ideas of two theorists who have tried to develop fairly general models of the rules or standards that govern communication or conversation. Paul Grice and Jürgen Habermas operate within the broad framework of speech act theory described in the previous section and are interested in developing explanatory models of the diverse uses to which we put language. In general, they ask what implicit understandings and agreements we share by virtue of our effort to communicate with each other; what does such an effort take for granted, and what does it require to be successful? While they are not considering the topic of dialogue directly, their insights will be helpful to us when we do.

Paul Grice (1989) provided one such account of communication, based on what he called the "Cooperative Principle": "Make your conversational contribution such as is required, at the stage at which it occurs, by the accepted purpose or direction of the talk exchange in which you are engaged" (p. 26). In attempting to characterize this rather broad principle more specifically, Grice offered a set of *maxims* (the examples are mine).

Quantity

- Make your contribution as informative as required (e.g., if a close friend asks where you went for vacation, you wouldn't normally reply simply, "Europe").
- Do not make your contribution more informative than is required (e.g., if someone asks you the correct time, you don't need to explain where you bought the watch).

Quality

- Do not say what you believe to be false (e.g., if you lost your friend's jacket, don't say it was stolen).
- Do not say that for which you lack adequate evidence (e.g., if you haven't read a book, don't offer an opinion about it).

Relation

- Be relevant (e.g., if asked about the qualifications of a job applicant, leave her choice of jewelry out of it—unless, of course, that relates to the job in some way).

Manner

- Avoid obscurity of expression (e.g., if asked about your great-est regret in life, don't just say "Rosebud").
- Avoid ambiguity (e.g., if you are discussing your siblings, don't begin a sentence with "my sister said," when you have four of them).
- Be brief (e.g., if asked about how your morning has gone, don't begin the story in 1974).
- Be orderly (e.g., if you are describing your qualifications for a job, don't repeatedly veer off on tangential topics).

While acknowledging that "there are all sorts of other maxims," Grice believes he has captured here the essence of communication, by which he means the "maximally effective exchange of information." Grice's maxims are suggestive of the kinds of communicative stan-dards implicit in our everyday conversations. However, they are clearly impoverished even as a characterization of information-based communication; they are too clear-cut about such issues as relevance, obscurity, or brevity, when these are obviously difficult assessments to make in many practical contexts. Moreover, they abstract commu-nication from any relational context of feeling or intimacy: Perhaps in some friendships one *should* say things that are not strictly true. By limiting himself to information-based communication, Grice explicitly excludes what he calls "aesthetic, moral, or social" considerations. Particularly in light of our present purposes, Grice's maxims fail to capture factors that are essential to teaching, such as the presentation of ideas, the posing of questions, or the modeling of methods of inquiry in a manner directly addressed to the needs and abilities of a particular student or group of students. Grice's maxims pertain to *telling* more than to teaching. They have no dialogical structure at all.

Such considerations are better accounted for by a different set of communicative standards, provided by Jürgen Habermas (1976, 1984), who has been working over a number of years to develop a comprehensive theory of communication. One of the basic distinc-tions in his work is that between "strategic" forms of communica-tion, where the purpose is one of *using* language in order to have certain effects on other people, such as getting them to do things, or not to do things, according to one's desires; and "communication oriented toward understanding," in which the speakers' primary purposes are to express their meanings and intentions to one another as clearly as possible. Strategic communication regards speech acts in a utilitarian, almost calculating, way to get what we want out of social situations (see, for example, the work of Erving Goffman, 1967, 1969, 1974, 1983).

The essential feature of communication toward understanding is that it entails an implicit commitment to certain standards (or "validity claims") that can be invoked by either partner in a conversation (Habermas, 1976, 1984).

- *Comprehensibility.* Make the statement grammatical, clear, and understandable.
- *Truth.* Select propositional content in such a way as to accurately represent an experience or fact.
- *Sincerity.* Express intentions in such a way that the linguistic expression accurately reflects what is meant.
- *Rightness.* Carry out a speech act in such a way that it satisfies recognized norms or accepted self-images.

This implied commitment means that these validity claims, when called up, must be "redeemed," like a promissory note (1976), leading to a dialogical interchange that seeks to resolve the difference or misunderstanding. I can ask you, for example, what you mean by what you just said, what evidence you have for it, whether you truly believe what you are saying, or whether you have violated certain norms by saying it; and you implicitly agree to provide a response—if not, then intersubjective understanding cannot be your primary purpose. These validity claims can refer to different aspects of the same utterance: If I say you are wearing an unattractive outfit, you might reply with any or all of the following: (1) What do you mean by "unattractive"? (2) What makes it unattractive? You don't know what you are talking about. (3) This isn't about my outfit at all, is it? You are simply trying to hurt my feelings because of what I said yesterday. (4) How dare you? I am your professional co-worker; you have no business commenting on my dress or appearance in any way.

A context in which these validity claims can be invoked and redeemed openly, and in which participants seek to resolve disagreements over these claims through reasoned discussion, characterizes what Habermas calls the "ideal speech situation." Habermas has been misunderstood on this point (for secondary analyses of this idea, see Benhabib, 1986, pp. 287–288; McCarthy, 1978, pp. 306–307; R. Young, 1990, pp. 71–78). The ideal speech situation never actually exists, or could exist—there are too many practical barriers to its full realization. Rather, it is a counterfactual hypothesis about what we ideally presume when we endeavor to speak together; so, for example, when we assert a belief that we hold, we also offer an implied promise to provide at least some of the evidence and reasons behind that belief, if asked. We may not be asked; we may not be able to provide those reasons fully; and we may not convince others if we do—but by making the assertion we commit ourselves to that broader obligation. By providing such reasons, in turn, we manifest an implicit faith in an ideal communicative relation in which reasons will be taken seriously and in which the weight of persuasive reasons or justifications will be granted credence (the fact that many real-world situations do not approximate this ideal does not change this commitment). If we did not assume something like this, then we would not offer reasons or justifications, or expect them to have any effect if we did. The ideal speech situation, therefore, is neither a portrayal of how communication actually happens or a prescriptive model of how it ought to be. It is "ideal" in the sense that it represents certain implicit norms that are *in fact* neither consistently recognized nor lived up to. Because ideological and institutional factors impede the attainment of the ideal speech situation, this ideal provides a critical lens through which *distortions* to communication can be identified and criticized.

Most of Grice's criteria pertain to the first two of Habermas's validity claims, comprehensibility and truth. What Habermas adds to our understanding of communication is that a bond of trust needs to be established within a communicative relation, through our confidence that the speaker's statements accurately represent his or her intentions and purposes in the relation (sincerity); and that the form of the communicative interchange is answerable to larger normative structures concerning appropriate social relations and personal obligations (rightness). Unlike Grice, Habermas wants to situate these standards not outside a "core" function of communication (for Grice, exchanging information), but within the communicative relation itself. Hence a statement might be true, but insincere; and to call a statement insincere is for Habermas as profound a basis for challenging it as would be challenging its truth. For example, political figures often cite statistics or polling data that are, strictly speaking, true, but that are clearly being invoked in a distorted and self-serving way; sincerity and rightness claims provide a basis for challenging them, even if the facts are "correct."

Habermas resituates communication in a relational context. What is appealing in his account is that it grounds our norms and standards, not in metaphysical certainties, or in transcendent reason, but in conversational processes of persuasion and intersubjective exploration. Claims of force, authority, tradition, or intellectual status hold no leverage in these sorts of conversations. The underlying value of such communication is simply the willingness "in principle" to subject all claims to discursive redemption, "whereby the phrase 'in principle' expresses the idealizing proviso: if only the argumentation could be conducted openly enough and continued long enough" (Habermas, 1984, p. 42). In this view, we try to resolve disputes about meaning, truth, intention, or appropriateness not by retreating into a pristine meta-discourse, but from within what may already be a confused and conflicted communicative situation.

Habermas's work has been revised and extended further by the feminist theorist Seyla Benhabib. What is most troublesome in Habermas's theory is the "quasi-transcendental" character of some of his conclusions. At some points he seems to say that the process of discursive redemption of validity claims is a process through-and-through; what counts as a final answer is nothing more than what the persuasive process, carried out by actual persons, settles on (Habermas, 1984, 1990a). At other times, he claims much broader and more universal consequences—that a truth claim is not only the result of the best arguments in a particular communicative setting, but that it should also be binding in other settings as well. A related concern is Habermas's rationalism; his continual reliance on the weight of reasons and arguments, as if these could be (or should be) conclusive in all validity contexts. What is needed, it seems, is to make Habermas's claims more pragmatic and to resituate them in concrete (and imperfect) communicative relations.

Benhabib (1986) questions Habermas's "rationalistic bias" and what she calls the "philosophy of the subject" that underlies it. While the force of communicatively secured agreement provides some grounding (for example, for the resolution of a legal dispute), this grounding is much more contextual and limited than Habermas seems to want it to be. Benhabib's (1987, 1990) key insight here is that communication occurs with a *concrete*, not *generalized*, other. These arguments, misunderstandings, negotiations, or agreements need to be worked out in *this* communicative setting, with *these* participants, ordinary people talking with one another in an ordinary (not ideal) speech situation. As a result, the generalizability of any outcome will be extremely bounded: To the extent that the parties are thoughtful, fair-minded, and convincing in their deliberations, their conclusions may be persuasive to others as well (for example, physicists studying the structure of a quark; or friends debating whether to encourage a mutual friend to file for a divorce). But this generalizability is, in Michael Kelly's (1990) phrase, a "weak generalizability," not a "strong" one, because it has nothing to do with having found the ultimately "true" or "right" answer, but simply with having found a persuasive case that knowledgeable and interested parties can agree upon. The reasonableness of this outcome is secured not by the fact that it conforms to certain rationalistic standards, but by the degree to which it is based on reasons that the participants agree to, not through coercive or manipulative strategies (Burbules, 1991a, 1992).

In light of these considerations, I believe we need to incorporate into this model of communication the role of those emotions, dispositions, and experiences that facilitate effective communication. As discussed in Chapter 2, emotional bonds such as respect, trust, and concern are frequently what draw people into a communicative relation in the first place; certainly they are essential to keeping people in the communicative situation when it becomes difficult, frustrating, conflicted, and so forth. Hence, some attention to fostering these emotions must be given within the communicative relation; such efforts do not take place "outside" the topic being considered but are inseparable from it. One theoretical path to pursue might be to broaden Habermas's sincerity condition to include attention to broader issues of emotional authenticity and empathy: Part of effective communication is in coming to feel certain ways about our partners in conversation.

Similarly, the success of a communicative relation depends on certain virtues that cannot be taken for granted in most cases, including patience, tolerance for alternative points of view, an openness to give and receive criticism, and—often neglected as a key element in dialogue—the willingness and ability to listen thoughtfully and attentively. I have been calling these "communicative virtues." These virtues are developed, reflexively, through the kinds of communicative relations in which we are engaged as children and into adult life. To develop these virtues is to be drawn into certain kinds of communicative relations; to have such relations, we need to exercise, to some extent, those virtues. Theoretically, it may be possible to incorporate such virtues into the category of Habermas's rightness criterion.

My reason for recounting in some detail Habermas's theory is that more than one commentator has seen in it the basis for a model of dialogue. Benhabib (1989) says, for example:

> The procedural constraints of the "ideal speech situation" are that each participant must have an equal chance to initiate and to continue communication. Each must have an equal chance to make assertions, recommendations, and explanations. All must have equal chances to explain their wishes, desires, and feelings. And finally, within the situation of dialogue speakers must feel free to thematize those power relations which in ordinary contexts would constrain the wholly free articulation of opinions and positions. Together these conditions specify a norm of communication that can be named one of *egalitarian reciprocity*. (p. 150)

Similarly, Jochen Mecke (1990) draws on Habermas to describe his own conception of dialogue.

> Thus dialogue presupposes, as Habermas declares in his theory of communicative competence, an ideal speech situation with the following features: (1) systematic and equal distribution of the opportunity to select and perform speech acts; (2) exchange of the dialogic roles of speaker and hearer; (3) equal distribution of choosing communicative, regulative, representative, and stative speech acts; (4) the possibility of putting in question all possible norms and opinions; (5) presupposition of good faith of the partners. (p. 208)

Without debating the adequacy of these descriptions as full-blown accounts of dialogue, they do exemplify those features of the Habermasian view that have appeal for any account of dialogue: the commitment to a communicative *process* to achieve understanding or to reconcile differences; the open-endedness of this process, in which the only justification for an assertion is in its capacity to be redeemed, according to the validity claims (a redemption that itself in turn is always open to question); an equality of status and respect, in which any participant has the right to pose questions or make assertions; and the avowal of a standard against which distortions to communication can be diagnosed and critiqued. When we say that a regime of power imposes certain "hegemonic" understandings on persons, when we criticize the "ideological" character of certain aspects of the curriculum, or when we condemn the tendency of certain groups (or persons) to "silence" the voices of others, it is important to acknowledge that these can be judged only against the background of an implicit set of beliefs about how communication *should* proceed. Habermas's framework for communication is only one among many, but it has a merit that few other candidates have: the willingness in principle to subject *any* of its assertions to question, and hence a reflexive integrity vis-à-vis its own principles.

THREE RULES OF DIALOGUE

Dialogue is one form of communication, and as such it is subject to all the general rules or normative standards of communication (such as, say, truthfulness). In fact, it has been argued, from a Habermasian standpoint among others, that in dialogue we see the *crystallization* of these standards.

> Communicative action is intrinsically *dialogical*. The starting point for an analysis of the pragmatics of speech is the situation of a speaker *and* a hearer who are oriented to *mutual* reciprocal understanding; a speaker and a hearer who have the capacity to take an affirmative or negative stance when a validity claim is challenged. (R. Bernstein, 1985, p. 18)

However, we cannot leave the matter at this, for dialogue is also in many ways *not* typical of communication generally. I introduced this perspective in Chapter 1, where I defined dialogue as a particular kind of pedagogical communicative relation, and explained how each aspect of this description places special conditions on what can count as dialogue and what cannot. The question that this chapter has been leading to is, What rules or principles characterize dialogue as a *particular* form of communication?

There have been several recent attempts to provide such an account, with varying degrees of systematicity and precision (Alexy, 1990; Carlson, 1983; Haroutunian-Gordon, 1991; Hintikka, 1982; Mukarovsky, in Mecke, 1990). On the one hand, some accounts exaggerate the formalism of their analysis to the point where dialogue becomes a bloodless object of dissection; the parts are all laid out on the table, but the patient has, unfortunately, died. On the other hand, some discussions of dialogue, wanting to preserve the creative and spontaneous quality of the teaching encounter, refuse to articulate any standards that even appear to be constraints on the free play of communicative actors. But as I argued earlier, the existence of rules is in itself no inhibition to a playful spirit; on the contrary, reflection shows that, at a deeper level, rules of some sort are necessary for play to proceed, and creativity and spontaneity are usually the result of "playing off of" well-defined norms or expectations. The challenge, then, is to identify rules that are plausible at a conceptual or explanatory level, but that are sufficiently flexible to tolerate a range of ways of fulfilling them; as Wittgenstein said, such rules are like signposts, indicating a general direction—how we pursue that direction is open to a diversity of approaches.

Corresponding to the three components of the characterization of dialogue as a pedagogical communicative relation are three kinds of rules.

The Rule of Participation

If dialogue is to be *pedagogical*, it requires the active participation of all participants. Active participation can take a range of forms, but since edification is the purpose of dialogue, there must be opportunities for engagement, questioning, trying out new ideas, and hearing diverse points of view. The chief threat to this end, as Freire describes so well, is *monologue*, the presentation of a single authoritative point of view that brooks no challenges and tolerates no participation in directing the course of investigation. I have already referred to the research that shows how learning requires an interaction between a learner and new information; and how diverse styles of assimilating this new information argue for a pedagogy that draws upon the interests and perspectives of different learners. Over and above these learning considerations, furthermore, there are social and moral ideals that make us favor a broad range of participation. But my point here is that even without these ideals certain conditions are entailed by the very fact that we aspire to educate.

The first rule of dialogue, therefore, can be called the *rule of participation*: Engagement in this type of communicative relation must be voluntary and open to active involvement by any of its participants. An obvious corollary of this principle would be that the forms of participation chosen by certain participants cannot be such that the participation of others is peremptorily excluded or discouraged. What this means in practice is that any participant should be able to raise topics, pose questions, challenge other points of view, or engage in any of the other activities that define the dialogical interaction.

The Rule of Commitment

Because dialogue is *communicative*, it is aimed at the pursuit of intersubjective understanding, which may or may not result in agreement. As discussed earlier, consensus may be too much to hope for in certain situations where differences or disagreements run deep. But some degree of understanding of one another's views, and the thoughts, feelings, and experiences that underlie them, is usually *not* too much to hope for. Whether this process takes the specifically Habermasian form of redeeming validity claims, or not, the communicative character of dialogue commits participants to a certain degree of openness about their positions and how they have come to hold them, as well as an open-handedness about their intentions within the dialogical relation itself. The chief threats to this end are manipulativeness and disingenuousness: of seeking to *use* the communicative engagement for purposes that one is not willing to admit, let alone explain or defend to one's interlocutors. Running a close second, however, as a threat to open dialogue is an inability or unwillingness to see the process through to some meaningful conclusion—not necessarily to agreement or consensus, but at least to an understanding and respect for differences. Because usually dialogue's pedagogical purposes can only be achieved over time, a willingness to stay with the process, even when its outcomes are uncertain or unclear, is essential for success.

The second rule of dialogue, therefore, can be called the *rule of commitment*: Engagement in this type of communicative relation must allow the flow of conversation to be persistent and extensive across a range of shared concerns, even difficult or divisive ones. This principle also requires sufficient commitment to, and confidence in, the communicative process to be willing to disclose one's underlying reasons, feelings, and motivations, when asked. Again, whether one adopts the Habermasian view of validity claims or not, "disclosure" means that in principle any communicatively relevant assertion can be raised for consideration *within* the dialogical relation; and this entails, in conjunction with the rule of participation, that individual participants cannot unilaterally determine when and if questions will be raised. In practice, this would mean, for example, that students should be able to raise question with a teacher who seems to be intolerant of students' taking positions that disagree with him.

Because such discursions are likely to be difficult, there will often be a temptation to set them aside for the sake of "getting on with the topic at hand." The problem with this avoidance is that such issues, though ostensibly ignored, will still tend to distort the communicative interaction. Besides, frequently they are *more important* than the topic at hand.

The Rule of Reciprocity

Because dialogue is a *relation*, maintaining the quality of communicative interaction and sustaining the conditions that make it possible must be a concern of all parties to the discussion. In Chapter 2, I discussed in detail how the creation and maintenance of such a relation requires attention not only to the form of conversation itself, but to the feelings and motivations of its participants. Because a dialogical relation needs to be sustained over time in order to be pedagogically beneficial, it inevitably involves an engagement that is more than purely cognitive. The capacities, or virtues, that foster an effective dialogical relation frequently need to be developed and improved among the participants as they learn together, not only about the topic at hand, but also about the communicative/pedagogical process itself.

The third rule of dialogue, then, is the *rule of reciprocity*: Engagement in this type of communicative relation must be undertaken in a spirit of mutual respect and concern, and must not take for granted roles of privilege or expertise. A corollary of this principle is that any dynamic within a dialogical relation must be *reversible* and *reflexive*. In other words, what we ask of others we must be prepared for them to ask of us; and what we expect of others we must expect of ourselves. If we ask others questions, they can ask us questions; if we are offended by others who do not pay attention to what we have to say, we ought to be sure that we have made the effort to listen to them. In practice, for example, this does not deny all forms of authority, but embeds any such claims in a broader relation of reciprocal regard and a willingness to see authority called into question.

A few caveats about these rules are in order. The first is that, as discussed previously, for many participants in dialogue they will not be experienced as "rules," but simply as extensions of their general communicative dispositions (what I have called "virtues"). Related to this point is that in a dynamic, ongoing dialogical encounter these rules will be largely unspoken, or even ignored. Indeed, a repeated need to invoke them is itself a sign of a dialogical relation gone bad. As in other forms of play, one might say, it's no fun when you're always arguing about the rules.

Furthermore, these three principles are obviously not expressed as strict, formal injunctions; I have purposely framed them in fairly broad, loose terms, partly because that is the state of my thinking on this subject, but also because such rules should be subject to flexible interpretation and judgment. In addition, these rules are highly interactive; problems or issues arising with one frequently carry over to the others.

Finally, these principles are not laid down as absolute mandates, and they are not presented here as conditions of communication generally. I have suggested that these help to characterize one sense of dialogue, and that if one wants to play the dialogue game, one must abide by some rules that are at least similar to these. Of course, some persons will not want to play this game, and it is important to note that there may be other *educational* activities (as well as other communicative activities generally) that are significant and beneficial, but that do not conform to these particular standards, or need to. But what is not possible is that they do not conform to any standards at all.

WHY DO WE NEED RULES FOR DIALOGUE?

In conclusion, I want to return to this question, but approach it from a different angle. Previously I stressed the need for rules as a positive condition of playing any game, such as the dialogue game. But there are other benefits as well in trying to clarify what, if any, implicit rules there might be underlying our practices and relations, some of which I have hinted at already.

First, if it is true that dialogue is the crystallization of our highest norms of communication (mutuality, openness, the cooperative pursuit of understanding, and so on), then reflecting on its rules might illuminate tacit assumptions of other communicative endeavors; and by attempting to change our habits to accord with those standards, we might find our capacities for a range of other communicative activities improving as well.

Second, having rules or standards serves a valuable *critical* function. Needless to say, many of our educational practices do not conform to these rules, even though we might aspire to them. In some cases the fault is in ourselves; in many other cases the fault is due to the kinds of circumstances in which our society has chosen to try to educate its children. Institutional constraints, power imbalances, cultural intolerance, unequal educational resources, and the threat (or reality) of physical and psychic harm all make the attainment of these sorts of dialogical relations unlikely for vast numbers of students. Yet the leverage we require to identify what has gone wrong, and why it is wrong, comes from having norms that tell us how education *ought* to be. Arguing for the value of dialogue, and the rules that characterize it, helps provide such critical standards, I believe.

Third, articulating rules as explicit principles, even if this means oversimplifying them somewhat, also plays an important role in our coming to learn them. Although after a while we may come to see numerous subtleties, complexities, and exceptions to these rules, we will have gotten to that point partly by having learned them, lived with them, and grown beyond them; there could not have been any more direct route to that outcome. Once a dialogical relation has been established, an explicit discussion about, or reliance on, rules will be rare; but the question is, How do we get to that point? How do we learn from our previous failures and false starts, without an explicit structure of expectations against which to judge our efforts?

Finally, there are what have been called "dialogue break-downs": "cases of manipulation, of misinterpretation of intentions and illocutionary force, of opposition of goals of communication, or of contradiction between divergent aims" (Marcondes, 1985, pp. 417–418). When something has gone wrong in a dialogical encounter, reflection on the implicit rules we have been taking for granted can often shed light on where things went off track and what we can try to do to change that.

Yet, despite such potential benefits, identifying rules for dialogue only takes us part of the way toward understanding it. Such rules have much more to do with why we value dialogue than with telling us how to go about it successfully. This is because rules, while they define the parameters of a game, do not address the more specific question of how participants should conduct themselves within it. We learn a game not only by learning its rules, but by also learning and practicing its *moves*. This is the topic of Chapter 5.

Moves in the Dialogue Game

There are many dangers of pressing the game analogy too far when discussing dialogue, and one of the most troubling of these is that the reader may get the impression that dialogue can be seen as simply a series of formal gestures, governed by calculated strategies, carried forth in order to "win," in one sense or the other of the word *win*. I hope that my comments up to now have made it clear that a relational conception of dialogue leads in an entirely different direction. In this sort of game we are "caught up," our moves and responses are actively engaged by the activities of our partners, the rules that we follow are only those that provide the loosest sort of guidance and direction to our choices, and, most of all, the chief goal is for the game to continue so long as it remains enjoyable and meaningful to all involved. At the point where dialogue becomes formal, calculated, and competitive, it ceases to be dialogue.

Similarly, the connotations of the term *move* in some game contexts can imply manipulation, clever deception, and subterfuge; and such strategic motivations certainly do enter into some communicative situations as well. But while there is a planful, deliberate character to moves—and while this is a crucial aspect of teaching and learning through dialogue—whether in fact the moves, and the motives behind them, are "within the spirit of the game" cannot be read off directly from the appearance of the move itself. Rather, we need to look at how a particular move fits into a sequence of moves and responses: "Just as a move in chess doesn't consist simply in moving a piece in such-and-such a way on the board—nor yet in one's thoughts and feeling as one makes the move: but in the circumstances that we call 'playing a game of chess'" (Wittgenstein, 1958, p. 17). Wittgenstein's insight here shows the limits of any purely behavioristic account of a "move."

As noted earlier, we need to consider and judge dialogical engagement from a *diachronic* and *developmental* standpoint: not just what is occurring at one moment, but how a particular statement fits into an ongoing pattern of statements. From this standpoint, what looks innocent within a short time frame might constitute part of an antidialogical trend in the longer term; and what seems to be flawed communication at first might develop into an effective dialogue. Hence it is impossible to analyze the significance of a move in a dialogue apart from how it is situated in a sequence of moves. For example, a literally false statement, while it may appear, from a "snapshot" perspective, inappropriate to communication oriented toward intersubjective understanding, might prove itself to be a valuable *pedagogical* move if in fact it leads to certain kinds of interchange and a more accurate state of understanding in the longer run.

Therefore, my main purpose in this chapter will be to describe in a general way some of the prototypical moves in dialogue—especially the central role of *questions*. I will suggest that it is primarily from the type of questions they comprise that most dialogues take their characteristic shape and tone. Finally, I will consider how sequences of moves can work to advance a dialogue in one of several ways, given the pedagogical purposes one has. I will conclude by noting four very different forms or genres of dialogue that can result from certain sequences of moves (these four types of dialogue, in turn, will be the central topic of Chapter 6).

DIALOGUE MOVES

As Searle, Gadamer, and others have pointed out, the *rules* of an activity (a game, an artistic creation, a performance) do not determine the specific conduct of persons engaged in that activity. Rather, rules provide a structure that is relatively stable and predictable, *against which* participants "play off" their own choices about how best to express themselves within those rules and even—occasionally—how and when to violate those rules, in a technical sense, as a way of serving the game. Spontaneity, creativity, and improvisation belie attempts to formalize or delimit particular choices players might make, within the rules. Nevertheless, repeated playings of a game do tend to fall into characteristic, recognizable, patterns of activity; for various reasons having to do with the criteria for success within a particular game, people develop certain ways of acting that, solely within the pragmatics of experience, they come to find effective and reliable. These artifacts of convention and tradition are passed along, through lore, observation, imitation, or direct instruction; sometimes they are learned entirely tacitly, by being caught up in certain patterns of activity with others, and gradually being drawn into similar dynamics. But in the process of learning them, and through a range of interactions with others, players often adapt these patterns further to suit their own personality, purposes, context, and style. Indeed, finding new moves or new uses for familiar moves is one of the intrinsic pleasures of a game.

Here I want to suggest a few of the typical moves, and sequences of moves, in dialogue, not with the expectation of generating an exhaustive list (which is impossible, in principle), or with the desire to prescribe them as a step-by-step technique; but simply to clarify some of the implicit options from which we can choose in dialogue. I suggest them as broad guidelines for reflecting on how we teach and learn through dialogue, and how we might do that more effectively (and more enjoyably).

In this section, I am going to describe five general types of utterances that we see in dialogical encounters: questions, responses, building statements, redirecting statements, and regulatory statements (for a different typology, see Dillon, 1983). I will describe different forms each might take and the various purposes they can serve in dialogue.

Questions

A partner in a dialogue may ask a question for a variety of different purposes. The simplest case is where a specific piece of information is sought in response ("What time is it?" "Have you read this book?"). Such questions rarely in themselves promote an ongoing dialogue, since they are usually entirely satisfied by the response—they do not lead anywhere. Nevertheless, they are an indispensable element in an ongoing pedagogical discussion. Often they help identify the conditions that situate a dialogue (such as the state of participants' knowledge on a particular subject). Sometimes they might introduce topics that receive more elaborated consideration later. Significantly, from the standpoint of establishing and *initiating* a dialogue, straightforward, simple questions may help create an interactive pattern of talk and may help to set the tone for a relation of mutual interest and trust. On the other hand, the repeated use of such one-sided and constrained questions can dampen any sense of enthusiasm or spontaneity in the exchange.

More elaborate questions might probe for understanding ("Can you explain this article to me?" "What did you think of that movie?" "What did you mean when you said he is 'old-fashioned'?"). Such questions are best seen as *invitations*, open-ended requests for opinions, beliefs, evaluations, interpretations, elaborations, and so on. The questioner is (or ought to be) motivated by an authentic desire to learn in some detail what the other thinks, knows, or feels about a subject. The question may be self-serving, in the sense that the questioner personally wants to know or understand something better than he or she does at present; or it may be probing, seeking to learn something about the other person, even when the answer is not particularly new or useful to the questioner. Even further along this spectrum, such a question may be diagnostic, aimed at encouraging the other to formulate and articulate a view that the questioner seeks to know, not for his or her own edification, but as part of teaching, advising, or otherwise assisting the other. Having set apart these various purposes analytically, we need to recognize of course that in real discussions they are rarely separate or mutually exclusive.

Yet another kind of questioning poses a challenge, or criticism, to the partner ("Why do you believe that?" "Is this consistent with what you said earlier?" "What should we do if what you say is true?" "What entitles you to make such an accusation?"). Such a question is not necessarily hostile, adversarial, or unsympathetic, but naturally in actual experience we find that the feeling or intention with which it is asked (or perceived to be asked) can influence the kind of answer, if any, it is likely to receive. There is sometimes confusion on this point: Some identify the very form of probing or critical questions as creating a "doubting game," attributing to their use in all cases a dispassionate, separating distance (Belenky et al., 1986; Elbow, 1986). Certainly there are instances in which the haste to criticize or disagree interferes with an accurate and sympathetic appreciation of what the partner is trying to say, or what stands behind what he or she says (such as experiences, beliefs, or feelings that underlie and grant validity to the claim). This "rush to judgment" can threaten the fabric of a dialogical relation, turning it from a cooperative to a competitive, from a trusting and respectful to suspicious, interaction. However, dialogue cannot explore certain levels of understanding if such questions are entirely barred from consideration; this is the central insight of Habermas's argument that in an "ideal speech situation," *any* validity claim can be questioned within the context of a relation oriented toward intersubjective understanding. Unless dialogue is to become the mere exchange of sedimented and complacent beliefs or casual first impressions, at some point the relation must be able to tolerate a dynamic in which interlocutors can pose skeptical questions and be willing to be questioned themselves, in turn. Working to create and maintain a relation in which such questions can be asked and answered undefensively, without jeopardizing the fabric of the relation itself, is one of the central challenges of dialogue.

The understanding that a questioner can be questioned in turn is one of the conditions that helps to create and maintain a dialogical relation of mutual respect and trust. I will return to this topic in Chapter 6. But the best known images of the "Socratic method"—such as Socrates interrogating the slave boy in the *Meno*, leading him through the steps of a geometric proof, or Kingsfield grilling his law students in the film *The Paper Chase*—are strikingly one-sided in terms of who does the questioning and who is being "taught" through the questions. In the *Meno*, Socrates asks, the boys answers. The questions are extremely narrow, usually permitting only a single, one-word response. Step-by-step, the interchange approaches a foreordained conclusion that Socrates had in mind from the very beginning. A similar analysis can be made of Kingsfield's pedagogy. While this method can be of definite benefit within an ongoing dialogue, taken alone it is sharply limited. Specifically, it threatens the rules of dialogue spelled out in Chapter 4: participation, shared commitment, and reciprocity. Such questioning is also of limited usefulness in areas where correct answers are not very clear and deductively certain (that is, in most areas of human concern). Furthermore, the asymmetry of such a relation reinforces a status and authority distance that, in the long run, is not conducive to continued dialogue. Finally, there is something paternalistic and potentially manipulative in asking questions solely in order to lead a partner down a path whose course and destination one has in mind but does not disclose. There is a valid use for such questions, and they can promote discoveries that partners might not ever reach developmentally on their own. But by themselves these questions cannot support an ongoing and sustainable dialogical relation.

Such leading questions also appear in a milder form, where the questioner is consciously tracing a line of inquiry, but without a definite outcome in mind. This use of questioning tends to preserve the dialogical form, since it requires active and creative responses by both parties, and since it more easily allows either partner to introduce new topics, to ask questions in return, or to change the direction of inquiry in unpredictable ways.

I will present a more detailed analysis of questions in the next section; but there are at least four other types of moves that recur in dialogue.

Responses

By "response" here I mean specifically statements made immediately following a question. Hence the patterns of response can be partly traced as parallel to the pattern of questions: Some are brief, direct, and informative; others are detailed elaborations of a view, or the experiences, beliefs, and feelings that underlie it. Some are attempts to "satisfy" an inquiry and so end the dialogue; others are more open-ended speculations that encourage another step in the discussion, in order to keep it going.

But the most interesting issue here is what it means generally to "answer a question." At a preliminary level, an answer can be the presentation of a pre-established, unreflective assertion: a fact, a cliché, a bit of conventional wisdom, or a set piece that merely reiterates an often-repeated position. What all of these (otherwise quite different) responses have in common is an offhandedness that is common in informal conversation, but that discourages dialogue because it implies a lack of interest or curiosity about the topic, about the partner's question, or about what led the partner to ask the question. Certain kinds of questions invite such responses (media political polling comes readily to mind). The flatness of such responses goes to show that either partner can have a "veto" over the direction and vitality of a discussion, simply by refusing to play within the spirit of the game. A skilled questioner (such as Socrates) may find a way to turn even truisms and trite platitudes to good purpose, by refocusing attention on the commonplace and conventional as a way of interrogating them. But even here the respondent must be interested and willing in pursuing this line of inquiry, or else it will go nowhere.

Other responses reveal a more active attempt to investigate a topic, develop a new view, or, at least, reformulate a long-held position in a manner that is responsive to the specific question, context, and partner at hand. Such answers indicate a desire, not to finish with the question, but to keep it alive; to explore new topics or to reflect on the familiar; to offer plausible evidence and arguments for what is said. Such responses invite further questions, or building statements, and in this they serve to maintain the to-and-fro movement of the game.

Finally, it should be noted that an important species of response to a question can be another question. Responding questions can take several forms, but some of the most important ones are those that raise validity concerns about the original questions themselves ("What do you mean by 'postmodern'?" "Why are you asking me about this?'' ''Am I going to be graded on my answer?''). Such responses can yield new understandings of the process—about what is meant by the original question, about why it is being asked, about what significance rests on the answer. They are also a direct attempt to create an *interlocutory* relation, as opposed to an entirely one-sided one (as is fostered by the *Meno* model, or certain models of direct instruction in which one partner does all the significant questioning). By creating more of a relation of mutual give-and-take, responding questions can be a direct challenge to unquestioned status and authority roles. Because of the power of a questioner to set an agenda and direct a discussion, and because repetitive questioning is also a way of shielding one's own positions from scrutiny, it is essential if a genuine dialogue is to come into being that neither partner claim a monopoly on questions (imagine, for example, the ways in which a lawyer's examination of a witness on the stand falls short of a dialogue). Responding questions are a healthy counterweight to such tendencies. This is especially important when the only ''correct'' response to a question is that it is the *wrong question*, a misleading question, an unfair question, or a question the other has no right to ask: Sometimes this should be simply asserted (a redirection), or raised by a skeptical or challenging question in response.

Building Statements and Redirecting Statements

Building statements and redirecting statements can be fruitfully discussed together, I think. Both types of statements are not direct responses to questions (although the latter can be an oblique response to a question, as just noted), but are statements following upon responses, or upon other building statements or redirecting statements. The basic difference between them is that a building statement tends to carry the discussion further along a particular line of development, while a redirecting statement seeks to introduce a new topic or lead the discussion along a different course.

Building statements raise the interesting question of what constitutes a connection of continuity in a discussion. One fairly obvious form is logical implication: ''If what you say is true, then such and such is also the case,'' for example. But there are other, nonlogical sorts of association as well: ''That reminds me of something my grandmother always used to say,'' or, ''What you say makes me realize that I might not have handled that situation very well.'' (Obviously, I am phrasing these examples in a more formal and explicit manner than we would use in most ordinary situations.) Sometimes the association is almost entirely juxtapositional and nonlinear (at which point such statements start to tend over more toward redirections): "You mentioned Goethe. You know, I had a teacher in high school who was always quoting Goethe." Contrasts and counter-assertions can also be building statements: "I don't think that's what he said. I thought he said 'no *man* is an island,'" or, "I liked the concert also, but that second piece wasn't performed very well, I thought." Again, though, if a contrast or counter-assertion is sharp enough, it begins to work more as a redirection than as a building statement; these sorts of examples show that the border between the two categories is somewhat fluid.

Redirecting statements, then, can be of the two forms just mentioned: juxtapositions of association that are tangential, or skewed, to the original direction of discussion; and contrasts or counter-assertions that drastically challenge the original terms of the discussion. But there are other types as well. Another type of redirection is a matter of avoidance: "No, I wasn't part of that conversation, so I'd rather not discuss it." Yet another type, an unintentional redirection, is the result of a misunderstanding, making a connection with what was said, but discontinuously, sometimes comically: "Yes, I've always admired the work of Macmillan and Garrison, especially their erotic theory of teaching" (their term is "erotetic," as I will discuss in a moment).

Now, within these two broad categories, there are two types of statements that are very common in dialogue, and that can fall under either heading. One type is initiating statements; dialogues, after all, don't always start with a question. Sometimes the beginning of a dialogue is in an assertion or set of assertions. Is such an initiation best considered a building statement, or a redirection, or something on its own? It seems most useful, I think, to judge an initiating statement as either a building statement or a redirect, depending on its content, tone, and the situation in which it is uttered. Some initiations comment on a situation, or invite a response, and so in that sense are in the spirit of building statements; others are so *sui generis* that they are almost disorienting—"out of left field," we say—and they are more in the spirit of redirections, even though they were not preceded by anything.

One type of initiating statement, by the way, can be a lecture—great or small. This book is not about lecturing, but about dialogue. Yet when a lecture is framed as a building statement—inviting responses, open to question, put forth in a way that encourages continual engagement and reflection, and so on—it can be seen as one phase in a larger dialogue. A lecture can also resist dialogue; it can be irrelevant, self-indulgent, and out of touch. Or it can be what Freire calls a *monologue*—an oppressive pronouncement about what is True and Right that does not invite, or even tolerate, response.

A similar analysis can be given for another type of statement, a disagreement: "No, I did not think her argument was convincing, and I'm a little surprised you did." Is this a building statement, or a redirection? Again, the content, tone, and the situation in which such a statement is uttered will have much to do with whether it has the effect of pressing a dialogue further along a particular line, or diverting it along an entirely different course (or, for that matter, ending the discussion, at least for a time).

Regulatory Statements

These are a separate category of statements within a dialogue, those directed not toward the substance of the discussion, but toward the process of communication itself: "I don't think you're listening to what I'm saying," or, more positively, "I can follow your argument up to now." Such statements have primarily to do with creating, or maintaining, the quality and spirit of the dialogical relation in which a discussion can proceed smoothly. However, as noted previously, while a certain amount of this intervention is necessary to encourage and motivate an ongoing dialogue, too much time spent reflecting and commenting on the process can interfere with the continuity of the dialogical interchange itself. It is a sign of artificiality or strain when one or both parties continually make external comments on their discussion, rather than contributing to the discussion itself.

Still, regulatory comments play an essential role in dialogue. There are many contexts, such as well-established friendships, in which conversation proceeds in an entirely spontaneous and effortless manner; but the more common experience, particularly in teaching contexts, is that the conditions of trust, cooperation, and mutuality essential for dialogue need to be monitored and consciously encouraged. Moreover, such comments can themselves contribute a teaching and learning element into the dialogue, since learning to communicate effectively happens no more automatically than does any other complex human practice. The acquisition and development of the communicative virtues, discussed in Chapter 2, depend in part on such explicit guidance and commentary.

Regulatory statements can include the following: explicit and pointed statements of agreement, praise, or reassurance ("Yes, that's an excellent point!''); commentary on the communicative process it-self (''You seem to be raising objections to everything I say''); or emotional assessments of oneself or one's partner (''I'm a little em-barrassed by this topic''). They are frequently concerned, as I have said, with the conditions of maintaining or developing the dialogical relation itself; they might even appear, in some contexts, to be *non sequiturs*, but apparent irrelevancies, humorous asides, and so on, can still play an important role in maintaining ''conversational involvement.''

Such examples, however, show that it would be a mistake to exaggerate the separateness of this class of statements; and as with other aspects of the model I am sketching here, particular statements belie these distinct categories. While, generally speaking, ''regula-tory'' statements should be seen as separate from ''content'' state-ments, we have just seen that they can constitute a kind of content themselves; and in many cases they are continuous with content statements: for example, ''I think we've gotten off the important issue here.'' Is that a regulatory comment, or a substantive contribu-tion to the discussion? Well, both, obviously. And by offering such commentary and contributing it to one's partner for consideration, or dispute (''No, I think this is precisely the issue we need to be talking about''), making regulatory statements is itself within the spirit of the dialogue game and can constitute an area of investigation and discovery. Regulatory statements are not necessarily ''outside the frame'' of the topic actually being discussed.

Because of this importance, a crucial consideration is *who* gets to makes such comments on the process, and whether this is a right implicitly or explicitly reserved for one party in the discussion—clearly in a dialogical relation of mutuality and respect it should not be. The latitude to offer such commentary often carries more weight, in terms of being able to guide the dialogue toward particular conclu-sions, than the force of one's statements within it; and as I will dis-cuss later, this is a primary area in which status or power differences can intervene to distort the dialogical relation and make it an instru-ment of something nonpedagogical (''*I'm* asking the questions here!''). We can see the force of this role by examining the Com-mander, the benevolent but authoritarian policewoman in Bruce Ack-erman's (1980) book *Social Justice in the Liberal State*, who has the role of intervening in the examples of liberal dialogue he cites. Her role is to impose regulatory ''conversational constraints'' on what people can and cannot say—but, as Michael Walzer (1990) points out, she does this so heavy-handedly that frequently people are left with noth-ing they can say at all!

Much, much more can be said about these five categories of statements in dialogue (questions, responses, building statements, redirecting statements, and regulatory statements) and how they work together to create and maintain an ongoing dialogue. But enough has been said about them here to suit our present purposes. These are, I believe, the basic "moves" that typify most dialogical interchange. They have characteristic purposes, and benefits, in light of keeping a dialogue moving forward; yet each can be misused in ways that actually impede the dialogue. Reflecting on when and how these kinds of statements can be helpful in dialogue, and being aware, within a dialogue, of whether one is using them appropriately, is a significant part of improving our practice as partners in dialogue.

Further Clarifications

In closing this section, let me add a few more clarifications that can avoid misunderstanding. First, by using the term *statements*, I don't mean that each of these is a unique and specific sentence uttered in a dialogue (although my examples have been). These statements can be of variable duration, and may span various utterances made over time within a dialogue; a "question" or a "statement" might actually comprise several separate sentences. Several types of statements will usually be combined together. Second, these are not entirely discrete classes of statements: Many statements will contain aspects of several of these moves, and can serve more than one purpose at the same time. Third, these are *functional*, not *formal*, definitions: A statement that may not have the form of a question can be taken as a question, in context; conversely, a statement that has the form of a question might actually be a thinly veiled assertion, and so on. Whether particular utterances operate as, say, building statements or redirecting statements is a highly contextual outcome, depending on myriad conditions of the topic, the content of the utterance, the circumstances of the dialogue, the state of the dialogical relation between participants, and much more—in short, it is a condition of *practice* and shows the complexity and depth of the judgments we need to make in contexts of practice. These cannot be stipulated in advance by the abstractions of an idealized model.

Nevertheless, a few general characteristics of dialogue *can* be partly formalized; and these moves, which are simply the attempt to generalize a range of choices participants actually make in dialogues, have distinct characters that we can usefully reflect upon. In the pedagogical circumstances that guide dialogue, these moves are the basic "links" that provide continuity and direction to an ongoing discussion. Given the diachronic and developmental view of dialogue I am emphasizing in this book, it is crucial that participants have an eye toward keeping the dialogue going, by relating what they say meaningfully to what has come before—and, as noted, this is a prerogative that all participants ought to have. When questions, redirections, or regulatory statements are the sole preserve of some members and not others, the direction of the dialogue is likely to be skewed, and the pedagogical benefits limited. The misuse of these moves can jeopardize the vitality of a dialogue, just as surely as can formally breaking the rules that govern dialogue.

In the next section, I want to focus a bit more on one class of statements, namely, questions. Hans-Georg Gadamer, among others, has argued that it is the structure of *questioning* that gives a particular dialogue its tone and character. Certain kinds of questions invite certain kinds of responses; some are more amenable to the sort of mutuality that we expect in dialogue; some are more likely than others to keep a dialogue going. By discussing this class of statements in more detail, I hope to provide a model of the kind of analysis that can be given to the other types of moves as well.

QUESTIONS IN DIALOGUE

As noted, Gadamer (1982) regards questioning as the heart of the dialogical process.

> To conduct a conversation requires first of all that the partners to it do not talk at cross purposes. Hence its *necessary structure* is that of question and answer. The first condition of the art of conversation is to insure that the other person is with us. . . . It requires that one does not try to out-argue the other person, but that one really considers the weight of the other's opinion. Hence it is an art of testing. But the art of testing is the art of questioning. For we have seen that to question means to lay open, to place in the open. As against the solidity of opinions, questioning makes the object and all its possibilities fluid. A person who possesses the "art" of questioning is a person who is able to prevent the suppression of questions by the dominant opinion. . . . The art of questioning is that of being able to go on asking questions, i.e. the art of thinking. (p. 330)

Gadamer may not be, strictly speaking, correct that a dialogue has the "necessary structure" of question and answer. We might imagine a dialogue entirely composed of initiating statements, responses, and building statements, which never includes questions; but at a deeper level there is still a questioning *spirit* to the process, since discovering and understanding the beliefs, values, and experiences of the partner remains part of what animates and sustains the dialogical engagement.

Types of Questions

In the same section of his book, *Truth and Method* (1982), Gadamer distinguishes "apparent" from "genuine" questions (pp. 325–341; see also Weinsheimer, 1985, p. 207). Apparent questions artificially delimit what can stand as a satisfactory answer, while genuine questions remain fundamentally "open": "The openness of what is in question consists in the fact that the answer is not settled. . . . [However, the] openness of the question is not boundless. It is delimited by the horizon of the question. A question which lacks this is, so to speak, floating" (p. 326). The chief challenge, therefore, in pedagogical questioning, as in dialogue, is to frame questions that are neither so broad as to be "floating," nor so narrow as to restrict the possibilities of generating original and creative insights—yet most pedagogical questions, Gadamer says, fail to navigate between this Scylla and Charybdis.

The complexity and difficulty of using questions in teaching can be inferred from the voluminous literature on the use of questions in the classroom (for example, D. Bridges, 1987, 1988b; Carlson, 1983, ch. 3; Dillon, 1983, 1987, 1988; Haroutunian-Gordon, 1991, ch. 3; Hunkins, 1972; Hyman, 1979; Manor, 1987; Morgan & Saxton, 1991, pp. 41–51; Potter & Andersen, 1963; Sanders, 1966; R. Young, 1992, pp. 89–121). There are as many different typologies and lists of questions as there are authors on the subject, and the ones I highlight here are only a sample of what is available. However, these accounts, in my view, go farther than most in being specific and clear, not only about the types of questions one can choose, but in how that choice stands against a broader scope of educational aims and purposes.

Earlier, I made a distinction between questions that are basically convergent, in terms of being directed toward a specific, definite answer, and those that are more divergent, or open, in terms of allowing a broader degree of uncertainty in what would constitute an adequate answer. This is similar to the distinction Gadamer makes between "apparent" and "genuine" questions. However, Gadamer goes too far in denying the pedagogical benefit of narrow, constrained questions for certain purposes; rather, the actual problem in education arises when these are the *only* types of questions asked.

More than one observer has commented that education is the only context in which one asks questions that one already knows the answer to, and there is a sense in which this does make such premeditated questions nongenuine. A common form, which rarely suits complex educational purposes, is the "guess what I'm thinking" sort of question. But specific, narrow questions, like other moves in dialogue, need to be judged as elements in an ongoing process; and there are many contexts in which such questions might be quite appropriate. Some of these uses were mentioned earlier. One is diagnostic, assessing the state of a partner's knowledge and understanding, in order to be able to frame more divergent and cognitively demanding questions afterward. Another is to establish a degree of confidence in the questioning process by trying to engage a student in dialogue in an unthreatening manner; some success in early, straightforward questions might encourage partners to feel secure in the dialogical relation, even later when questions may become more difficult, uncertain, and challenging. Finally, within certain constraints, these sorts of questions can serve the end of "leading" a student through the sequential steps of a complex argument (as in the *Meno*); and as I will try to show in Chapter 6, this approach to instruction has definite benefits, although it has potential limitations as well. The most constrained expression of this sort of questioning can be seen in the rather mechanical I.R.E. (Initiation-Response-Evaluation) pattern, so often recommended in models of direct instruction (Cazden, 1986). Because such techniques tend to be presented to teachers and adopted by them in ways that drive alternative forms of pedagogy off the agenda, we ought to be suspicious of them. If there is one thing that can be said with confidence about teaching and learning generally (and it might be the only thing), it is that there is no one approach that will work for all subjects, all teachers, and all students—that pluralism in methods and approaches is the only intelligent attitude to adopt. Yet certain models of questioning within the direct instruction literature, such as I.R.E., are put forth as the basis for *all* teaching, and teachers frequently apply them in that mechanical spirit (Alvermann & Hayes, 1989; Cazden, 1986, 1988; Gall, 1970, 1984; Good & Brophy, 1973; Guszak, 1967; Pearson & Gallagher, 1983; Wilen, 1982, 1984). Such reductionism is to be regretted (just as it is to be regretted, by the way, when proponents recommend something called the "Socratic method" as the ideal form of *all* teaching).

By far the more complex and interesting class of questions are those that are probing in a more open-ended way. An important way to get at these questions is to ask, not which of the *questioner's* purposes are served by a question, but which of the *questionee's* purposes are served. Wade and Armbruster (1990) suggest that questions with the following goals can be beneficial to students:

- *Setting a purpose*—identifying in advance a particular defined sphere of inquiry (Note that what Gadamer calls "floating" questions do not do this well.)
- *Guiding cognitive processing*—framing a particular line of inquiry, and cueing, often through key words in the question, the kinds of thought called for ("Explain how that works, please" or "What did you think about the camera movement in that film?")
- *Activating prior knowledge*—linking a line of inquiry to familiar knowledge, experience, and so forth ("Does this seem similar to anything you read last week?")
- *Focusing attention*—pointing out salient aspects of a problem ("Have you noticed any changes in the leaves since yesterday?")
- *Promoting cognitive monitoring*—helping students reflect on the state of their own understanding and thought processes ("Did this make sense, or do you need another explanation?")

David Bridges (1988a) suggests an even more detailed list of potential questions that can promote open-ended discussion.

- Asking why someone holds a particular opinion
- Asking how one point follows from another
- Asking what is the relevance of some point to the issue at hand
- Asking what alternative opinions might be presented
- Calling for more clarification, explanation, illustration, precision, conciseness, reasons, evidence, or argument
- Seeking a more systematic pooling of information; a more sympathetic hearing of divergent opinions, a more imaginative and open-minded conjecture, a more vigorous critical attack, a more ready and tolerant adjustment of one's own opinion to other people's
- Encouraging orderliness, reasonableness, and respect for different points of view

Purposes of Questions

What is most helpful about the accounts by Wade and Armbruster and by Bridges is not only their thoroughness but their attention to the matter of what purposes of benefit to *students* questions serve. The most important of these is whether questions are framed in ways that promote the capacity and disposition in students to become more effective questioners themselves. This is a valuable pedagogical outcome that is frequently ignored in these times of laundry lists of "cultural literacy" facts students are expected to know, with tests to enforce them; and it is an outcome that dialogue is uniquely qualified to promote.

The primary factors in helping students become more effective questioners themselves have already been mentioned: Does the structure of dialogical engagement encourage the formulation of questions in response; and does the status of teacher authority permit such questions? Can one's partner answer a question with a question, especially a skeptical or challenging one? Can one's partner initiate a line of inquiry through his or her questions, rather than solely in response to one's own? Are questions and responses encouraged among students (in a classroom discussion setting) and not only between teacher and individual student? Clearly, both the form of teachers' questions, as well as institutional constraints that define the social dimensions of appropriate questioning, make this outcome doubtful in many classrooms. In such circumstances, dialogical relations cannot arise or endure.

C. J. B. Macmillan and James Garrison (1983, 1988) address this problem in their "erotetic" theory of teaching: "On the erotetic concept it is the intention of teaching acts to answer questions that students *ought* to ask concerning the subject matter with which the teacher and student are engaged" (1988, pp. 15–16). In distinguishing the questions students ask from those they ought to be asking, the erotetic model proposes an "epistemological ought"; in other words, what kinds of questions are likely to lead to the kinds of knowledge students need, and how can teachers translate these idealized questions into questions students actually will be able and willing to ask? Macmillan and Garrison discuss a broad range of pedagogical approaches toward this end, including dialogue. But it is clear from their discussion that the central influences that develop the capacity for questioning in students are the sorts of questions teachers model in interchange with them; the manner in which teachers respond to the questions *they* are asked; and the sorts of questions teachers encourage students to ask themselves and one another. David Bridges (1987, 1988a) agrees that one of the chief purposes in adopting discussion methods is for "the development of people's ability to discuss" (1987, p. 35).

In other words, we teach through dialogue, and engage students with questions in dialogue, partly because of the specific insights we hope to develop, in ourselves as well as in our students, through such exchanges. But we *also* adopt such an approach because it helps to foster in our partners, and in ourselves, the capacity for asking genuine and productive questions. There is no way to develop this by being told about it, or by looking at a list of effective questions; these serve at most as hints or reminders of some of the possibilities before us. We learn to ask, and to answer, effective questions—as with any other communicative skill—through practice, through engagement with others similarly concerned. As Gadamer (1982) says, "It is more difficult to ask questions than to answer them" (p. 326). Dialogue provides a context in which what Gadamer calls "the art of question-asking" can be practiced and improved, for our students and for ourselves.

As with the other moves described in this chapter, questions cannot be given a purely formal characterization. Some utterances that look like questions actually are not ("Do you really expect me to believe that?"); utterances that are not in the form of questions can have the same effect as questions ("Please tell me about the central arguments in the article"), and sometimes the significance of a question will be apparent only after the fact. In other words, we need to be aware of both *explicit* and *implicit* questions (Pearson & Johnson, 1978). Or, to generalize the point, "To hear an utterance as a question is . . . as much a matter of situational factors as of its formal properties" (Benyon, 1987, p. 40). A corollary of this insight is that many aspects of a situation can prevent even well-formed and well-intended questions from being effective. As Philip Jackson (1986) notes, students often perceive questions to be "intrusive," "threatening," and "unnatural," *especially* when they perceive that the teacher is merely "fishing" for a predetermined answer (pp. 62–66).

As a result, pedagogical uses of questions raise many of the general concerns of creating and fostering a certain kind of authentic relation between partners in a dialogue: a relation of concern, trust, respect, and so on. When questions are seen outside such a relation, they can be deprived of their capacity to prompt serious thought and reflection; and here, as elsewhere, nonverbal as well as verbal accommodations need to be made to create and foster such a relation.

Some of these are familiar to all teachers: working to create a context in which the pressure to come up with the "right" answer, or the teacher's desired answer (which may be confused as the same thing), is minimized; waiting for a substantial period after asking a question to allow partners to consider and formulate an answer they feel secure offering; adopting a tone of voice that shows the question to be an authentic question, if indeed it is one; and, perhaps most important of all, showing through eye contact and attentive listening that the answer one's partner gives is of real and serious interest (Costa, 1990). Questions that are not expressed in such a nonverbal context might just as well not have been asked at all.

Finally, we can illustrate Gadamer's point about how one's choice of questions can shape the form and direction of a dialogue. Let me mention four examples: (1) a dialogue in which the questions are predominantly interpersonal, so that the tendency is to focus on aspects of intersubjective understanding, rather than the examination or criticism of external ideas or issues; (2) a dialogue in which the questions are predominantly open-ended, "genuine," to use Gadamer's phrase, so that the general tendency is to investigate together novel and uncharted ideas; (3) a dialogue in which the questions are predominantly skeptical and challenging, so that the general tendency is toward criticism and response; and (4) a dialogue in which the questions are predominantly of the leading variety, so that the general tendency is for the questioner to direct where the dialogue is headed. These four types of dialogue will feel quite different to the participants, are directed toward very different sorts of aims, and will yield quite different patterns of interaction. And while the form of questions is not the only difference among them, it is a *central* difference that gives these types of dialogue their unique characters.

SEQUENCES OF MOVES IN DIALOGUE

While dialogue has a spontaneous, immediate character to it—a relational interaction that catches us up in ways that we are barely aware of at the moment—in contexts of intentional teaching and learning we want to be able to adopt a dialogical approach as a way of serving more or less definite goals. Just as moves are prototypical actions and choices players make in the "dialogue game," so too there are some fairly coherent *sequences* of moves that can serve our purposes. By far the most detailed and perceptive analysis of these sequences is that of Allan Collins and Albert Stevens (Collins, 1977;

Collins & Stevens, 1982, 1983). Drawing from a body of previous research observing teachers in a variety of dialogical teaching situations, ranging from preschool to university, Collins and his colleagues gradually came to identify a series of basic dialogical patterns. I want to recount them here as a useful general map of some of the paths a dialogical interaction might follow in pursuing particular educational goals. What is most attractive about these approaches is that they are addressed to "higher order" cognitive processes, and not simply to answering questions to show recall of information. Collins and Stevens (1983) discuss these processes as follows:

> The most frequent goal is for the student to derive a *specific rule* or theory that the teacher has in mind. . . . Along with trying to teach a particular rule or theory, teachers often try to elicit and *debug incorrect rules* or theories. . . . Another goal that frequently pairs with teaching a given rule or theory is teaching students how to make *novel predictions* based on the rule or theory.
>   The other top-level goal of inquiry teachers is to teach students *how to derive* a new rule or theory. . . . One related ability is knowing *What questions to ask* in order to derive a new rule or theory on your own. . . . A goal that underlies many . . . dialogues is to teach students *what form* a rule or theory should take. . . . Occasionally in . . . dialogues teachers pursue a goal of teaching students how to *evaluate* a rule or theory that has been constructed. . . . Finally, it was a clear goal of [some teachers] . . . to get their students to *verbalize and defend* their rules or theories. (pp. 258–259)

I understand that the precise language of Collins and Stevens—a highly formalized language derived from theories of artificial intelligence, a language of strategies, techniques, and debugging—and their scientific theoretical and methodological orientation will be alienating for some readers. But we should consider whether in fact these goals, expressed in different words perhaps, are not goals we actually share, in some dialogical teaching contexts at least.

Similarly, their analysis of sequences of moves is highly suggestive of useful ways to plan one's questions and contributions to a dialogical encounter in order to pursue, with one's partner, new theoretical and conceptual insights about a subject. While Collins and Stevens (1983) describe these sequences primarily in the context of "Socratic" encounters, where the teacher questions and the student is led through these questions to specific conclusions the teacher has in mind, one need not have that purpose to find these sequences helpful. I will alternate their ten descriptions with my own commentary and examples.

1. "Selecting positive and negative exemplars. Teachers often choose positive or negative paradigm cases in order to highlight the relevant factors" (p. 260). By suggesting examples that clearly fall inside or outside a category, and then questioning students about why these do or do not count as instances of that category, it is possible to discover the characteristics by virtue of which we define them. For example, "What makes *this* an instance of sexual harassment, and that, not?" or "How many of the institutions of democracy does a country need to have before we are prepared to *call* it a 'democracy'?" Then responses to these questions might be followed by further examples: "Okay, if you count *that* as an instance, what would you say about *this*, which shares some, but not all, of its characteristics?" This suggests the next pattern.

2. "Varying cases systematically. Teachers often choose cases in systematic sequences to emphasize particular factors that they want the student to notice" (p. 262). One way to do this is to take an instance that clearly falls within a definition, then to vary its characteristics, one by one, until it clearly falls *outside* that category, and to inquire which changes were essential to this difference. Note, however, that if Wittgenstein's "family resemblance" argument is correct, for at least a certain class of concepts there will not be a determinative set of criteria for falling within or outside a definitional category. What is useful about this approach, however, is that it can *show* when such is the case. For example, a teacher may explore the concept of "indoctrination" with students by removing or altering one feature after another in a teaching situation until students agree that "teaching" has ceased and "indoctrination" has begun.

3. "Selecting counterexamples. A third method of choosing cases that teachers use in dialogues . . . is selecting counterexamples" (p. 263). Once a provisional set of criteria has been put forth, a very important dialogical move is to introduce problematic cases that test those criteria and may require their modification. For example (to adapt an example Collins and Stevens use): "Earlier, you said that all revolutions are wrong, because they involve killing innocent civilians and destroying private property. But then what do you think about the American Revolution?"

4. "Generating hypothetical cases. These teachers often generate hypothetical cases to challenge their students' reasoning" (p. 264). These hypothetical cases are generally also tests of proposed criteria, although unlike the other counterexamples they are not real

cases. For example, "Earlier, you said that any student who hits another student should miss recess for punishment. But what if the student doesn't *like* recess anyway?"

5. "Forming hypotheses. The most prevalent strategy that teachers use is to get students to formulate *general rules* relating different factors to values of the dependent variable" (p. 265). Better than for the teacher to formulate cases that fit the characteristics under consideration, in order to test them, is for the students themselves to actively generate them. For example, "Okay, so far we've established that wool is a good insulator, and a thermos is a good insulator, and a down comforter is a good insulator. Now what do you think makes these all good insulators?"

6. "Evaluating hypotheses. Sometimes teachers follow up the hypothesis-formation stage by trying to get students to systematically test out their hypotheses" (p. 267). In thinking about these recommendations, it is important to reflect (as Collins and Stevens do) on nonscientific, as well as scientific, contexts where learning can be enhanced by such dialogical approaches. For example, "You said that you thought Robert Frost's poetry was about the love of nature. Can you think of passages in his poems that might not fit that pattern?"

7. "Considering alternative predictions. Hypothesis formation is concerned with identifying *different factors* and how they relate to values of the dependent variable. . . . Encouraging students to consider other values of the dependent variable forces them into the more powerful methods of differential diagnosis or comparative hypothesis testing as opposed to the more natural tendency to consider only one alternative at a time" (p. 268). One of the most important challenges to a teacher interested in influencing students' schematic understanding through dialogue is not only to show that there may be exceptions to the models or beliefs students generate, but also to consider ways in which more than one hypothesis can account for any finite set of conditions. For example, "Our working assumption here has been that Lincoln worked to free the slaves because of doubts about the morality of that institution. But can we find other ways of accounting for his actions and statements?"

8. "Entrapping students. The teachers we have analyzed often use entrapment strategies to get the students to reveal their underlying misconceptions" (p. 269). One might not care much for how this is phrased, but the lesson here is a valuable one. Sequences of questions and responses often lead to impasses, self-contradictions, or points beyond which our explanations cannot go. It is often at

these very points that major flaws or limitations in our understandings become apparent to us, causing us to rethink in fundamental
ways our assumptions and frameworks. The give-and-take of dialogue (as Socrates's efforts certainly showed) can often serve this
end. For example, "Earlier you said that you thought lying was never
justified between friends. But now you say that false compliments
can be a 'nice gesture' between friends. Which is it? Are false compliments not lies, or are some lies between friends justified after all?
And if some lies are justified, why not others as well?"

9. "Tracing consequences to a contradiction. One of the ways
teachers try to get students to correct their misconceptions is to trace
the consequences of the misconceptions to some conclusion that the
students will agree cannot be correct" (p. 271). The key to this approach is that it must be an *internal* contradiction that the students
feel; it must be a clash with their own values, not simply a matter of
being told that they have a misconception. For example, "Joseph,
you just argued that the government should provide welfare pay-
ments only to people who are willing to work. Would you still hold
that position if it meant that the children of some families were mal-
nourished, even starving?"

10. "Questioning authority. A striking aspect of [some of these]
dialogues is the effort these teachers make to get the students not to
look to the teacher or the book for the correct answers, but rather to
construct their own theories" (p. 273). This reveals the underlying
spirit that makes the recommendations of Collins and Stevens so
appealing for dialogical teaching. It allows a teacher to resist providing a single definitive answer, while serving an active role in helping
students construct their own. For example, "Well, I simply don't
know why it doesn't work. Let's think about it together. What hap-
pened just before it broke down?"

Finally, Collins and Stevens summarize three overarching principles that can apply across all these examples.

1. Select cases that illustrate more important factors before less important factors.
2. Select cases to move from concrete to abstract cases.
3. Select more important or more frequent cases before less important
   or less frequent cases. (p. 274)

These principles are, of course, at an extremely high level of abstrac-
tion; their primary benefit, I think, is in helping us decide on the

kinds of examples or topics used to encourage some of the hypothe-sis-generating or testing procedures.

I believe that these general dialogical approaches provide an ex-tremely thorough and useful set of guides for planning questions and sequences of moves in dialogical interchange. Collins and Stevens make three bold claims for these uses of dialogue: (1) that they foster such "higher order" cognitive skills as forming and testing hypothe-ses, generating counterexamples, distinguishing between necessary and sufficient conditions, and knowing what kinds of questions are useful to ask; (2) that they are "exceptionally motivating for stu-dents"; and (3) that "students come out of the experience able to attack novel problems by applying these strategies themselves" (p. 276). While these are not the only goals we want to pursue through dialogue, they are certainly important goals. Collins and Stevens show how the planful use of moves available to a teacher in dialogue can develop specific insights and generalizable skills that, in turn, enable students to become more independent learners and problem solvers. Moreover, although it is not their purpose, these outcomes also address many of the intellectual habits we want to encourage in students when we engage in "critical pedagogy": questioning where social categories come from; looking for exceptions to hegemonic norms; formulating independent interpretations of political events; detecting contradictions; questioning authority; and so on. While, as I have said, Collins and Stevens describe these planful teaching sequences in terms one might not agree with, their insights are per-ceptive; and it may be interesting to note that all of these move sequences can be found repeatedly in Socrates's own dialogues.

LIMITATIONS OF THE "MOVE" ANALOGY

In conclusion, I want to reiterate what the analysis of dialogue in terms of the five basic kinds of moves (questions, responses, building statements, redirecting statements, and regulatory statements) does *not* provide. Dialogue is, after all, situated within the context of com-munication generally; and there are numerous kinds of utterances that are common in practical discourse but cannot simply be assigned to one of these five categories. Deborah Tannen (1989), for example, describes a number of examples of utterances that are directed toward maintaining "conversational involvement" (in my terms, maintain-ing the dialogical relation), which cannot be analyzed simply as meaningful contributions to a linear, logical sequence of statements. A particularly clear example that she cites is *repetition*, restating what one's partner has just said. Repetition serves a number of valuable purposes: It shows one's partner that one is attending carefully; it is a way of checking the accuracy of one's understanding by restating or rephrasing what one has heard, in order to give the speaker a chance to correct the understanding; and it can help create a mood of intimacy and sympathy that can reinforce sentiments, such as trust, that are necessary for dialogue, especially about difficult topics, to proceed. Tannen's analysis includes a number of other examples of utterances as well. The general point is that any actual conversation will contain repetitions, discontinuities, irrelevancies, casual asides, interruptions, *non sequiturs*, and redundancies that may be, strictly speaking, irrelevant or unnecessary for the topic under discussion, but have much to do with creating and maintaining the fabric of a communicative relation. (This shows again, by the way, why Grice's criteria are inadequate.) These kinds of statements are not easily as-signed to the five categories of moves I have described here. Nothing I have said implies that these categories are exhaustive; nor that *all* of our utterances in an ongoing dialogue are planful, logical moves in a direct linear sequence. But to the extent that we *do* have conscious pedagogical aims in mind when engaged in dialogue with a partner, attending to these moves, and thinking about when and how they can be useful for our purposes, can improve our dialogical practice.

Such practice requires judgment and experience as well. Choices about the moves that we adopt in a dialogical relation—such as the kinds of questions we ask—arise from explicit or implicit decisions about such things as a view of knowledge, a conception of authority, or assumptions about our partners in the relation. Because such choices rely on a range of contextual judgments, the use of moves in dialogue should never be seen as a technique or step-by-step recipe. Many of these judgments have to do with the appropriateness of particular moves for particular purposes (for example, when it is not advisable to try to "entrap" students). Another dimension of such judgments, I believe, is in knowing which sorts of moves work well for oneself, given one's skills and personality; exercising moves by rote, without a sense of enthusiasm or confidence in them, will rarely gain desired pedagogical aims. An important factor here, as Gadamer (1982) says, is knowing what one does not know; so that at least some of the questions one asks can arise from sincere curiosity and interest, not from a fishing expedition.

Thus, reflecting on the variety of moves, and combinations of moves, one can actually adopt in dialogue (or in different dialogues with different sorts of partners) begins to move us away from seeing the "Socratic method" as one simple thing. There are different styles or genres of dialogue: each with different affective tones, different patterns of verbal interaction, different aims or purposes, and possibly appropriate to different kinds of subject matters. The skillful playing of dialogue, then, appears as a *repertoire* of moves and sequences of moves, along with a sense of when and how each might be beneficial for our purposes. Different combinations of such moves and sequences of moves will yield dialogues with quite different patterns. This is the topic of Chapter 6, in which I will discuss four different types of dialogue: dialogue as conversation, dialogue as inquiry, dialogue as debate, and dialogue as instruction.

Four Types of Dialogue

From the four passages quoted at the beginning of the Introduction to this book, I have repeatedly drawn examples to show that dialogue is not just one thing; that it depends on a variety of communicative approaches, which I have called "moves"; and that these moves can be seen as falling into fairly regular prototypical patterns. I believe we can identify at least four such patterns that are—in any real dialogue— combined and overlapping in multiple ways, but that retain discrete characters. The idea that the so-called "Socratic method" is not a single process has been argued most persuasively by Gadamer (1980) in his book, *Dialogue and Dialectic*, where he distinguishes a variety of dialogical approaches in Plato's dialogues, arguing that the real genius of the teacher Socrates, as we encounter him there, is in his capacity to choose and adapt these approaches to the audience, context, and topic under consideration. Many of my arguments in this chapter, although not my analysis of four types of dialogue, are centrally beholden to Gadamer's insights (there are also some related distinctions made in Rorty, 1979).

The four types, or genres, of dialogue I will describe are dialogue as conversation, dialogue as inquiry, dialogue as debate, and dialogue as instruction. Before I describe them and their differences in detail, I should explain the genesis of these four categories and their relation to one another.

I have repeatedly made two kinds of distinctions in discussing dialogical situations in this book. The first distinction bears primarily on the conception of dialogue and its relation to knowledge. One view, which has been termed "referential" or "teleological," assumes that the dialogical process is aimed toward a particular epistemic end point: a final answer or conclusion to the argument (Dascal, 1985a, p. 3; Petit, 1985, p. 431). I want to term this position a *convergent* view of dialogue, since it assumes that the various positions of the interlocutors are, as least in principle, resolvable into a consensus around a correct answer.

The other view of the relation of dialogue to knowledge is most strongly expressed by Bakhtin (1981) in his view of "heteroglossia," discussed earlier. For Bakhtin, dialogue is necessarily *divergent*, and each statement in it is irresolvably plural.

> Alongside the centripetal forces, the centrifugal forces of language carry on their uninterrupted work; alongside verbal-ideological centralization and unification, the uninterrupted processes of decentralization and disunification go forward. . . . Every concrete utterance of a speaking subject serves as a point where centrifugal as well as centripetal forces are brought to bear. (p. 272)

While this tends to overstate the point, it presents an important insight about the "internal dialogization" of language: that plural meanings, complex and ambiguous connotations, and the myriad associations speakers have for the terms they use, often put their utterances at cross-purposes, multiplying possible interpretations rather than narrowing them toward a single correct one (Daelemans & Maranhão, 1990; Fraser, 1989). Here we have a distinction between *convergent* and *divergent* views of dialogue. However, one need not adopt one of these positions or the other universally; and it is conceivable that one may hold a convergent view of dialogue in some subject areas, but regard dialogue in other contexts divergently.

The other distinction that has recurred in this text is one expressing two different attitudes toward one's partner in dialogue, and basic orientations to what he or she says. This distinction was framed by Peter Elbow (1986) as "the believing game" and "the doubting game," and by Mary Belenky and her coauthors (1986) as "connected knowing" and "separate knowing." I will call this distinction one of adopting either an *inclusive* or a *critical* orientation toward one's partner in dialogue. Whatever terms are used, in each of these distinctions the first attitude is one of granting at least a provisional plausibility to what one's partner says, simply by virtue of the fact that the partner asserts it. The initial task of a partner in dialogue, taking the inclusive stance, is to understand what has led the other person to his or her position: what beliefs, feelings, or experiences underlie the position and give it veracity, at least in the mind of the speaker. The second attitude in each of these distinctions is more skeptical, questioning; it emphasizes a judgment about the objective accuracy of the partner's position, and does not hesitate to test it against evidence, consistency, and logic. Again, as with the first pair, one need not hold to one attitude or the other exclusively (although by constitution many persons seem predisposed to one approach or the other);

one may hold different attitudes with different partners, or with different subject matters, or at different points in an ongoing dialogue. A person may, for example, begin by playing the "believing game" for as long as possible, to make sure that the best and most sympathetic case has been granted to the partner's claims, *before* then turning a more critical lens on those claims. Indeed, this may not be a bad general rule of thumb (Garrison & Phelan, 1990).

I have now defined two distinctions: that between *convergent* and *divergent* views of knowledge; and that between *inclusive* and *critical* attitudes toward one's partner in communication. Imagine, now, a two-by-two grid, with each distinction along one dimension. The result is four pairs of combinations; and these pairs characterize each of the four types of dialogue I have discussed so far.

Inclusive-divergent	Dialogue as conversation
Inclusive-convergent	Dialogue as inquiry
Critical-divergent	Dialogue as debate
Critical-convergent	Dialogue as instruction

In the remainder of this chapter, I will describe each of these four genres in greater detail and consider possible domains of application for each. I will suggest how each of these approaches can take educationally beneficial and educationally detrimental forms, and conclude by discussing how they might be combined in an overall approach to teaching.

DIALOGUE AS CONVERSATION

An inclusive-divergent dialogue has two characteristics: a generally cooperative, tolerant spirit, and a direction toward mutual understanding. It does not necessarily aim toward agreement or the reconciliation of differences. We engage in this kind of dialogue when we are primarily interested in understanding the outlook and experiences of a partner in dialogue. An example might be a discussion between two friends about their relations to their respective families; learning more about what made them each the people they are today. I label this kind of exchange a "conversation," not to suggest that all conversations are dialogues, but to stress the continuity of this view of dialogue with the ideas of Gadamer, in whose work (at least in translation) the term *conversation* is frequently used to denote dialogue per se. The central notion for the Gadamerian view of dialogue is its goal of *understanding*. For Gadamer (1982), understanding begins with a question.

> The close relation that exists between question and understanding is what gives the hermeneutic experience its true dimension. However much a person seeking understanding may leave open the truth of what is said, however much he may turn away from the immediate meaning of the object and consider, rather, its deeper significance, and take the latter not as true, but merely as meaningful, so that the possibility of its truth remains unsettled, this is the real and basic nature of a question. (pp. 337–338)

A kinship with Elbow's "believing game" and Belenky and coauthors' "connected knowing" should be apparent here. For Gadamer, what matters most "is the mutuality, the respect required, the genuine seeking to understand what the other is saying, the openness to test and evaluate our own opinions through such an encounter" (R. Bernstein, 1986, p. 113).

The result of such a dialogical engagement is what Gadamer (1982) calls a "fusion of horizons," the basis for intersubjective understanding (pp. 273–274, 337, 358). Conversation in this sense seeks a language and manner of communication that can make speakers comprehensible to one another. Two aspects of Gadamer's account are crucial: The first is that "understanding is not based on 'getting inside' another person, on the immediate fusing of one person in another" (p. 345). It is a serious misreading of Gadamer to think that this "fusion" can be satisfied by the imposition of one person's understandings as the dominant or only correct ones. Such an outcome may only maintain prejudices, without raising them for mutual scrutiny. The second, following from this point, is that this "fused horizon" is not *found*, but *created*; it is established in the conversational exchange itself. Gadamer relates this process to one of translation: not of converting A to B, but of "finding a common language" (pp. 346, 349).

This translation can be made difficult in situations of broad cultural difference, as discussed earlier. Attempts at dialogue across such differences can run up against linguistic, experiential, or paradigmatic incommensurabilities. The frustrating experience of radical misunderstanding or nonunderstanding is familiar to us all. In certain cases this gulf of misunderstanding might be so serious that on specific points no meeting of the minds is possible, even at the level of mutual comprehension, let alone fused horizons. But the ordinary experience of translation across natural languages tells us that the *usual* case is that effective common meanings can be established, and that sufficient equivalencies can be built over time so that speakers of any two languages can achieve a significant degree of mutual understanding. Translation does not need to be complete or perfect for this to occur: In any ongoing attempt to understand one another, we will need to build upon what has previously been established in common as a way of bridging additional areas of difference. This process may involve analogy, metaphor, paraphrase, or indirect reference; and it may or may not be successful—this is something to be discovered in practice. As Gadamer (1982) points out:

> The translator is often painfully aware of his inevitable distance from the original. . . . And, as in conversation, when there are such unbridgeable differences, a compromise can sometimes be achieved in the to and fro of dialogue, so the translator will seek the best solution in the toing and froing of weighing up and considering possibilities—a solution which can never be more than a compromise. (p. 348)

This point about natural languages can be extended to other cultural and paradigmatic systems as well. The occasional experience of radical incommensurability should not obscure the much more important point that, despite enormous diversity, our ways of thinking and speaking about our world also exhibit striking commonalities. These commonalities give us some reason to pursue attempts at overcoming misunderstandings or nonunderstandings when they do occur, rather than abandoning the effort because it is assumed to be futile.

> To use the language of incommensurability, we can say that the incommensurability of different forms of life or different historical epochs always presents a challenge to us, a challenge that requires learning to ask the right questions and drawing on the resources of our own linguistic horizon in order to understand that which is alien. For Gadamer, it is not a dead metaphor to liken the fusion of horizons that is the constant task of effective-historical consciousness to an ongoing and open dialogue or conversation. (R. Bernstein, 1983, p. 144)

Furthermore, even when the pursuit of understanding fails, dialogue as conversation can promote tolerance and respect across difference. There is no reason to assume that dialogue across differences involves either eliminating those differences or imposing one individual's or group's views on others; dialogue can *sustain* differences within a broader compact of toleration and respect (Burbules & Rice, 1991).

The matter of understanding and misunderstanding needs further clarification here. One often encounters what might be called a "positivistic" conception of understanding: If the object of understanding is taken as a given, then one must "get it right," and anything short of understanding *exactly* what is being understood is unacceptable. But once one adopts a Gadamerian outlook on this process, and realizes that understandings are constructed, that all attempts to bridge difference are imperfect translations, the dichotomy of "understanding" versus "misunderstanding" drops away. We come to realize that *understanding and misunderstanding always occur together*. Every understanding is partial and established through a process of interpretation that necessarily transforms what was initially said or meant into terms that are salient for the listener. Every misunderstanding results from something that *is* understood, but then extended or inferred into something that is not. Thus, understanding and misunderstanding should not be dichotomously opposed to one another: no communicative process is perfect; no intersubjective understanding, even among partners who share a language, culture, and set of experiences, is ever complete. Moreover, it is often by the very process of "misunderstanding" others, that is, interpreting their claims and beliefs in slightly different terms than they do themselves, that the process of communication actually moves forward to new understandings—this is partly why we engage in conversation (Dascal, 1985b).

Sometimes an external perspective is helpful *precisely because* it is different from one's own. Both as individuals and groups, we can broaden and enrich our self-understanding by considering our beliefs, values, and actions from a fresh standpoint. This does not require embracing the other standpoint or letting it supersede our own, but it does stress the value of incorporating that perspective into a more complex and multifaceted framework of understanding.

In the model of dialogue as conversation, then, understanding is conceived "as part of the process of the coming into being of meaning" (Gadamer, 1982, p. 147). Partners in the dialogue proceed interactively, cooperatively, not toward a specific common goal, but in a *process* of mutual engagement directed toward shared understanding. I am drawn to *this* sort of dialogue with *this* person because in *this* process I see an opportunity to supplement and refigure my own understandings (and presumably my partner is motivated similarly). We speak with and listen to one another in a pedagogical communicative relation whose divergent aim is not a correct and final answer, but a heightened sense of sensitivity and understanding of other persons, and through understanding them, newly understanding ourselves.

DIALOGUE AS INQUIRY

An inclusive-convergent dialogue aims toward the answering of a specific question, the resolution of a specific problem, or the reconciliation of a specific dispute; it is convergent in its aim to produce an outcome agreeable to all. An example might be a group of young students trying to figure out why the plants on one side of the classroom are dying, while those on the other are flourishing. I label this a kind of "inquiry," since it typically involves the investigation of alternatives, the weighing and testing of different potential answers, within a dialogical structure that encourages a range of perspectives and approaches to the problem at hand. One phase of this process, in fact, may be divergent, "brainstorming" as many ideas as possible. But the point of doing so, in this sort of dialogue, is to provide substance for a further process that compares, evaluates, and builds upon these different views, in order to make choices among them. On the other hand, because there are often many possible answers to a question, or solutions to a problem, encouraging a variety of approaches, without seeking to reconcile them or choose one single answer from among them, can be a valuable educational goal as well—but the spirit of inquiry is still convergent in the sense that these alternatives are all tied to addressing the same question or problem.

One form of this kind of dialogue involves an investigation into an issue or question with the hope of finding an answer to it. Here, the educational benefit of dialogue is in people "attempting, together, to learn more than they now know" (Freire, 1970, p. 79). The contributions of knowledge and insight made by different members can become synergistic, generating new understandings through the process of building ideas upon one another. However, there is also a questioning aspect appropriate to this kind of dialogue, not with the critical purpose of rejecting these alternatives, but directed toward determining the reasons, evidence, and experiences that underlie them, as a way of understanding and assessing them more accurately.

A second form of this kind of dialogue involves problem solving: approaching a difficulty or conflict that requires the development of workable, and perhaps novel, solutions. Here, too, generating an initial range of alternatives might be a useful starting point; but, again, it also requires a process by which these alternatives are tested or evaluated, and either elaborated or rejected as inadequate. Identifying varying experiences that the participants might have had with potential proposed solutions, generating unexpected or unconventional approaches, and considering together how these various solutions might affect diverse populations, are all elements of an inclusive dialogical process that makes a better and more feasible solution likely.

A third form of this kind of dialogue involves working to achieve a political consensus. Persons, at least in a democracy, often need to engage in a dialogical interchange in order to work through conflicting social or political demands. While it is sometimes the case that these conflicts cannot in fact be resolved (dialogue here, as in all other contexts, is fallible), this *process* of respectfully weighing alternative views and the merits of the cases that can be made for them is the essence of the democratic spirit.

A fourth form of this kind of dialogue involves coordinating actions to achieve some common purpose: "What should we do next?" Even after identifying common social or political purposes, say, there may still remain the question of how best to achieve them, and these are matters that persons will usually disagree about. The benefit of an inclusive dialogue here is that coordinating activity will require different persons to see their efforts in relation to those of others, in the context of some coherent larger plan. Yet to the extent that persons also feel that they have had a legitimate voice in the process by which this plan was generated, they will act to fulfill their role with greater enthusiasm and sense of purpose.

A fifth form of this kind of dialogue involves adjudicating moral differences; acknowledging strong grounds for disagreement, perhaps, but by discussing and comparing them seeking a basis on which these views can become, if not reconciled, at least expressible in ways that are compatible with and tolerant of one another. Various real-world experiences—the current debate over abortion rights, for example—show how very difficult, and possibly intractable, such disputes can be. However, *if* they are going to be resolvable at all (some will and some may not be), it must be through a process that involves the open presentation of different alternatives, the articulation of the beliefs and values that give rise to them, and an attempt to find a common ground.

Clearly, these five forms of dialogue as inquiry are closely linked, and other versions might be imagined. But the central point for my purposes here is that they all depend on the same inclusive, convergent process: fostering a spirit of tolerance and respect for a range of views, with the *intention* of addressing some sort of question or problem, and with the *hope* that these differences can be reconciled into at least partial and provisional commonalities. This process underlies all five of these different forms.

Moreover, as Habermas's theoretical work has shown us, in its emphasis on the simultaneity of the four validity claims (comprehensibility, truth, sincerity, and rightness), the various dimensions of establishing common evidentiary grounds and arguments, reconciling moral differences, building a social and political consensus, finding common purpose, and coordinating actions are *all* likely, in any complex social debate, to be dimensions of the problem at hand. Thus, attempts to resolve any one of these sorts of disputes will frequently invoke criteria or standards that need to be adjudicated, or "redeemed," to use Habermas's phrase, along other lines of inquiry. So, for example, a debate about the relative merits of certain environmental protections and the interests of employment and economic development within a particular community will range over all these sorts of issues in a very complex way. The only general principle that can be proposed in such cases is to realize *which* sort of dispute is at stake, and which methods of resolution may be appropriate to it: for example, that questions of fact can (at least) sometimes be resolved apart from moral disputes; or that the likely consequences of policies often might need to be predicted before those policies can be fairly judged and compared, and so on.

The use of questions in this kind of dialogue, as noted earlier, is quite different from the use of questions in dialogue as conversation. Here, many of the questions will be more externally than internally directed—in other words, referring more often to states of events in the social and natural world, and less often solely to the internal beliefs and values of participants. Dialogue toward understanding can be largely satisfied with identifying the underlying elements of belief and value systems; dialogue toward inquiry, because it is usually addressed to some broader practical purpose of investigation or effective activity, must try to find ways to compare and evaluate these differences. Nevertheless, this approach is much less critical than the following form of dialogue, dialogue as debate.

DIALOGUE AS DEBATE

A critical-divergent dialogue has a sharply questioning, skeptical spirit, but does not have any necessary aim toward agreement or the reconciliation of differences. An example might be two panels of students discussing the relative merits of two political candidates. The primary potential benefit of such an exchange, for the participants, is in seeing their respective positions receive the most difficult challenge possible, in being pressed to articulate and defend those positions as clearly and thoroughly as they can, and in seeing the merits of alternative views presented from a strong advocacy position. This process may or may not take the form of what we consider a "debate," which has connotations of competitiveness, winning, and losing. The debating spirit of this form of dialogue is in its dedication to contrasting the merits of alternative positions from the strongest positions available. For nonparticipants to this process, who are not necessarily committed to an advocacy role toward any particular position, a potential benefit can be in observing the respective cases made for each view and gaining a better sense of the number and strength of arguments available to them, pro and con on each position. There are also potentially counterproductive forms that this kind of dialogue can take (as there are for all four of the types described in this chapter—I will return to this point), but my concern here is to show how and when this type of dialogue *can* be educationally beneficial (see Walton, 1990).

The skills of debate were a primary focus of the teaching of the rhetoricians in classical Greece. One of the most famous of these was Isocrates, who taught his students to "stand up to the fire and cunning of an opponent in public debate, and vanquish him by the arguments and style of delivery appropriate to that particular case" (Johnson, 1959, p. 29). Now, this is a variety of the "dialogue game" that may not appeal to many readers; and, as noted in Chapters 2 and 3, a spirit of aggressive competitiveness can interfere with the spirit of the game.

In this context, however, my concern is with how a rhetorical approach to debate can interfere with or support the *dialogical* aims of communication and pedagogical growth. If the purposes of debate are the generation of new information, better arguments, and a clearer general understanding of the issues at stake, these are not served when participants to that debate engage in obfuscation, manipulation, or selective use of information simply for the sake of winning the case. On the other hand, even dialogue as debate can have a cooperative and respectful spirit in the sense that each part-ner—as in the dialogue game generally—agrees to play by certain common rules for the sake of the overall pleasure and benefit of the game. When the desire to "win" the argument becomes exaggerated enough to interfere with these aims, it is that desire that should be questioned, not the vitality and spirit of the game.

The questions that contribute to this kind of dialogical interaction are obviously probing and challenging; but they are directed toward the positions at issue and the arguments being put forth for them. There are many contexts in which teachers can use this kind of ques-tioning in interchange with students, or create settings in which stu-dents are encouraged to adopt, in earnest or perhaps in role-playing, the positions of advocates in a debate setting. (And as many teachers have found, one fruitful exercise can be to assign advocates to posi-tions *against* the grain of views that they actually hold.)

DIALOGUE AS INSTRUCTION

A critical-convergent dialogue involves the use of some of the same sorts of critical questions that a critical-divergent dialogue does, but with a different aim. In this type of dialogue, the use of questions and other statements is to move the discussion toward a definite conclusion. An example might be a teacher talking a young student through the steps of searching for a book in the library. This is the "leading" form of dialogue, most familiar in the context of Plato's dialogue the *Meno* and other exemplars of the "Socratic method." Dialogue in this genre is a highly directive form of teaching, but one that operates through indirect processes of instruction that require the student to work actively to make conceptual connections in re-sponse to teacher questions.

Socrates, in one his most famous metaphors, compares the role of the teacher with that of a midwife: a person who does not create, but labors to draw forth the creations of others (Plato, 1961d; see also Haroutunian-Gordon, 1989). In the *Meno* (Plato, 1961b), we observe Socrates leading a young boy through the steps of a geometric proof, apparently never asserting anything himself, but asking questions at just the right level of difficulty to keep the student making active connections without needing to make conceptual leaps he was not prepared to make. One of the central features of this dialogue, and of Socratic interrogation generally, is the phase—Socrates says it is an essential phase—of inducing a state of *aporia*, or deep conceptual confusion, before the reconstruction of a new and more accurate understanding is possible. For Socrates, when people already think they understand something, their mistaken but firmly entrenched presumptions themselves become an active obstacle to learning. Hence in order to be introduced to a drastically different way of thinking, the learner must first be brought to a state of puzzlement and uncertainty. This explains the frequent instances in the dialogues in which we see Socrates methodically leading partners into self-contradictory positions, until, as Meno puts it, they feel numbed, as if stung by a stingray (Plato, 1961b).

Again, there are many aspects of this characterization of "leading dialogue" that are inappropriate to the model of dialogue I am proposing in this book. But what this Socratic legacy has given us is the insight that one valuable process of teaching through dialogue can be a give-and-take that is planful and directed by one of the parties in order to assist and guide the other through the steps of complex and developmentally novel cognitive processes (Petrie, 1981).

The model of dialogue as a mode of instruction, however, is not limited only to the Socratic methods illustrated in the *Meno* and other dialogues. One widely discussed current approach to instruction, reciprocal teaching, has a similar dialogical structure. Drawing on constructivist views of knowledge and Vygotskyan models of development, this approach relates teacher and student in a highly interactive process of questioning, modeling, and what is often termed "scaffolding." Although the label "reciprocal teaching" has been used to refer to many different kinds of teaching, having varying degrees of success (Rosenshine & Meister, 1991), this approach, because of its close affinity with several theories of dialogue, is worth consideration here.

The connection between Vygotsky's ideas on the relation of thought to language and some models of dialogue was discussed in Chapter 1 (see also Wertsch, 1980). Anne-Marie Palincsar (1986) makes a similar point about teaching.

> Critical to the teaching-learning process is the role of dialogue: it is the means by which support is provided and adjusted. . . . When children engage in problem solving, they display the kind of behaviors that are characteristic of dialogue, posing and responding to their own questions, essentially internalizing the dialogue they have experienced in the initial stages of problem solving when they were collaborating with a more expert individual. It is this dialogue, occurring with initial in-

struction regarding the strategy, that enables learners to participate in strategic activity even though they may not fully understand the activity and would most certainly not be able to exercise the strategy independently. The relationship between the learner and teacher in this supportive dialogue is to be contrasted with that observed when students are left to discover or invent strategies independently or when students are passive observers who receive demonstration and are "talked at" regarding strategy use. (p. 75)

One important element in this process is its appropriation of the Vygotskyan idea of a "zone of proximal development," a state of readiness in which a student will be able to make certain kinds of conceptual connections, but not others: anything too simple for the student will quickly become boring; anything too difficult will quickly become demoralizing. Palincsar (1986) asks, "How can educators best aid learners in the zone of proximal development, nudging them from one level of competence to the next and eventually to independent application of the instructed skill?" (p. 74). It is interesting to consider that the Socrates of the *Meno* seems to be operating within a similar framework of questioning, asking stepwise questions that are challenging, but not too discouraging for his partners in dialogue.

However, *reciprocal teaching*, as Palincsar (1986) describes it, is less exclusively constituted by questioning processes.

The term reciprocal was chosen because in reciprocal exchange one party acts by way of response or reaction to the other party. Reciprocal teaching is best represented as a dialogue between teachers and students in which participants take turns assuming the role of teacher. (pp. 77–78)

Palincsar and Ann Brown (1984) describe four strategies as part of this interchange: prediction, question generation, summarization, and clarification (it is important to note that they are referring here primarily to developing the skills of comprehension for written texts). What is important, and generalizable, about this process is that the teacher in this relation is engaged in two important processes, the first of which is *modeling*.

Initially the adult teacher modeled the activities, but the students had great difficulty assuming the role of dialogue teacher when their turn came. . . . With repeated interaction with an adult model performing appropriate questioning and paraphrasing activities, the students became able to perform these functions on their own. (pp. 124, 135)

The second aspect of reciprocal teaching is the process called *scaffolding*. Here, the teacher not only models a process, but intervenes actively to provide just sufficient structure and guidance to allow the student to apply the strategies effectively. But this support is gradually withdrawn over time (as with a scaffolding that is dismantled as a structure can stand on its own). Scaffolding approaches have three chief benefits, according to Courtney Cazden (1988).

> They make it possible for the novice to participate in the mature task from the very beginning; and they do this by providing support that is both adjustable and temporary. . . . If, in fact, the novice takes over more and more responsibility for the task at hand, . . . then we can infer, retrospectively, that our help was well timed and well tuned, and that the novice was functioning in his or her zone of proximal development, doing at first with help what he or she could very soon do alone. (p. 107)

My motivation in discussing these views of Palincsar, Brown, and Cazden in detail is that they all refer explicitly to dialogue as the paradigm of this interactive model of teaching: for example, "dialogue has a critical role to play in scaffolded instruction, facilitating the collaboration necessary between the novice and expert for the novice to acquire the cognitive strategy or strategies" (Palincsar, 1986, p. 95). Specifically, the interactive structure of dialogue makes possible two elements of a complex instructional process. First, as noted, modeling provides an external, expert, and explicit example of the strategies being learned, and in the interaction between student and teacher these processes can be repeated, or accompanied by step-by-step explanations. Second, when students are engaged in such interaction, teachers have an immediate, accurate basis for judging their competence and providing appropriate feedback (Palincsar & Brown, 1984). The dialogical model provides some useful criteria for judging the effectiveness of reciprocal teaching.

> (a) The extent to which there was teacher support of the students' contribution to the dialogue . . . ; (b) the extent to which there was a deft use of student ideas and linking of those ideas to new knowledge; (c) the extent to which there was focus and direction to the dialogue; (d) the extent to which the point of instruction was made explicit to the student and seemed explicit to the teacher; and (e) the way in which evaluative statements were made that changed the complexion of a student response from negative to constructive. (Palincsar, 1986, p. 96)

In this section I have described two dialogical approaches to instruction: that of Socrates, driven largely by questions and leading a dialogical partner through the logical steps of complex arguments or proofs; and the reciprocal teaching model, which involves a much more complex process of modeling, scaffolding, questioning, and providing feedback through a close, ongoing interaction between teacher and student. Both are instructional, in that they are directed toward specific learning goals: knowledge, skills, and a greater degree of cognitive self-sufficiency. Each may have only specific spheres of applicability, namely, those in which a highly "explicit" modeling of "strategies" of sequential reasoning is possible. They assume an "expertise" on the part of the teacher that, given my previous discussions of authority, may be problematic in some instances. Yet for some domains at least, these approaches have been shown to be much more effective than either simply lecturing or "showing," on the one hand, and unguided, "free" discovery learning on the other. Finally, both *can* operate within the structure of the dialogical relation, accommodating the values of mutuality and open communication that dialogue demands—although, as with the other types of dialogue I have described here, they can each take antidialogical forms as well. This is the main topic of the next section.

REFINING THE TYPOLOGY OF DIALOGUE GENRES

The major danger in offering a typology like this one, in my view, is the risk of having it be seen as a reified and exhaustive set of categories to which all forms of actual dialogical practice must conform. To forestall this tendency, I would like to make some explicit clarificatory comments about these four types.

First, they may not be exhaustive of all potential forms. There is, for example, frequent discussion of "therapeutic" dialogue in the literature, which may or may not be classifiable in terms of these four types (Daelemans & Maranhão, 1990; Keeney, 1990). Similarly, there are varieties of dialogue across cultural settings (Fisher & Abedi, 1990; Urban, 1990), which again may or may not fit within these genres. While the structure of the two-by-two pattern I have described seems flexible enough to encompass the similarities and differences of a wide range of specific dialogical styles, I am making no special claims for comprehensiveness here. One central reason for avoiding such a claim is that, as in other activities of practice, the practice of dialogue is the primary creative domain, not our theoretical models—and whether or not such practice has given, or will give, rise to unusual and unanticipated possibilities is something that cannot, in my view, be prejudged.

Second, these are "ideal types," not rigid categories; any actual dialogue may be a hybrid of various elements from each. Moreover, in an ongoing dialogue there will be phases it moves through, at some points being more argumentative, perhaps, at other points more oriented toward intersubjective understanding (Wilen, 1990). In fact, given the diachronic and developmental conception of dialogue I have presented in this book, where establishing and maintaining the conditions of a dialogical relation are primary elements of the communicative process, it will often be *necessary* to move from one type of dialogue to another—some of the more critical modes of dialogical interaction, in particular, probably cannot sustain a long-term relation all by themselves.

Third, in presentations of these ideas with others, I have previously encountered the attitude that two of these forms, conversation and inquiry, are morally preferable to the other two, instruction and debate. A general concern about the potential for critical modes of interrogation to become argumentative and insensitive seems to be behind this response. Certainly, there are points at which the latter two forms of dialogue can pass over into modes of verbal interaction that begin to threaten the rules and relational conditions that make dialogue possible. However, a deeper analysis of the issue seems to me to suggest that all four of these types can take both beneficial and pernicious forms; that while each has an appropriate purpose and domain of expression, all four have the potential to become antidialogical as well.

Dialogue as conversation, for example, is clearly guided by a spirit of sympathy and tolerance for alternative points of view, and in this it can express some of the most important communicative virtues, discussed previously. But the exercise of any virtue can become a vice when it is exaggerated, or exercised in inappropriate contexts. The prime risk in this sort of dialogue is that of relativism, of turning dialogue into a kind of interview, in which *anything* can be said, but not questioned. *Dialogue as inquiry*, on the other hand, is animated by a pursuit of new knowledge, consensus on moral or political issues, and the solution of problems. But it is possible for such an approach to focus too strenuously on "settling the issue," to rush too hastily to embrace a single answer, or to reify that answer as a potentially "final" one. At such points it, too, threatens the conditions of dialogue.

Dialogue as instruction, clearly, can take forms that are manipulative, excessively one-sided, and narrowly restrictive of the possibilities of open investigation. Calvin Trillin (1984), discussing this mode of instruction in the context of law schools (the mode we see exemplified in the character of Kingsfield in *The Paper Chase*), describes

> the style of teaching in which the professor singles out some unfortunate in a large lecture hall and puts him through difficult and perhaps humiliating exercises in order to extract the correct answer—a method that one student . . . called "Socrates gone mad." (p. 64)

No one could endorse this as legitimate dialogue. However, as the teaching of Socrates and the research conducted on reciprocal teaching show, there are situations in which it can be extremely helpful to students, and entirely within the spirit of dialogue, for the teacher to engage a partner in a planned sequence of questions and other statements in order to induct him or her into a method of reasoning or line of investigation. I have mentioned some of the conditions that make this sort of practice consistent with dialogue: that the student's involvement be consensual and guided by his or her own interest in learning; that the questioning process be, in principle, reversible; that withdrawing from this mode of interaction, or attempting to change it into some other form of dialogue, be a prerogative open to either partner, and so on. But I think it leads to an impoverished conception of dialogue, and pedagogy, to assume that there are no contexts in which dialogue as instruction might be appropriate. Furthermore, even within a planned sequence of questions, surprises and novel insights are possible; and if nothing else the questioner stands to learn more about the student and his or her thinking processes.

Similarly, *dialogue as debate* can have antidialogical effects. Some of these have been analyzed well by Janice Moulton (1983). Moulton points out how the aggressive and argumentative style typical of much academic discussion, and particularly common in philosophical discourse, actually *impedes* the discovery and development of new insights. Hence, her criticism goes beyond, although it also includes, the more conventional criticism that the form of competitive debate excludes and discourages potential participants, and biases the criteria of "high status" professional interaction against the verbal styles most comfortable for many women and the members of some cultural or ethnic subgroups. It is not entirely clear from her essay, however, whether she is concluding that this mode of interaction is inherently and necessarily illegitimate as a form of dialogue, or that it simply needs to be complemented by a tolerance for other forms of verbal interaction as well. The view I am proposing is that debate can have beneficial dialogical forms, although it also can pass over into argumentative, competitive, and intolerant forms. Debates can remain dialogical when the respective postures of advocacy are taken in the spirit of advancing a mutual understanding of the issues, not primarily in order to "win" or make one's partner look bad; and when they are adopted in a "playful" attitude, that is, with a certain provisional distance from the interaction, keeping in mind that the process of questioning and challenge is directed toward positions, not primarily toward persons. Of course, such a dispassioned distance will not be easy for some people on some issues; and in such cases dialogue as debate will be difficult, perhaps impossible, to sustain.

These characterizations of beneficial and antidialogical forms of each of the four types of dialogue can be summarized concisely: Some practices within a dialogical relation tend to maintain the relation and move the discussion forward; others threaten to finish it, end it. As Richard Bernstein (1986) notes about this orientation:

> It means taking conversation seriously (and playfully) without thinking that the only type of conversation that is important is the type that aspires to put an end to conversation by reaching some sort of "rational consensus," or that all "genuine" conversations are really inquiries about "truth." (p. 86)

In this statement, Bernstein is taking the Rortyan, or more pragmatist, view over the Habermasian view: that the prime benefit of conversation is in creating and maintaining the conditions for more conversation. This does not mean that provisional resolutions cannot be settled, but merely that they should never be regarded as "final." Nor does it mean that more talking, or more persistent efforts at talking, are always the best thing. There are many practical communicative situations in which the only possibility of attaining the conditions of dialogue between persons requires a delay of dialogue among them, or a temporary avoidance of certain kinds of issues or topics within a dialogue. Yet once a dialogue is embarked upon, a primary sign of success (although not the only one) is the extent to which participants see a personal and mutual benefit in working to make the dialogue move forward.

Clearly, some dialogues do reach an end point. But Bernstein is correct: These cannot all be defined in terms of a "rational consensus" or settling on the "truth." In fact there is a range of outcomes that dialogue can attain, including

1. Agreement and consensus, identifying beliefs or values all parties can agree to
2. Not agreement, but a common understanding in which the parties do not agree, but establish common meanings in which to discuss their differences
3. Not a common understanding, but an understanding of differences in which the parties do not entirely bridge these differences, but through analogies of experience or other indirect translations can understand, at least in part, each other's positions
4. Little understanding, but a respect across differences, in which the parties do not fully understand one another, but by each seeing that the other has a thoughtful, conscientious position, they can come to appreciate and respect even positions they disagree with
5. Irreconcilable and incommensurable plurality (Burbules & Rice, 1991)

Many have written as if the first and last alternatives were the only two options; and this has led them to some extremely superficial analyses of the possibilities and limits of communication in contexts of difference.

TEACHING WITH THE FOUR TYPES OF DIALOGUE

I have tried to avoid, in this chapter and throughout this book, the language of calling dialogue a "method." Clearly, there are skills and specific planned interventions a dialogical partner might invoke as part of trying to advance the discussion. This is particularly true when one partner has a mutually identified role as the teacher, which carries with it certain responsibilities for helping to manage the dialogue and promote its pedagogical possibilities (although the student in this relation will have similar or reciprocal responsibilities as well). But regarding dialogue as a method threatens to turn it into a more strategic, directive, and less open-ended process; and it exaggerates the teacher's responsibility for the dialogue (Neiman, 1991). Considering dialogue as a relation that can "catch up" its participants in the ongoing flow of an interchange, and that can change its tone, its purpose, and its direction through the choices of either of its participants, belies regarding it as a method that can be "used" by either one.

Moreover, as should be clear by now, dialogue is not a *single* method. The four types of dialogue have quite distinct characters and purposes; and a good teacher, or a skillful player of the dialogue game generally, is one who is aware of these various forms and their specific characteristics, so that he or she can make an intelligent choice from among them when dealing with particular kinds of students, particular communicative contexts, or particular subject matters. Such a choice requires experience, judgment, and a sensitivity to others. If an ongoing dialogue will move through different phases of communicative interaction, then recognizing these changes, and how new and varied "moves" will be appropriate for some situations and not others, is an important part of how one can remain within the spirit of the dialogical relation while being flexible about just what that entails from moment to moment. This relational element assumes as well that these choices should never be entirely unilateral.

What are some of the considerations that come into play in choosing from among these four types of dialogue? A complete account of these very complex issues is beyond the scope of the current project, but many of the dimensions of choice are clear. These different types of dialogue manifest different views of how knowledge is attained; of the nature and justification of authority; of the appropriate style and use of questions; of the learning processes that characterize the subject matter under consideration; about the possibility or likelihood of attaining consensus or an answer to the problem at hand; of the moral responsibilities that one has toward one's partner; of the status and limitations of one's own knowledge about a subject, and the knowledge of one's partner; of the context and circumstances in which the dialogue is taking place; and, of course, other issues as well. My point here is that choices among these different types of dialogue reflect implicit or explicit decisions about such factors; and a major reason for the lack of success in many dialogues is that one misjudges the appropriateness of a particular dialogical approach for the partner, context, or subject matter at hand. It is a major benefit of dialogical approaches that they provide a context in which these sorts of judgments need not, and often should not, be made by one partner alone—and it is often through the engagement of one's partner over such questions that the conditions of the dialogical relation itself can be strengthened.

Hence, for the dialogical partner, and especially for the teacher, a degree of flexibility and pluralism in dialogical approach is essential for dialogue across a range of partners, situations, and issues. Just such a pluralism and flexibility was behind Socrates's genius as a teacher, not an inflexible reliance on a single "Socratic method"— and in this, I would say, resides his primary educational lesson.

In the following Interlude, Ladd Holt and I have tried to illustrate, both in form and in content, the range of problems that dialogue can encounter, and the different forms of interchange—some more successful than others—that can characterize an ongoing dialogical engagement. Two characters, Pat Richards and Sal Torres, discuss their different roles, their different views of teaching, and the relevance of dialogue to their work situations (the university and the public school, respectively). While in no way an "ideal" dialogue, it is meant to illustrate briefly some of the key concepts from this chapter and throughout this book.

A Dialogue on Teaching

WRITTEN WITH LADD HOLT

Scene: A faculty office in a college of education. Professor Pat Richards is seated at a desk, writing an article on a computer, pecking at the keys somewhat feverishly; it is 2 days past the deadline when the paper was due. A tap on the open door interrupts. "Excuse me, Professor Richards? I was wondering if I could come in and speak with you for a few minutes."

PR: Well, actually, it's . . . yes, sure, okay. You were in my class last semester—Sal, isn't it?

ST: Sal Torres. I teach at Jefferson Elementary.

PR: Yes. How can I help you?

ST: I'm not sure it's help that I want, exactly. You see, I've been teaching for 8 years, and I really love teaching—I'm a good teacher, I think. But despite that, I'm thinking of quitting. I don't see how I can keep doing it.

PR: Damn. Burnout. I see it all the time.

ST: No, that's not it at all. Actually, I guess, you're partly the source of the problem. You see, since I took your class, a lot of things have been bothering me, things about my job, my school, my students, my colleagues, things that never bothered me before. We read those articles by Apple, and Bowles and Gintis, and by you, too, and what it all added up to, for me, was that schools are harming a lot of students—not intentionally, but in small ways, day after day, however much good we try to do for them. I try to put it all in some big balance-scale, and I just can't do it. I feel like an accomplice in some . . . some mindless conspiracy.

PR: Well, Sal, it sounds as if you're asking important critical questions about the school system. I work hard to get people to start asking those questions. But they're difficult to find answers for, I agree.

ST: Maybe I'm not being very clear about this, Professor Richards. My problem isn't that I'm struggling with new questions, or pondering some complex sociological issue. I'm talking about my life, my job, my feelings about myself and the place I work. I feel guilty. I feel compromised. I feel I shouldn't keep doing something I enjoy, something I'm good at. I feel robbed, to put it bluntly, robbed of something that was very important to me. And I think you're partly responsible.

PR: Calm down a second, Sal. You're a little upset right now, and it's going to be difficult to talk if we continue like this. I didn't expect to get into a long conversation right at this moment, but I'll put the time into it if you'll meet me halfway.

ST: Okay. But I can't imagine what you'll say that will make me feel any better.

PR: Fortunately, I'm not trying to make you feel better. I wouldn't begin to know how to do that. It may be that guilt, and anger, and a sense of loss, are just what you ought to be feeling. I can't say. But what I can do is talk with you and listen, more carefully than I have up until now, to what you're telling me. Let's see if we can come to a clearer understanding of your situation. If you have to leave teaching, it better be for reasons we can look back on without regret.

ST: As the old joke says, what do you mean *we*? I'm the one on the battle lines. I'm the one whose job is at stake.

PR: I'm not sure it's that simple, Sal. See, you've come in here and confronted me with a very upsetting dilemma. You're one of the more enjoyable students I've worked with. Your comments in class and in your papers were great. I liked seeing you grapple with ideas and questions that most students try to ignore or rationalize away. You have a deep conscience about what you're doing, you're reflective and thoughtful, you're smart—all the things I could wish for in a student. More to the point, you're exactly the sort of person we need more of in schools. Now, just because you're all those things, and because I seem to have succeeded in what I was trying to achieve in my course, you're about to leave your job. That isn't what I wanted at all. But if this is the outcome with my very best students, what am I supposed to make of that?

ST: In a way, we have the same problem, don't we? We both want to make schools better, me from the inside, you by teaching teachers. And the thing is, does what we do make any difference?

PR: Well, Sal, I must admit that these days "making schools better" seems pretty daunting as an objective. Sometimes I think we're doing all we can just to keep them from becoming worse, and not doing too well at that. I get pretty discouraged at times.

ST: But Professor Richards, how can you stay in teaching if you feel that way? What makes it worthwhile for *you*?

PR: I think that's a topic for another time. I've probably said more in that direction than I ought to already. Tell me specifically, what are the things that are bothering you about teaching?

ST: Well, there are countless headaches involved with the job itself: I don't get the support and resources I need to do my job well, decisions are made by other people that determine what I can and can't do, there are many petty sorts of ways in which I'm made to feel that what I do isn't valued. But I can put up with a lot of that; I have for 8 years. The positive seemed to outweigh the negative—at least, that's what I told myself. Now, after taking your class, and thinking about a lot of things, the compromises don't seem worth it any more. I look at my students, and I see so many different faces, some bright and alert, some sleepy, some resentful, some absolutely unreadable, and I wonder, "Am I making a difference to you, and is it a difference for the better?" Everyone has bad days, but I could get through mine because I thought the balance tipped to the positive side in the long run. Now I think about the hidden curriculum, most of which I have no influence over, and the biases built into the standard curriculum, which excludes and discourages so many students whom we then label "failures," and I think about the enormous influences on the students that are completely outside the school, some of which undermine or undo our best efforts. And now it seems to me that it isn't an issue of balance or trade-offs at all, that it's a whole system out of whack, and there's no way to be part of it and do real good for more than a few isolated cases; meanwhile, the vast majority are silently slipping away, whatever I try to do.

PR: I've felt that way.

ST: But something else is worse: the way my feelings toward my fellow teachers have changed. The ones who seem to be going through the motions now seem to me part of some evil conspiracy; the ones who are happy in their job seem dupes; some of them feel like enemies to me now. These are people I want to feel close to in some professional, collegial sense. I wish . . . well, I wish I was having this conversation with some of *them*.

PR: So, why aren't you?

ST: When? No one seems to have the time, and when we do talk it's usually chatting, filling in a few minutes over coffee. I've tried starting up serious talks more than once, sometimes around these sorts of issues. They don't seem to go very far. They turn into gripe sessions, with each person taking a turn complaining. Or someone will say, "Gee, I wish I could talk, but I've got to run." There are so many ways to stop a conversation, or to keep it from reaching any serious level, and sometimes I think we've become expert at them all.

PR: Why do you think that is?

ST: Are you playing professor with me now? Damn it, why do *you* think it is? When the topic gets close to what you think, or feel, or worry about, it veers off suddenly. Isn't that just another way of avoiding real conversation?

PR: Well look, Sal, you're the one who came in here with a problem. We're talking about *you*, and trying to figure out some things that are bothering *you*, and I don't think it will be helpful from that standpoint to get into a long digression about what I think, or feel, or worry about.

ST: But don't you see, I don't want to be just a student coming in here with a question that you can Socratically lead me to answering. And I don't want to be analyzed; I can pay for therapy if I want it. I'm looking for someone to talk with about these concerns I have, someone who will understand and respond to what I'm feeling, and here you are, a supposed expert in the subject, and I can't even get you to level with me.

PR: Fine, let's level a little bit, then. I think you're taking the easy way out, Sal. There isn't a person working in any job in the world who doesn't sometimes feel that they're not making enough of a difference for the better, that other people are making their jobs more difficult for them, that it isn't all that they'd hoped it would be, and on and on. Most of them are in much worse shape economically than you are. You've chosen a pretty decent calling, compared with a lot of others. You're good at what you do. What's the grief, when you really get down to it? That it's not perfect?

ST: Professor Richards, I'm 32 years old. I don't need a night light, and no one reads me fairy tales at bedtime. If the best justification you can give me—you, whose career is based on preparing and inspiring teachers—if the best justification is, "Hey, kid, it's a hard world and nothing's perfect" . . . I mean, is that it?

PR: I'm getting pretty uncomfortable with where this conversation is going. I think you're asking things of me I never promised to offer. The purpose of this conversation, I thought, wasn't to solve your problem—it may not be solvable—but to understand better what the problem is and what options you might have.

ST: Okay, fine.

PR: Now, I'm learning something from the way this conversation has gone so far. I've learned that I can't simply "play professor," as you put it, because you're asking for a more personal level of response. I've learned that this conversation will take my own best efforts to think through the problem with you, because it touches on a concern I feel too. And I've learned that since I'm partly responsible for this crisis, I can't—right now I'd say shouldn't—simply act the detached interrogator.

ST: For the first time, I feel as if you're working *with* me in all this. Now, where were we?

PR: Well, you said before that the worst part of this whole thing was feeling alienated from your colleagues; some of them seem like "enemies," I think you said. You can't talk with them about the things you are worrying about. Now, I feel that way often in my job here at the university; so many of my colleagues are either fixated on their own professional advancement, or are content with piecemeal accomplishments that occupy a lot of attention day to day, but don't add up to much. I have a few good friends here, but I rarely feel part of some larger effort to make a difference.

ST: Yes, yes! That's the sort of thing I'm talking about, a feeling of common purpose. If I felt that with the people I work with, it would be easier to press some of my concerns with them; as it is, I feel awkward asking for their time and attention, and just accept it when they brush me off.

PR: Well, it isn't going to be quite as simple as feeling a sense of common purpose, though. Even when you have a basic sense of agreement with people, good serious, far-reaching conversation isn't easy.

ST: No, it isn't, but it's *easier*.

PR: I'm not sure. Maybe you have it backward; you're saying you can't talk with your colleagues because you don't feel a sense of community with them. But maybe it's more accurate to say you don't feel a sense of community with them because you don't talk—

ST: —But I *do* initiate conversations; others just don't seem to have the time to listen carefully, or to engage their brains more than it takes to spread the latest school gossip.

PR: What I was going to say is that it may take a shared belief in the value of certain kinds of conversation and the idea that one stands to gain from the endeavor. A serious talk—the kind of thing we're having here, for example—is real work: It takes thoughtful effort by both parties, as you say. But even more than that, it takes a kind of persistence, a desire to see the process through to some outcome; and it may not be clear sometimes what that outcome is going to be. I think this is more important than a shared sense of agreement on the issues. Sometimes we can learn the most from people we strongly disagree with, if we approach the conversation in the right way.

ST: I just noticed that "communication" and "community" come from the same roots. Maybe you're right that the sense of common purpose or group feeling I'm talking about comes more from our efforts at communication than by how much we agree or disagree on any particular issue. But what gets the process of communication off the ground—what you called "a shared belief in the value of conversation"?

PR: Let's start with the tough case: where people know they disagree about some important things. Why should they bother talking to one another? One typical motivation is trying to convince or change the other person.

ST: But that's dishonest, isn't it, if one doesn't consider the possibility of being convinced or changed oneself?

PR: I think that's true. But who's going to create that degree of honesty, if it isn't generated out of the conversation itself? There's nothing particularly wrong with person A trying to convince person B; but A often *needs* B to point out that it may be the opposite. Or, sometimes B will redirect the conversation by choosing only some of A's issues to respond to, or will send them back across the net with a different spin. In a way, you've been doing this with me, right?

ST: I suppose so. There are some things that interfere with what you're talking about. One is our tendency to view differences in opinion or judgment as a good guys/bad guys issue. You're only going to approach conversation one way if you're certain the other person is mistaken, and not only mistaken, but somehow bad for it. At the other extreme, a kind of relativism interferes too: "Oh well, you have your opinion, I have mine. Nobody's wrong, let's drop the subject."

PR: That's interesting—so both absolutism and relativism are impediments to conversation.

ST: Somewhere in between is trying to talk across differences, talk *through* them, like when we're translating from one language to another. In fact, as you said, these are often the most interesting conversations. We need to keep the differences alive, keep them in tension. Still, differences keep getting in the way, despite good intentions . . . like this conversation, for example.

PR: What do you mean?

ST: I mean, here we are in your office, on campus. I call you "Professor Richards," and you call me "Sal." I feel like a *student* coming in here, feel a little guilty about taking up your time.

PR: You can call me "Pat," if you'd like. Many students do.

ST: That really isn't the point, is it? It's the *presumption* that I come in here with; the name thing just symbolizes it.

PR: Point taken. But you *are* one of my students, you know; I can't help feeling a little responsible for you.

ST: I don't mind the fact that you know things I don't, and maybe have thought some issues through more than I have. That's partly why I came to talk to you. I just don't want to be treated like another "case." Even if you know a lot about these general issues, my situation is special; it's unique, it's about *me*, not anyone else.

PR: You're saying that familiar social roles, stereotypes, comfortable clichés also block the possibility of real communication. We assume too much about each other, assume that we already know what the other person has to say.

ST: Well, partly that, but also that those roles often interfere with our ability to focus on the *content* of the conversation, whether we agree or disagree, without it taking on a false significance because of those roles. This makes me wonder why we, here, seem willing to be persistent in this conversation. It hasn't been easy, for either of us, and it's almost broken down a couple of times. It seems to me that part of the answer is that we do share a progressive outlook on schools; it's not the majority view, so maybe we're thrown together somewhat by feeling a commitment to something that "they," whoever they are, don't understand.

PR: That's certainly a factor in this case, I agree. But even agreement can be a barrier to conversation: "Well, you and I see eye to eye on this already, so why go any further?" In the end, agreement or disagreement can't be the key factors. We don't always know if we agree or disagree before embarking on a conversation. Besides, *either* agreement or disagreement can be an excuse for cutting conversation short, if one is looking for an excuse. I think a person has to basically believe that talking about common concerns is a good thing. It takes a certain kind of curiosity and interest in others, a kind of trust, too, and a belief that this is how understanding is achieved: by people talking, even arguing, about things they are wondering about. You have to talk with people because that's what you believe in doing, and because you each see that you stand to gain from it. This goes back to what you were talking about before: People have to be similar enough to make conversation possible, and different enough to make it worthwhile.

ST: That's a nice way of putting it. Still, "commitment to the value of conversation itself" seems awfully abstract to me as an explanation of real people's motives. The people I work with may be perfectly willing to have serious conversations with their family members at home, or with their pals over a beer, or with their religious group, or whatever, but not in school. . . . So they aren't committed to conversation in the abstract, divorced from context. Maybe the problem is that in those more consensual contexts there's an identifiable group they feel part of, and so they *want* to understand each other, even when it leads to disagreements. They feel safe enough to risk that, because the basic bond won't be jeopardized if an argument breaks out. But since we don't feel that kind of bond at school, the possibility of disagreement—which seems inevitable once a serious talk gets going, even for people who basically agree about some things—is too risky. You still have to deal with the person day in and day out, you know? What happens if they decide you're a jerk?

PR: I'm not sure how often true conversation takes place even in those consensual settings. Even when people are inclined to work at understanding, they often seem to lack the ability to converse effectively. Teachers are no exception.

ST: That seems like quite an indictment of teachers, if it's true. In one sense, all teaching *is* just carrying on a conversation. And you're saying teachers don't know how to do it well?

PR: I don't mean to blame teachers for that. They hardly get the chance to learn to do it well; we certainly don't teach it to them in our university programs. And it doesn't rate very high on the state list of "teaching competencies."

ST: So maybe the lack of real conversation among teachers isn't just because we don't value it, or because there isn't time, but because we don't know how.

PR: Conversation is assumed to be such a natural thing that we never teach *anyone* how to do it well. We take it for granted that conversation just happens.

ST: In one sense, I suppose, conversation *is* natural—it happens all the time. But what you seem to mean by conversation has a lot more in it, like the notion of *dialogue*: an attempt at understanding, at questioning the positions of others and ourselves, of exploring certain ideas together. That's not easy to do.

PR: I wonder what it would mean to teach good conversation or "dialogue" as an explicit skill?

ST: Well, for one thing, I'm not sure it's possible to learn it in a step-by-step set of rules. There may be some guidelines: be honest, stick to the topic, listen before you speak, don't be defensive about questions or criticisms, and so on. But a conversation's not going to be critical or insightful because of a list of procedures; participants have to bring to the conversation a willingness to look at things critically.

PR: It's something they have to make happen.

ST: Rig..t. In the end it seems a pretty clear case of learning by doing. It takes at least two willing participants, and it also takes opportunities. Yet often we need to *make* the opportunity, or it will never happen at all, especially when there are so many roadblocks and hurdles to prevent conversation happening easily—some of which seem almost intentional with teachers, keeping us so busy that it's difficult to find time.

PR: Part of creating the opportunity is engaging the attention of a partner. You said both parties to a conversation have to be willing, but they often aren't—Socrates collaring people in the public square, or you with your colleagues, or even you and me, initially.

ST: I think Socrates was especially good at taking a question or puzzle the other person had and turning it to his own purposes. Teachers need to do that with students all the time. Participants may not both be committed to the conversation at first, but they can gradually *become* committed.

PR: So, sometimes the joint purpose is established by a common set of values or prior relationships—you mentioned this earlier. But sometimes the joint purpose needs to be established by the conversants themselves, by discovering points of common concern.

ST: But whether they have points of common concern is a result of pre-existing conditions, too. A third possibility is that sometimes they need to *create* a common concern as they talk about it. In some ways this is what I face with my fellow teachers; most of them aren't troubled by the things that trouble me. Can I get them interested?

PR: You mean can you worry and upset them the way I've worried and upset you? Or the way you've worried and upset me?

ST: The key to popularity, eh?

PR: Well, I suspect you'll find out you're not the only one to worry about these things.

ST: But what about the rest of it? I mean, let's say I can get my colleagues to talk with me. Fine, that would be great. But there's still the rest of what troubles me about schools, my job, my students, and all. Is conversation going to change any of that?

PR: I think we need to go back to the basic question that seems to be bothering you. Wasn't it that you don't have the same sense of value about your teaching that you did before, that you want to feel that what you're doing is worthwhile, has a progressive purpose? Mightn't talking with your colleagues help in making sense of your feeling of loss, and perhaps in creating a new sense of purpose?

ST: That doesn't seem to be it, exactly, or maybe my thoughts are clarifying as we talk. Since I've come back to the university, I've learned a lot about the effect of schools on kids and on society. I always believed it was basically good, though of course I knew there were some lousy teachers and other serious problems in schools. Now it all seems inverted: I think most of what schools do is to buttress the status quo, keep minority and poor kids in their place, pander to the Least Common Denominator; the good teachers I know seem few and far between, and a lot of them are quitting, though not usually for the reasons I'm describing. I'm beginning to doubt the whole system of education. In what ways do I fit into that larger pattern? Am I aware of the actual effects of my teaching?

PR: You know, sometimes I think we do our students at the university a great disservice: We provide ideas, perspectives, new approaches to teaching that are all virtually guaranteed to make them feel like misfits in schools, as they exist. We tell ourselves, as faculty, that if we keep producing enough right-thinking folks, the schools will change. But it's clear that just putting our students out there doesn't fundamentally change the schools; it just makes them feel isolated and weird. And maybe changing schools fundamentally isn't possible at all, right now.

ST: What keeps you in teaching, then? Do you ever feel trapped or compromised by the system?

PR: Of course I do. And I don't kid myself that it's likely to change substantially in the near future. But I have the belief that what I'm doing—educating—is an intrinsically worthwhile thing.

ST: But maybe you're also perpetuating the system you're criticizing.

PR: If the only two options are to overthrow everything or to be utterly co-opted, then I'm utterly co-opted, I guess. But I think it's worth something to keep alternatives alive, to try to represent a different, better set of educational values, even if there's little you can do to get them established across the board.

ST: For example?

PR: Well, conversations like this. I lost track a long time ago of whether I'm trying to teach you something or you're teaching me, but I do know that we're both learning some crucial things by going through this process, especially learning something about conversation itself. Call it what you will, but I think we need this in our lives, whether we do it for a living or not. I suppose in some ways this is an argument for quitting, too, since we need to have people doing this in lots of other contexts, not only the special place and time we call "school." But we need them in school especially, because it's the one institution formally dedicated to having this happen.

ST: Your school, perhaps, the university. Not mine.

PR: What would it take to change that?

ST: It would take more time, for one thing. More academic freedom, and personal freedom, to say what we really think. The feeling that we're trying to make a difference and that "we're all in this together," which we don't have much of at the moment. And more time—did I already say that?

PR: Maybe you need to look to other places besides your school for those sorts of opportunities. Maybe your professional organization or union, whichever you want to call it. Maybe other neighborhood groups—the conversation certainly shouldn't be limited just to other teachers.

ST: Then we're back to the question of how a sense of community gets formed, and the chicken-and-egg problem of getting people started in these sorts of conversations. I see now that conversations about teaching are *part* of teaching. I see that I need help from others in recognizing the effects of what I'm doing, and vice versa. And I see that I can't rely just on other teachers to do this. But how does it get started?

PR: You're asking me? I don't have any recipes. But isn't what we've just been doing an example of how it can happen? We didn't start out understanding each other. We've both gotten a little touchy and defensive at points. We aren't members of the same community—

ST: —Maybe we are now, in a way that we weren't before. Instead of teacher and student, we are beginning to see ourselves as both part of a broader community of "educators."

PR: Or part of an ongoing conversation about teaching, which is also a way of learning about conversation itself. In fact, if the only way to learn how to have serious conversations is to have them, then by extending conversations to more and more people, including our students, we improve our capacities, we improve their capacities, and we keep an alternative approach to education alive. But all the same barriers to creating such conversations still exist.

ST: I know that. But this whole discussion is based on the assumption that lots of things are built into schools that keep us from doing what we want to do, what we believe is needed. The only way we'll even come close to dealing with that reality is by creating a critical understanding of what we're doing, of what interests we serve. Then perhaps we can challenge some of those barriers and create niches of radically different possibilities. But we can't do that on our own; we need to talk to each other.

PR: So, what are you going to do about this in your school setting?

ST: What are you going to do about this in *your* school setting?

CHAPTER 7

Why Dialogues Fail

My purpose in exploring the structure and dynamics of dialogical relations is to contribute to a better understanding of what dialogue is and how it can contribute to teaching and learning activities. If this book provides an impetus for reflection and further discussion on the possibilities of dialogue, and motivates teachers and students interested in dialogue to consider how it can become more a part of their educational practice, then my project will have succeeded. But this is not a utopian book. Since I do not consider dialogue a "method," nothing here should be taken as a blueprint or "how to" manual. Given my view of dialogue, the most that an investigation such as this can provide is an introduction and stimulus to further discussions, which I am certain will amplify, modify, or reject at least parts of what I propose here. In this, my view differs from that of advocates for a particular type of dialogical teaching and learning as the highest form of pedagogy; like Wittgenstein's signpost, this book suggests a direction of pedagogical exploration, not a map of how to get there.

Dialogue is no panacea. As should be clear from my arguments here, dialogue is an enormously flexible, adaptive approach to teaching and learning. It comprises a range of different moves, and sequences of moves, and so can be suited to many different types of subject matter, different teachers, and different types of students. Yet, dialogue can fail. Every form of dialogical engagement can fall into patterns that become antidialogical, as discussed in Chapter 6: Debate can become an argument; inquiry can become an obsessively narrow, ends-driven endeavor; conversation can become a meandering chat that leads nowhere important or interesting; instruction can become manipulative. We engage in dialogical approaches not because they are methods guaranteed to succeed, but fundamentally because we are drawn to the spirit of equality, mutuality, and cooperation that animates them.

THE FAILURE OF DIALOGUE

What does it mean for dialogue to fail? Because dialogue is not a means toward a specific end, the failure to achieve certain kinds of outcomes (a "correct" answer, a final consensus, a workable solution, and so on) cannot itself be taken as a failure of dialogue. In fact, as discussed in Chapter 6, and illustrated in the dialogue between Pat Richards and Sal Torres, dialogue may produce a heightened sense of the differences among participants, may show how difficult the solution to a problem is, may reveal that there is no single correct answer to a question—and these can be taken as signs of success for the dialogue itself. A better sense of understanding of oneself, one's partner, or the world or situation in which one lives clearly does not guarantee a sense of satisfaction about what one will find. Hence, the success of dialogue must be assessed through the quality of communicative exchange that develops within the dialogical relation, not only through its outcomes. Conversely, the failure of dialogue pertains primarily to damage done to the fabric of the dialogical relation itself: what cuts the discussion short, what pre-empts certain areas of investigation, or what silences or overwhelms certain points of view within it. If the value of dialogue is in facilitating the possibilities of future conversations, then interactions that inhibit those possibilities must be seen as signs of failure.

This claim can be illustrated with a simple example. Sometimes an ongoing dialogical investigation will yield an incorrect or unworkable answer to a problem; persistent, careful thought does not guarantee solutions. This is an inherent possibility, but frustrating and discouraging as it might be, it is not a sign of failure, *if* there is an opportunity to reconsider that error, learn from it, and continue the investigation further. Making errors is obviously part of the process of learning and creating new knowledge; what matters is whether the investigative process itself can continue in light of an error. For dialogue, this example shows that maintaining the relational conditions for further discussion is frequently more important, in the long run, than settling the specific question at hand. Answers, solutions, and agreements are fleeting things in human history—while the fabric of dialogical interchange sustains the very human capacity to generate and revise those provisional outcomes.

Impediments to the conditions of dialogue itself give rise to what some authors have termed "dialogue breakdowns."

It characterizes a dialogue breakdown in the sense that communication becomes one-dimensional; its function ceases to be cooperative as

> speakers do only what is expected of them. There is a mechanical exchange of messages, but no real possibility of dialogue; since the power structure reflecting itself in this use of language is asymmetrical and unequal, people have only restricted possibilities of using language and performing speech acts. (Marcondes, 1985, pp. 420–421)

This condition can be summarized briefly as "not taking seriously what one says oneself, what the other says, or what constitutes the object of the discussion" (Petit, 1985, p. 430). Notice that this failure cannot be analyzed in terms of any particular pattern of speech act, although some are typical of dialogue breakdowns (extended monologues, careless interchange, bitter argument, "talking past" one another, and so on). Rather, the breakdown is at the level of performative intentions that underlie participation within the spirit of the game. When these break down, even attempts to correct or redirect the course of speech acts *within* the relation may become impossible.

Marcondes (1985) discusses perceptively a range of factors that can contribute to such breakdowns.

> Manipulation, misinterpretation of intentions, opposition of goals in communication, contradictions between divergent aims in performing speech acts . . . , interruptions. . . . As if in communication we really had to decipher and interpret some secret intention of our interlocutor, whose objective is to try to hide something from us or mislead us by what he says. (pp. 417–418, 419, 421)

In such instances, dialogue can become a kind of "jurisdictional controversy concerning the ultimate authority in treating . . . questions" (McKeon, 1990, p. 25). It ceases to be an intersubjective exploration of a problem or question, and instead becomes a struggle over whose voice and perspective will be the dominant one. While there are ways of trying to repair a dialogical relation that has broken down, my point of emphasis here is that, once damaged, the very nature and purpose of the dialogical relation comes to be doubted, and because this relation is the very fabric of dialogue, any communicative outcome that may be achieved is compromised.

Hence, an exploration of the possibilities of dialogue would be incomplete without an acknowledgment of the social conditions, including especially conditions in schools, that contribute to "dialogue breakdowns," making dialogue difficult or impossible. As Richard Bernstein (1983) points out, this is one of Habermas's chief criticisms of Gadamer.

In his analysis of dialogue, Gadamer emphasizes the type of mutuality, sharing, respect, and equality required for a genuine dialogue, and the principle of dialogue is universalized when Gadamer endorses the principle of freedom that encompasses all of humanity. Habermas agrees with all of this, but what he emphasizes is that there are structural societal barriers that systematically distort such dialogue and communication. (p. 190)

For Habermas it is a "fiction to believe that Socratic dialogue is possible everywhere and at any time" (quoted in R. Bernstein, 1986, p. 93). Here we see a second, crucial purpose that an investigation of dialogue can play. Exploring the possibilities of dialogue also makes us become aware of *limits*. An investigation of an ideal, while it can inspire us, can also make us aware of how far from that we remain—indeed, how we often create and maintain conditions that work against it. It is as this sort of critical reference point that Habermas's "ideal speech situation" should be seen (Thompson, 1981); and it is how the analysis of dialogue I have presented here is intended to be understood. In this chapter I will examine some of the barriers and impediments our society has created—especially those in schools—that interfere with the goal of developing dialogical approaches to education.

THE ANTIDIALOGICAL SOCIETY

In discussing the factors that impede or discourage dialogue, I want to begin with a small focus and then widen it to consider broader social factors as well. Speaking narrowly, many of the impediments to dialogue concern the active choices of participants within that situation. These can sometimes be analyzed as violations of the three rules, described in Chapter 4, that constitute the "dialogue game": the rules of participation, commitment, and reciprocity. In the first instance, participants often act in ways that exclude or discourage the participation of others: by shouting them down, embarrassing them, or talking *at* them, for example. In the second instance, participants fail to engage the dialogical process seriously. They leave, or end it, when it fails to serve their personal, immediate purposes, and often fail to honor the intention within dialogue of allowing underlying commitments, motives, or assumptions to be raised for scrutiny. Refusing to see the discussion through, they can gain, or offer, only the most shallow of insights. In the third instance, participants arrogate to themselves privileges within the communicative encounter that they are unwilling to see extended to other participants; they ask of others what they are unwilling to have asked of themselves; they have agendas that they wish neither to disclose nor to have questioned. Naturally, no one can avoid certain mistakes or misjudgments within an ongoing dialogue; but the consistent violation of such rules threatens to produce a "dialogue breakdown"—a destruction of the relation that underlies dialogue itself.

Often these actions and choices cannot be understood as strict rule-violations; they are better seen as a failure of participants to exercise the "communicative virtues" I discussed in Chapter 2—careful listening, tolerance for other points of view, taking time to explain oneself carefully, and so on (see also Burbules & Rice, 1991, 1992; Rice & Burbules, 1993). These are not rule-governed activities, but aspects of character that persons who care about communication manifest in their conduct in relation to others. Although these virtues are not a primary focus of this book, many people do not acquire them; or they exercise them only very selectively, in some situations, with some partners, but not with others; or they live and speak in relational contexts that fail to foster or encourage the exercise of such virtues at all (the blame is not necessarily on them as individuals). The breakdown of many dialogues occurs, not because of serious epistemological incommensurability, but for the simple reason that at the level of communicative practice, virtues such as tolerance or patience are wanting. These are difficult to compensate for if the participants to a dialogue do not possess them and act on them, or if the relations among people effectively discourage their exercise (as when children grow up in homes of silence and familial abuse). Admittedly, in some cases this failure must be seen as a lack of willingness by communicative partners to acknowledge their own responsibility for the success of the dialogical relation. However, this judgment of responsibility must also be imbedded in the context of a *social critique* that asks what social conditions encourage or punish the exercise of these communicative virtues. For many people, in many situations, it is simply not realistic or safe to ask them to be more patient, more tolerant, or more understanding of certain views.

Slightly more general than the specific actions of participants in dialogue are their attitudes toward their partners or toward the subject under consideration. In the first case, assumptions that one's partner is ignorant about a subject, is morally obtuse, is dull-witted and needs everything spelled out very carefully, and so on, will all tend *against* dialogical engagement. The discussion, if it proceeds at all, will proceed as a monologue—or what Freire (1970) calls the "banking approach," in which the expert "deposits" knowledge into a passive and dependent recipient. This constitutes a violation of the spirit of reciprocity that is essential to dialogue. Clearly, this problem, in more or less subtle forms, is a particular temptation for educators, who are routinely placed in situations in which they know some things that their partners do not. Given such attitudes, a commitment to dialogue as a more open-ended investigative activity is made less likely. However, it is important to put this problem in a relational context; for it is equally true that when some participants regard others as "experts," and adopt a passive, recipient attitude toward them, this too interferes with the possibilities of dialogue.

The other set of attitudes involves how the participants regard the subject matter under discussion. When it is seen as an already-settled question, as a cut-and-dried moral dispute, or as a common-sensical problem with an easy solution, then deep, committed exploration of the topic through dialogue is also much less likely to happen. An excessive objectivism tends to encourage jumping to conclusions, or taking provisional outcomes as final ones. Yet, at the same time, an excessive relativism can undermine dialogue as well: For if one truly believes that one position is as good as another, and that arguments and reasons cannot be expected to convince others of one's position, then engagement in dialogue will always be half-hearted and easily abandoned. I will return to both of these topics in detail later.

Opening the focus out still further, the sorts of actions, choices, and attitudes described here cannot be seen simply as failures of individual character or intelligence. Various social dynamics and institutions tend to reinforce certain ways of thinking and acting, and to discourage others. For example, social systems of power and privilege tend to reinforce asymmetries within dialogue, vitiating the kind of mutuality and respect that dialogue requires. Experiences of harm or intimidation tend to "silence" certain voices, even in apparently open settings (Delpit, 1988; Ellsworth, 1989; Fine, 1987). There are greater risks for some partners than for others to broach certain subjects or disclose their beliefs, feelings, and experiences for dialogical consideration. There are inequalities even in terms of who is included in certain dialogues, or what tacit or explicit criteria might be operating that *effectively* exclude potential participants. There are prejudices and presuppositions that foreclose certain subjects, privilege certain points of view for reasons that are not open to negotiation, or color and distort the shape that a dialogue takes—and these are frequently not subjected to the process of disclosure and "redemption" within dialogue that would allow them to be questioned, challenged, or modified by the participants.

Finally, it must be said that in certain contexts this foreclosing of dialogical possibilities is intentional: that individuals or groups seeking to maintain their advantage over others seek ways to suppress communicative possibilities among those whom they seek to keep in their place, and between those others and themselves. Freire (1970) labels these as forms of "antidialogical action" and discusses four in detail: *conquest* (imposing upon "the oppressed and subjugated a world of deceit designed to increase their alienation and passivity"); *divide and rule* (suppressing "any action which even in incipient fashion could awaken the oppressed to the need for unity"); *manipulation* ("depositing myths indispensable to the preservation of the status quo"); and *cultural invasion* (imposing one's "own view of the world upon those [invaded] . . . and [inhibiting] the creativity of the invaded by curbing their expression"). These broad dimensions of oppression certainly have noncommunicative dimensions as well, such as the use of force; but they constitute direct and intentional limits placed on the form, content, participation, and possibilities of dialogue.

Yet the more striking fact, in the modern world, is how rarely the constraints on communication work through conscious manipulation or the imposition of some group's or individual's wishes upon others; how invisible and tacit these sorts of limitations actually become, to the point where no one is planning or steering them, and where they begin to work on *everyone*, not only one group to the benefit of others. Here we return to Habermas's critique of Gadamer: that the possibilities and limits of dialogue cannot be read simply off the intentions and prejudices of individuals, which they might be able to change or modify, but also from contexts of power and ideology that are beyond their immediate awareness or control. What a critical theory provides is a study of the systematic distortions and elisions that compromise the very conditions for communication. Habermas (1977) calls this study a "depth hermeneutics" (see also Misgeld, 1985; O'Neill, 1985).

In a sense, this insight was anticipated by Bakhtin: that we do not choose the language that we use; that the connotations and silences built into language are given to us by the voices that have spoken it before us; and that for this reason there are limits to our ability to analyze and articulate our social circumstances. We see an extreme illustration of this phenomenon in George Orwell's *1984*, where the gradual impoverishment of political discourse into an increasingly schematic and dualistic set of simple categories leaves citizens with the choice of either expressing themselves within the conventional grooves the language allows them, or remaining frustratedly inarticulate. If, as Dewey and many others argue, communication is the essential means of constituting and sustaining democratic life, then constraints on language are, straightforwardly, constraints on the body politic. There are many obvious examples of this process at work in a modern society characterized by pervasive media influences, including manipulative advertising; "spin doctors" and commentators who immediately interpret political events for us; books, magazines, and newspapers that are purposely written in a stylized, oversimplified vocabulary; a political culture of visual codes ("photo ops") and cliché-ridden speeches ("sound bites"), and so on and on. What must be seen about such influences is not only their direct effects in shaping the concerns and values of many citizens, but also their systemic effects, over time, in shaping a thin and facile style of social and political discourse. Power and ideology work not only through obvious suppression and propaganda, but also through more implicit, silent intrusions into our intellectual and emotional lives. What is required, then, is what Seyla Benhabib (1989) calls a "meta-politics of dialogue."

> Identifying the present social relations, power structures, and sociocultural grids of communication and interpretation that limit the identity of the parties to the public dialogue, that set the agenda for what is considered appropriate or inappropriate matters of public debate, and that sanctify the speech of some over the speech of others as being the language of the public. . . . The res publica can be truly identified only after the unreasonable constraints on public conversation have been removed. (pp. 155–156)

Yet, following upon this insight comes the recognition of how far from such conditions our society currently resides. Dialogue, unfortunately, comes to be seen as an extraordinary and fortuitous exception to the rule; sincere and successful attempts to engage one another's thoughts and feelings are rare or—where successful—relegated increasingly to a "private" sphere, and not to matters of public social and political concern. I believe that where dialogue endures it is largely *in spite of* dominant social and cultural influences. Yet at the same time, it is in the persistence of dialogue, despite the conditions of an antidialogical society, that we observe the centrality of communicative practices to our humanity and sense of self. What is most striking, to my way of thinking, is that our personal and social aspirations return again and again to the ideal of dialogue, even in circumstances that tend to discourage it; and it is by keeping such aspirations alive, at the level of practice, that we maintain the possibility of recasting society within a more inclusive, democratic, and open-ended communicative spirit.

> A community or *polis* is not something that can be made or engineered. . . . There is something of a circle here. . . . The coming into being of a type of public life that can strengthen solidarity, public freedom, a willingness to talk and listen, mutual debate, and a commitment to rational persuasion presupposes the incipient forms of such communal life. But what then is to be done in a situation in which there is a breakdown of such communities, and where the very conditions of social life have the consequences of furthering such a breakdown? More poignantly, what is to be done when we realize how much of humanity has been systematically excluded and prevented from participating in such dialogical communities? (R. Bernstein, 1983, p. 226)

Bernstein's question perfectly frames, I believe, the primary challenge to education in our time. Our fundamental educational problem today is not one of turning schools into better engines of increased economic productivity and growth, or of finding more and more directive ways to inculcate students with a body of "basic facts" that we presume they need to know. It is in finding ways to involve schools in creating and maintaining conditions in which inclusive, democratic, and open-ended dialogue can thrive. Such an endeavor is *basic* to our individual flourishing and to fostering the social-political development of equality and freedom. But what do we find when we look at typical school practices?

THE ANTIDIALOGICAL SCHOOL

One of the most striking facts about schools is that even as educators hold forth models of dialogue and a "Socratic method" as the ideal form of education, we tolerate institutional structures and routine practices that make dialogue unlikely for most teachers and most students, most of the time. In this section I will discuss some of these conditions and their effects on the possibility of dialogue.

Discouraging the Communicative Virtues

First are the conditions that discourage the expression and development of the "communicative virtues." Many of these supersede schools per se: When persons in their home lives, friendships, and communities outside the school are prevented from developing the capacities and dispositions for listening carefully, considering alternative points of view, tolerating criticism or disagreement, or expressing themselves straightforwardly and reasonably, it is unlikely that school experiences, however conducive, will counterbalance those tendencies. Nevertheless, what is even worse is when school influences reinforce those tendencies, as they so frequently do. When teacher–student interchange becomes primarily a matter of telling, or a matter of asking extremely narrow, one-way questions, the capacities of both participants to listen, think, question, and consider alternatives atrophy. When instruction is geared toward "correct answers," the inclination toward discussions that pertain more to investigation and divergent points of view is suppressed. When student–student dialogue is actively discouraged, or relegated only to very specific legitimate domains (the lunchroom, the playground), particular communicative skills and dispositions are certainly deterred. But more than this, a tacit message is expressed that these dialogical skills and dispositions are not themselves educationally (or socially, or politically) significant; because, clearly, if they were significant, the curriculum would acknowledge them. Finally, by inhibiting certain kinds of relational bonds between teachers and students (as well as among students), these school practices *also* inhibit the development of the communicative virtues in teachers, who frequently find after years in the school setting that their own capacities for spontaneous and enthusiastic engagement in dialogue with students (or with colleagues, or with parents) have atrophied as well. Because the development of the communicative virtues is time-consuming, deeply personal, and intertwined with other emotional as well as intellectual factors, formal educational settings are not well equipped to develop them when they are lacking.

Yet, even more serious are those aspects of the school situation that make it unsafe and threatening for those who *do* possess and practice the communicative virtues to manifest them in that setting. Because the communicative virtues are context-sensitive, what might constitute a virtue in one situation may become a vice in another. Listening and tolerance, for example, although generally regarded as virtues, are punitive when practiced in situations of offensive speech.

Educational contexts foster some circumstances that implicitly punish the exercise of certain virtues, or reward their violation. For example, the academic culture often rewards an aggressive style of communication, epitomized by an "adversary method," which assumes that the best way to evaluate another's ideas or arguments is to attack them (Moulton, 1983). Therefore, we should reflect on the institutional arrangements and practices in our schools that either (a) ignore the exercise and development of the communicative virtues, (b) marginalize them and treat them as insignificant educational goals, or (c) actually work to inhibit them. Where the communicative virtues are lacking, dialogue cannot occur.

Antidialogical Instructional Practices

Current tendencies in instructional practices are antidialogical as well. Pressures from the public and from state agencies, as well as some attitudes of teachers themselves, have led to

1. A content-driven conception of curriculum, in which "coverage" of material becomes a primary goal
2. A test-driven conception of educational aims, in which outcomes that cannot be measured in this way are pressed further and further into the background of educational aims
3. A management-driven conception of the teacher's role, in which maintaining conditions of order and discipline become, not means to educational ends, but ends in and of themselves

Many studies have shown how these factors are directly antagonistic to the possibilities of dialogue in the classroom. As one study concludes, "Dialogue does not currently play a very significant role in student–teacher verbal interaction" (Palincsar, 1986, p. 95).

Such technical conceptions of instruction tend to drive teacher–student comments primarily in the direction of "control talk": "When students initiate questions or stray from the topic, teachers view this behavior as evidence of their own loss of control, and they take action to restore order" (Alvermann, O'Brien, & Dillon, 1990, p. 320). When teachers do ask students questions, they tend to conform to the classic Initiation-Response-Evaluation pattern (Alvermann & Hayes, 1989; Cazden, 1986; Goffman, 1983). These "pseudoquestions" manifest a very narrow conception of knowledge and a lack of commitment to truly open-ended and exploratory dialogue. They serve to maintain the crude appearance of a "discussion"-

oriented classroom, while maintaining the teacher's desire for actual control. Thus even when teachers do engage in apparently dialogical practices, they often skew them through a need to control and direct the precise course of conversation. Alvermann and Hayes (1989) provide an all-too-familiar example (from the transcript of a discussion of *Antigone*).

> Teacher: "So is it a feminist or antifeminist play?"
> Students: "Anti!"
> Teacher: "Anti?"
> Student 1: "Anti."
> Teacher: "Huh?"
> Student 2: "Do you want us to say feminist?"
> Teacher: "Huh?"
> Student 2: "Because every time we say anti, you say—"
> Teacher: [Interrupting] Okay. No, I want—I want examples. I want something to support your opinion. (p. 321)

Although the teacher here, to his credit, eventually tries to shift gears to adapt to the unexpected response, it is clear that he had a specific answer in mind when first asking the question. Asking such questions, while potentially useful in what I have called dialogues of the instructional, "leading" variety, is obviously counterproductive in generating open-ended dialogical exchanges generally. Pseudo-questions communicate the implicit messages of fixed answers, of teacher expertise and student naivete, and often are perceived as manipulative and disingenuous. Given such serious shortcomings, I would suggest that if a teacher is disposed to lecturing, he or she should simply do so, and do so openly and as well as possible, rather than pretending to be engaged in discussion when he or she really is not.

Similarly, student–teacher communication is sharply truncated in most classrooms. Most student to teacher comments take the form of "recitation rather than give-and-take dialogue between teacher and students" (Alvermann & Hayes, 1989, p. 313). In such settings, "meaning was also constructed within the teacher's frame of reference. . . . Students rarely questioned that meaning; nor did they initiate questions that might have bridged the gulf between their frame of reference and that of their teachers" (p. 331). When students *do* initiate comments, furthermore, they tend to be requests for help (Cazden, 1986).

Finally, there is a striking paucity of student–student discussion in most classrooms. "Peer talk," as Courtney Cazden (1986) calls it, is in most classes a "rare event" (pp. 442–443). This circumstance is particularly striking given teachers' rhetorical commitments to valuing classroom discussion, even as they act in ways that inhibit it (Alvermann, O'Brien, & Dillon, 1990). Because classroom discussions often happen spontaneously and unexpectedly, if teachers are open to them, it seems to take an effort, conscious or otherwise, to suppress them (Cazden, 1988).

Now, it must be said that the unfavorable image of teachers emanating from such studies is not entirely the teachers' fault. Various institutional pressures, including conflicting expectations from different constituencies outside the classroom, often put teachers in a "no-win" situation. The current pressures for coverage of "basics" and test-based evaluations of student (and teacher, and school) performance are hardly teacher-driven initiatives. The constraints created by such demands, as well as the persistence of certain teacher attitudes and habits, are so intractable that even planned interventions to change teaching practices in the direction of more discussion have failed.

> Although we worked with teachers over 6 months to modify these discussion practices, the teachers and students in this study established a marked stability in their patterns of verbal exchange. . . . Overall, the intervention was not effective in modifying classroom discussions to allow for more meaningful give-and-take between teacher and students. (Alvermann & Hayes, 1989, p. 331)

These discouraging findings do not demonstrate that an increased use of dialogue among teachers and students in classrooms cannot occur, but they suggest that the barriers and impediments to doing so are severe. In the face of such evidence, simple prescriptions or perorations about the value of "dialogue," as many critics and commentators on schools are wont to offer, seem sadly out of touch.

Cultural Diversity in Schools

The diversity of students and teachers in classrooms, while in many ways creating wonderful educational opportunities for dialogue across difference, as I have emphasized throughout this book, also creates some impediments to dialogue. Different cultural groups obviously possess different languages (a concrete difficulty, as my discussion of translation suggests), but even where they have a common language they may have different styles of expression; what is acceptable communicative conduct within one cultural group may not appear to be acceptable to another (Heath, 1983). As a result, people in these groups often misunderstand and talk past one another; and so may respond to a situation of difference by rejecting the value of dialogue entirely. Similar differences in styles of communication have been noted between males and females (Tannen, 1990). Moreover, these differences do not reside all at the same level; contexts of power, prejudice, and intimidation make some people regard such *differences* as *inadequacies*. In such instances, speaking across differences no longer becomes a matter of goodwill or effort (if it is ever that simple), but of speaking against the grain of status differences and, often, personal histories of intolerance and harm. In some of these circumstances, as Ellsworth notes, dialogue may be too much to expect.

It is unrealistic and unfair to ask groups already put upon to take on also the burden of trying to understand, and make themselves understood by, those who harm them or benefit from their deprivation. In numerous unrecognized ways, specific features of the dialogical situation in classrooms may be perceived as intimidating (the presence of certain groups of people, the institutional setting, the threat of criticism)—and major, significant changes may be necessary to ameliorate such intimidating factors.

Another factor that inhibits dialogue in contexts of difference is the "silence" that excludes certain participants from speaking their hearts and minds, or from being heard if they do (Delpit, 1988; Fine, 1987). However, there are many kinds of silence, and they portend very different kinds of prospects for dialogue. Some silence, the silence that concerns Paulo Freire, for example, comes from an actual incapacity to express oneself, either through illiteracy or through such severe intimidation that fear of retribution prevents people from "speaking the word." Silence can also be a form of protest, willfully withdrawing from a discussion that has become irrelevant or offensive. Sometimes silence is actually a sign of thoughtful listening, where such listening and reflecting are forms of active participation that can help sustain an ongoing dialogue. Sometimes silence can be itself an eloquent mode of self-expression, as Wittgenstein (1961) noted, in the face of certain kinds of moral or religious insights: "What we cannot speak about we must pass over in silence" (p. 151)— which for Wittgenstein were the most important things (Monk, 1991). In still other cases, silence on the part of some persons might be an active choice, because speaking out may simply be too risky for them; or it may constitute a necessary phase of self-protection before future communication can occur (Lewis, 1990). Obviously, it is risky to *assume* that persistent silence reflects a conscious preference, and the typical case is that silence reflects a problem in the dialogical relation—but this cannot be inferred simply from the behavior.

A very different kind of silence is revealed in the work of Basil Bernstein (1971, 1982, 1990; see also Apple, 1992). Bernstein argues that different cultural and class groups, because they do not have equal access to the means of linguistic production (in schools and elsewhere), evolve patterns of speech that are not only different in style, but in *capacities*. He terms this a difference between "elaborated" and "restricted" linguistic codes. In this view, there are, between different linguistic communities, disparities of vocabulary and syntactic or semantic complexity and flexibility that have the effect of making it difficult if not impossible to express certain kinds of ideas within them. These "restricted codes" constitute a particularly insidious kind of silence, since it is not a matter of not being able (or willing, or comfortable) to speak, but of being able to speak only within certain limits that are largely invisible. Bernstein argues that while some of these differences in codes are features of social and cultural groups regardless of schools, schools exacerbate these problems when, through policies such as tracking, they segregate these speech communities and further limit their access to diverse, alternative, and more complex modes of expression. Bernstein has been accused of ethnocentrism, and of fostering a "deficit" model that labels cultural *difference* in linguistic style as an *inadequacy*. Yet Bernstein seems sympathetic to this concern, and has addressed it directly in his recent work (1990).

For this reason, it is important to note that not all cases of linguistic difference *are* cases of linguistic inadequacy; and that many minority dialects or speech patterns have highly developed levels of complexity and subtlety (Labov, 1972). In many cases the problem is not "linguistic inadequacy," but the intolerance of school settings for culturally diverse modes of self-expression.

> Because of prior experiences in their home community, students would be better served if teachers took difference more into account than they now do; and teachers now differentiate among their students in ways that may continue, even increase, inequalities of information and skills present when students start school. (Cazden, 1986, p. 445)

Because of these many forms of silencing—some active, some tacit—members of disadvantaged groups may have internalized the message from previous experiences in schools that their concerns, feelings, or world views are not important. In such cases, Lisa Delpit (1988) recommends:

> We must keep the perspective that people are expert on their own lives. There are certainly aspects of the outside world of which they may not be aware, but they can be the only authentic chroniclers of their own experience. We must not be too quick to deny their interpretations, or accuse them of "false consciousness." We must believe that people are rational beings. . . . We may not understand their rationales, but that in no way militates against the existence of these rationales or reduces our responsibility to attempt to apprehend them. And finally, we must learn to be vulnerable enough to allow our world to be turned upside down in order to allow the realities of others to edge themselves into our consciousness. (p. 297)

Despite these barriers of difference, however, there must be *some* forums in which such discussions are seriously undertaken, and there must be *some* individuals from each group who are prepared to take on the burden (and risk) of attempting some degree of communication and translation across the gulf that divides them. Among many reasons for this, one is that such discourse is a condition of democratic life.

> Democratic politics is an encounter among people with different interests, perspectives, and opinions—an encounter in which they reconsider and mutually revise opinions and interests, both individual and common. It happens always in a context of conflict, imperfect knowledge, and uncertainty, but where community action is necessary. The resolutions achieved are always more or less temporary, subject to reconsideration, and rarely unanimous. What matters is not unanimity but discourse. (Pitkin & Shumer, 1982, p. 47)

Schools are one public context established, ostensibly, to prepare young people for such democratic discussions; but this cannot occur without active interventions by teachers and others to encourage and facilitate that process (J. White, 1990). One of the factors that determines this process is the attitude of the participants, not only to the particular differences that distinguish them, but toward the very fact of difference itself. Sometimes there are tendencies to approach opposing points of view with suspicion, fear, or scorn; these may arise from intolerance and prejudice, or from previous painful encounters with such points of view. There may be a tendency to infer from certain differences the likeliness of other kinds of conflict; to prejudge, for example, that others will be unreasonable or insensitive to one's concerns because they are members of a particular group. There may be a tendency to judge alternative forms of expression against one dominant standard, and so to reject prematurely what might in fact constitute an adequate, but different, form of self-expression. Such attitudes are a serious constraint to the possibilities of dialogue, and education generally. Yet it is precisely because of the difficulty of such situations of difference that we stand to learn from them. There are benefits to be derived from dialogues with those like us; but there are benefits as well to be gained from persisting in dialogues with those not like us.

In light of such considerations, dialogue must take into account the diversity of communicative styles. Nancy Fraser (1989), for example, distinguishes between a *monological* conception of dialogue "in which interlocutors share a sense of what counts as a problem or question, as a well-formed or serious hypothesis, and as a good reason or argument" and a *polylogical* conception of dialogue that "involves a plurality of differentiable if not incommensurable voices, and . . . consists in an exchange among them that is lively if somewhat disorderly" (pp. 102–103). As I discussed in detail in Chapter 6, these two tendencies, convergent and divergent, are fundamental to any exchange of meaning. Every understanding is practical and is established through a process of interpretation that necessarily transforms what was initially said or meant into terms that are salient for the listener. In the context of dialogue, this means that what begins as an unfathomable difference can become an occasion for deeper self-understanding, seeing oneself as a stranger through the understandings of another—and this can be seen as an important educational opportunity.

The Outlooks of School Participants

The possibility of dialogue in educational contexts, especially in contexts of disagreement or difference, is limited as well by the attitudes that participants take toward their own and each other's perspectives: "Dialogue is interrupted in controversy . . . by dogmatism that refuses to submit opinions about . . . reality or the compelling evidence of experience or thought to the test of other opinions and hypotheses" (McKeon, 1990, p. 42). Richard McKeon, however, tells only half the story: for dialogue is interrupted not only by dogmatism, but by relativism as well. Bakhtin summarized this problem perfectly: "It should be noted that both relativism and dogmatism equally exclude all argumentation, all authentic dialogue, by making it either unnecessary (relativism) or impossible (dogmatism)'' (quoted in Morson, 1981a, p. viii). This problem is not hypothetical. Some current trends in educational theory tend to encourage relativistic thinking that abandons the ideals of dialogue and consensus: I discussed some of these issues in Chapter 2. Specifically, skepticism about the possibilities of dialogue has been raised by some postmodern writers. Given some of the doubts expressed in this chapter, it should be clear that I find many of these concerns credible. But at some point this postmodern critique passes over into an *antimodern* rejection of the value of dialogue itself (Burbules & Rice, 1991).

On the one hand, postmodernism provides strong reasons for valuing diversity, for not assuming homogeneity when it does not exist, and for avoiding modes of discursive and nondiscursive practice that implicitly or explicitly exclude subjects who do not participate in dominant modes of thought, speech, and action. This position might even be pushed a step further, to insist that given occasions of conflict and misunderstanding, we ought to err on the side of respecting the self-identification and world view of others, especially for members of groups who have been traditionally *told* who they are, what is true, and what is good for them. However, at some points in the literature, this position lapses over into claims that are much more problematic. Specifically, the celebration of difference becomes a presumption of incommensurability, a denial of the possibility of intersubjective understanding, and an exaggerated critique that *any* attempt to establish reasonable and consensual discourse across difference inevitably involves the imposition of dominant groups' values, beliefs, and modes of discourse upon others. When pushed to this extreme, these views are antimodern in their rejection of such goals as dialogue, reasonableness, and fair treatment of alternative points of view; such legacies of the modernist tradition are regarded not only as difficult and sometimes impossible to attain—which they are—but as actually undesirable ends.

My purpose here is not to engage this antimodern critique directly, but simply to point out that it has the effect of unilaterally prejudging the possibilities of success and failure in dialogue. In place of an antimodern presumption that dialogue must fail, or an Enlightenment faith that it must succeed, I would recommend a pragmatic, contextual, fallibilistic perspective that regards the possibilities of dialogue with persistence and hope, while being prepared as well for its possible failure and breakdown. We should not allow theoretical abstractions to obscure or override the ordinary experiences of our daily lives. It will not be evident, a priori and at a purely intellectual level, whether dialogue in a particular circumstance will or will not be possible; or *how much* understanding can be achieved through dialogue. We may remember vividly the frustrations and pains caused by previous failures of understanding. But the presumption that incommensurability is inevitable threatens to be self-confirming, since when efforts at understanding are not made, are made half-heartedly, or are abandoned when they become difficult or discouraging, then incommensurability does indeed result. Yet it results as a psychological/social consequence, not because of any inherent necessity. The presumption of consensus, on the other hand, threatens to ride roughshod over legitimate differences and disagreements, and to coerce conformity with dominant ideals.

On a related point, there is a range of commitments or oppositions among administrators, teachers, and students to the value of critical thinking. Dialogue has affinities with the processes of reflection and questioning that define this capacity; Richard Paul (1987), for example, defines critical thinking as a kind of "internal dialogue," in which we consider possible points of view, question them, and modify them, performing in effect both roles of a dialogical investigation within our own minds. Yet such capacities for critical thinking are often constrained by what Habermas refers to as "suppressed dialogue"(1971, p. 315), or elsewhere as "systematically distorted communication" (1984, p. 332). In his view, the insulation of certain positions from being questioned or subjected to interpersonal justification is what characterizes them as "ideological." Ideological positions, in this sense, stand at the opposite pole from critically derived ones; and their difference can be seen in terms of their relation to dialogue. Positions that are derived from dialogical interchange, or that can be subjected to it, are reasonable in a way that positions insulated from dialogical reconsideration and testing are not. In a society that harbors myriad ideological sects and clans, as ours does, it is essential that contexts remain where dialogue is valued as a critical counterweight to such tendencies. Educators, above all, should be models of dialogue as a means of reasoned inquiry, critical questioning, intersubjective understanding, and nonindoctrinatory instruction. Yet little in schools encourages them to do so, and many concrete features of schools discourage them.

The Kinds of Schools We Have Made

My final category of impediments to dialogue includes these concrete conditions: the circumstances in which we bring teachers and students together in schools. Dialogue on any general scale is simply

impracticable given such conditions. These factors are familiar to anyone who spends time in schools, and some of them have been noted
previously in this book.

- Pressures to cover material for the sake of "high stakes" stan-
  dardized tests
- Too little time in the day, and too few days in a year, to develop and sustain open-ended discussions with most students
- Absurdly overcrowded classrooms
- Evaluations of teachers based on "control and discipline"
  rather than on student enthusiasm and spontaneity
- Formal and informal practices that encourage competition
  among teachers, or among students, rather than dialogical cooperation
- Authority and privileges that accrue to teachers, which they
  believe will be threatened if they subject themselves to questioning by students

Indeed, it appears that if we were designing institutions from scratch
with a primary goal of *guaranteeing* that there would be few incentives
to pursue dialogue and even fewer opportunities to do so, we could
not do much better than the typical public school.

Of course, not all students go to large, overcrowded public
schools. Smaller and more affluent public schools, and many private
schools, do feature more dialogical interchanges between teachers
and students, and among students. This means, of course, that in
most cases the "right to have a small discussion begins as a class
privilege. The more elite the student, the more likely that he or she
will have a personalized, discussion contact with the professor or
teacher" (Shor & Freire, 1987a, p. 12). Similar comparisons can be
made among university teaching situations as well. If, as the research
I have discussed in this book suggests, dialogical modes of teaching
are linked with the development of higher cognitive capacities; if
they tend to generate the *internal* processes of dialogue that promote
critical thinking; if they have a strong influence on promoting students' self-esteem, as teachers and fellow students treat one another
with interest and respect; and if they are part of developing the character and disposition for active democratic participation—then where
access to and involvement with dialogue are class-biased privileges,
these learning outcomes tend to be as well. And that is an inequity, I
believe, that schools ought to take very seriously.

CONCLUSION

As I said at the beginning of this chapter, this is not a utopian book. It is appealing to imagine an educational system, and a democratic polity in general, founded on the basis of dialogical relations. But a frank recognition of the social trends, and specifically the features of schools, that discourage and inhibit such possibilities should counterbalance any such idealism. Instead, we might regard the dialogical model as a measuring stick against which to compare and judge our actual practices; *to what extent* are we successful or not in approaching its values of mutual respect, interest, and concern? The cause for hope is that we do return to these values again and again in our communicative relations; by continually seeking them out, and striving to maintain them in at least some domains of our lives, we keep alive both the ideal and the communicative virtues that help sustain it. As Richard Bernstein (1983) notes:

> What we desperately need today is to learn to think and act more like the fox than the hedgehog—to seize upon those experiences and struggles in which there are still the glimmerings of solidarity and the promise of dialogical communities in which there can be genuine mutual participation. (p. 228)

The persistence and pervasiveness of dialogue as a human practice give us reason to believe that it expresses something basic and essential about our human character; and as long as this is so, barriers and impediments will reveal themselves to us as such—though, of course, whether we can and will do anything to overcome them is a question yet to be answered.

Henry Giroux and Peter McLaren repeatedly urge upon educators a "language of possibility" and a "pedagogy of hope" (for example, Aronowitz & Giroux, 1985; McLaren, 1991). In this, they draw from the spirit of Freire's struggles to overcome the despair and fatalism of oppressed groups who have been shut off from the full range of their human potentialities. I understand and am sympathetic with such a commitment, but this sort of optimism does not come easily to me. I am too strongly aware of the persistent antidialogical features of the society, and schools, we have created—features many people seem intent on maintaining, even exacerbating. In the face of such obstacles, rhetorical flourishes about how dialogue will create the possibility of a new democratic equality and vitality seem sadly empty.

Nevertheless, Freire's work with illiterate and demoralized groups in the Third World, and elsewhere, stands as inspiring proof that dialogical relations can be created even under the most unfavorable conditions. Recent authors in the United States have shown how dialogical encounters *can* be fostered among teachers and students in real school settings, leading to valuable pedagogical opportunities. Sophie Haroutunian-Gordon (1991), for example, in her recent book *Turning the Soul*, gives many examples of creative and ingenious teaching through dialogue in an inner city high school. Andrew Gitlin (1990), in his work with teachers, shows how dialogical engagement can create supportive communities of practice. Kathleen Weiler (1988) provides a number of inspiring examples of feminist teachers struggling within existing institutional constraints to create a more dialogical pedagogy. Robert Young (1990, 1992) describes an innovative approach to pedagogy based entirely on Habermasian premises.

What we need, then, is not a matter of either optimism or pessimism. Instead, we ought to adopt a realistic, pragmatic approach that recognizes and seizes upon the opportunities for dialogue that we do have, and builds upon these, in full cognizance of the obstacles and prospects for failure, without succumbing either to empty hope or despair.

> There is no guarantee, there is no necessity, no "logic of history" that must inevitably lead to dialogical communities that embrace all of humanity and in which reciprocal judgment, practical discourse, and rational persuasion flourish. If anything, we have or should have learned how much the contemporary world conspires against it and undermines it. (R. Bernstein, 1983, p. 231)

In this endeavor, effort and goodwill alone are not guarantees. Dialogue can fail; yet even when this happens, it also can teach us something—that persistence does not resolve all conflicts, that some problems are not "solvable," but only "manageable," and that a level of mystery and perplexity accompanies all attempts at human understanding. Such realizations should foster in us a healthy modesty about the possibilities and limits of our communicative efforts (Burbules, 1990).

It is only at the level of practice that we can demonstrate our implicit commitment to dialogue and the values that animate it. The benefit of communicative norms such as dialogue, as Seyla Benhabib, Richard Bernstein, and Jurgen Habermas argue, is not that they represent abstract ideals to which we should aspire, but that they exemplify *implicit* values that we actually do hold, that are latent in the practices in which we are actually engaged. In this, they function as reminders of standards that are necessarily implied by what we do and by what we say we want. This book, on dialogue, is an exercise in this sort of investigation: I have tried to extract some consistent norms and patterns of dialogical engagement and re-present them for consideration. I have tried to clarify my own understanding of what dialogue is and how it works (when it does), and have suggested some categories and rules that give structure to the broad range of activities that are actually involved in dialogical relations. My only claim for this analysis is that it can provide some useful heuristics for further reflection on the problem of dialogue. In this, it is simply one stage of an ongoing dialogue itself, one now involving you, the reader, and others who will comment on this book, as well as myself.

Of course, I certainly do hope that teachers and students engaged in dialogical practices will recognize themselves and their efforts in parts of this book, and I will be pleased if the suggestions offered here help them, and others, find more effective ways to bring dialogue into their educational activities. But I am not trying to preach or to set standards for others to achieve. As I have argued repeatedly, we learn to engage in dialogue *by* engaging in dialogue. We improve through practice, by persisting in our efforts with a range of others and by trying to learn from their experiences, as well as from our own. Dialogue is, I have suggested, a "bootstrapped" endeavor; our errors and failings in dialogue can be corrected only through more dialogue—and we need to maintain and develop our communicative relations with others for this to occur.

References

Ackerman, B. (1980). *Social justice in the liberal state.* New Haven: Yale University Press.

Ackerman, B. (1989). Why dialogue? *Journal of Philosophy, 86,* 5–22.

Alexy, R. (1990). A theory of practical discourse. In S. Benhabib & F. Dallmayr (Eds.), *The communicative ethics controversy* (pp. 151–190). Cambridge, MA: MIT Press.

Alston, K. (1991). Teaching philosophy, and *Eros:* Love as a relation to truth. *Educational Theory, 41,* 385–395.

Alvermann, D. E., & Hayes, D. A. (1989). Classroom discussion of content area reading assignments: An intervention study. *Reading Research Quarterly, 24,* 305–335.

Alvermann, D. E., O'Brien, D. G., & Dillon, D. R. (1990). What teachers do when they say they are having discussions of content reading assignments: A qualitative analysis. *Reading Research Quarterly, 25,* 296–322.

Anderson, R. C. (1977). The notion of schemata. In R. C. Anderson, R. J. Spiro, & W. E. Montague (Eds.), *Schooling and the acquisition of knowledge* (pp. 415–431). Hillsdale, NJ: Erlbaum.

Apple, M. W. (1982). *Education and power.* Boston: RKP.

Apple, M. W. (1992). Education, culture, and class power: Basil Bernstein and the Neo-Marxist sociology of education. *Educational Theory, 42,* 127–145.

Aristotle. (1973). *Nichomachean ethics.* In R. McKeon (Ed.), *Introduction to Aristotle* (2nd ed., pp. 346–581). Chicago: University of Chicago Press.

Aronowitz, S., & Giroux, H. (1985). *Education under siege.* South Hadley, MA: Bergin & Garvey.

Austin, J. L. (1962). *How to do things with words.* Cambridge, MA: Harvard University Press.

Bakhtin, M. M. (1981). *The dialogic imagination.* Austin: University of Texas Press.

Bakhtin, M. M. (1986). *Speech genres.* Austin: University of Texas Press.

Barber, B. (1984). *Strong democracy: Participatory politics for a new age.* Berkeley: University of California Press.

Bauer, D. M. (1988). *Feminist dialogics: A theory of failed community.* Albany: State University of New York Press.

Belenky, M. F., Clinchy, B. M., Goldberger, N. R., & Tarule, J. M. (1986).

Women's ways of knowing: The development of self, voice, and mind. New York: Basic Books.

Benhabib, S. (1986). *Critique, norm, and utopia: A study of the foundations of critical theory.* New York: Columbia University Press.

Benhabib, S. (1987). The generalized and concrete other: The Kohlberg-Gilligan controversy and moral theory. In E. F. Kittay & D. T. Meyers (Eds.), *Women and moral theory* (pp. 154–177). Totowa, NJ: Rowman & Littlefield.

Benhabib, S. (1989). Liberal dialogue versus a critical theory of discursive legitimation. In N. L. Rosenblum (Ed.), *Liberalism and the moral life* (pp. 143–156). Cambridge, MA: Harvard University Press.

Benhabib, S. (1990). In the shadow of Aristotle and Hegel: Communicative ethics and current controversies in practical philosophy. In M. Kelly (Ed.), *Hermeneutics and critical theory in ethics and politics* (pp. 1–31). Cambridge, MA: MIT Press.

Benhabib, S., & Dallmayr, F. (Eds.). (1990). *The communicative ethics controversy.* Cambridge, MA: MIT Press.

Benyon, J. (1987). An ethnography of questioning practices. *Questioning Exchange, 1,* 39–42.

Bernstein, B. (1971). *Class, codes, and control: Vol. 1. Theoretical studies towards a sociology of language.* London: Routledge.

Bernstein, B. (1982). Codes, modalities, and the process of cultural reproduction. In M. W. Apple (Ed.), *Cultural and economic reproduction in education: Essays on class, ideology, and the state* (pp. 304–355). New York: Routledge.

Bernstein, B. (1990). *Class, codes, and control, Vol. 4: The structuring of pedagogic discourse.* London: Routledge.

Bernstein, M. A. (1981). When the carnival turns bitter: Preliminary reflections upon the abject hero. In G. S. Morson (Ed.), *Bakhtin: Essays and dialogues on his work* (pp. 99–121). Chicago: University of Chicago Press.

Bernstein, R. J. (1983). *Beyond objectivism and relativism: Science, hermeneutics, and praxis.* Philadelphia: University of Pennsylvania Press.

Bernstein, R. J. (1985). Introduction. In R. J. Bernstein (Ed.), *Habermas and modernity* (pp. 1–32). Cambridge, MA: MIT Press.

Bernstein, R. J. (1986). *Philosophical profiles.* Philadelphia: University of Pennsylvania Press.

Bohm, D., & Peat, F. D. (1991). *Science, order, and creativity.* New York: Bantam Books. Quoted in *Utne Reader, 4,* p. 82.

Bransford, J. D., & McCarrell, N. S. (1974). A sketch of a cognitive approach to comprehension: Some thoughts about understanding what it means to comprehend. In W. B. Weiner & D. S. Palermo (Eds.), *Cognition and the symbolic processes* (pp. 189–229). New York: Wiley.

Bridges, D. (1987). Discussion and questioning. *Questioning Exchange, 1,* 34–37.

Bridges, D. (1988a). *Education, democracy and discussion.* New York: University Press of America.

Bridges, D. (1988b). A philosophical analysis of discussion. In J. T. Dillon (Ed.), *Questioning and discussion: An interdisciplinary study* (pp. 15–28). Norwood, NJ: Ablex.

Bridges, J. (1973). The paper chase. Screenplay from the novel by John Jay Osborn, Jr. Twentieth Century Fox.

Bruner, J. (1971). *The relevance of education.* New York: W. W. Norton.

Buber, M. (1958). *I and thou.* New York: Scribners.

Burbules, N. C. (1986). A theory of power in education. *Educational Theory, 36,* 95–114.

Burbules, N. C. (1990). The tragic sense of education. *Teachers College Record, 91,* 469–479.

Burbules, N. C. (1991a). Rationality and reasonableness: A discussion of Harvey Siegel's *Relativism refuted* and *Educating reason. Educational Theory, 41,* 235–252

Burbules, N. C. (1991b). Varieties of educational dialogue. In D. P. Ericson (Ed.), *Philosophy of education 1990: Proceedings of the forty-sixth annual meeting of the Philosophy of Education Society* (pp. 120–131). Normal, IL: Philosophy of Education Society.

Burbules, N. C. (1992). The virtues of reasonableness. In M. Buchmann & R. Floden (Eds.), *Philosophy of education 1991: Proceedings of the forty-seventh annual meeting of the Philosophy of Education Society* (pp. 215–224). Normal, IL: Philosophy of Education Society.

Burbules, N. C., & Rice, S. (1991). Dialogue across differences: Continuing the conversation. *Harvard Educational Review, 61,* 393–416.

Burbules, N. C., & Rice, S. (1992). Can we be heard? A reply to Leach. *Harvard Educational Review, 62,* 264–271.

Carlson, L. (1983). *Dialogue games: An essay in formal semantics.* Boston: Reidel.

Carroll, L. (1916). *Alice in wonderland and Through the looking glass.* Kingsport, TN: Grosset & Dunlap.

Cazden, C. B. (1986). Classroom discourse. In M. C. Wittrock (Ed.), *Handbook of research on teaching* (3rd ed., pp. 432–463). New York: Macmillan.

Cazden, C. B. (1988). *Classroom discourse: The language of teaching and learning.* Portsmouth, NH: Heinemann.

Cherryholmes, C. (1988). *Power and criticism: Poststructural investigations in education.* New York: Teachers College Press.

Collins, A. (1977). Processes in acquiring knowledge. In R. C. Anderson, R. J. Spiro, & W. E. Montague (Eds.), *Schooling and the acquisition of knowledge* (pp. 339–363). Hillsdale, NJ: Erlbaum.

Collins, A., & Stevens, A. L. (1982). Goals and strategies of inquiry teachers. In R. Glaser (Ed.), *Advances in instructional psychology* (Vol. 2, pp. 65–119). Hillsdale, NJ: Erlbaum.

Collins, A., & Stevens, A. L. (1983). A cognitive theory of inquiry teaching. In C. M. Reigeluth (Ed.), *Instructional design theories and models: An overview of the current status* (pp. 247–278). Hillsdale, NJ: Erlbaum.

Costa, A. (1990). Teacher behaviors that promote discussion. In W. W. Wilen (Ed.), *Teaching and learning through discussion: The theory, research, and practice of the discussion method* (pp. 45–77). Springfield, IL: Charles C. Thomas.

Crapanzano, V. (1990). On dialogue. In T. Maranhão (Ed.), *The interpretation of dialogue* (pp. 269–291). Chicago: University of Chicago Press.

Crowell, S. G. (1990). Dialogue and text: Re-marking the difference. In T. Maranhão (Ed.), *The interpretation of dialogue* (pp. 338–360). Chicago: University of Chicago Press.

Daelemans, S., & Maranhão, T. (1990). Psychoanalytic discourse and the dialogical principle. In T. Maranhão (Ed.), *The interpretation of dialogue* (pp. 219–241). Chicago: University of Chicago Press.

Dascal, M. (1985a). Introduction. In M. Dascal (Ed.), *Dialogue: An interdisciplinary approach* (pp. 1–8). Philadelphia: Benjamin's.

Dascal, M. (1985b). The relevance of misunderstanding. In M. Dascal (Ed.), *Dialogue: An interdisciplinary approach* (pp. 441–459). Philadelphia: Benjamin's.

Delpit, L. (1988). The silenced dialogue. *Harvard Educational Review, 58,* 280–298.

Dewey, J. (1916). *Democracy and education.* New York: Macmillan.

Dillon, J. T. (1983). *Teaching and the art of questioning.* Bloomington, IN: Phi Delta Kappa.

Dillon, J. T. (1987). Question-answer practices in a dozen fields. *Questioning Exchange, 1,* 87–100.

Dillon, J. T. (Ed.). (1988). *Questioning and discussion: An interdisciplinary study.* Norwood, NJ: Ablex.

Elbow, P. (1986). *Embracing contraries: Explorations in learning and teaching.* New York: Oxford University Press.

Ellsworth, E. (1989). Why doesn't this feel empowering? Working through the repressive myths of critical pedagogy. *Harvard Educational Review, 59,* 291–324.

Ellsworth, E. (1990). The question remains: How will you hold awareness of the limits of your knowledge? *Harvard Educational Review, 60,* 396–405.

Emerson, C. (1981). The outer word and inner speech: Bakhtin, Vygotsky, and the internalization of language. In G. S. Morson (Ed.), *Bakhtin: Essays and dialogues on his work* (pp. 21–40). Chicago: University of Chicago Press.

Fay, B. (1977). How people change themselves: The relationship between critical theory and its audience. In T. Ball (Ed.), *Political theory and praxis: New perspectives* (pp. 200–233). Minneapolis: University of Minnesota Press.

Feinberg, W. (1990). A role for philosophy of education in intercultural research. In R. Page (Ed.), *Philosophy of education 1989: Proceedings of the forty-fifth annual meeting of the Philosophy of Education Society* (pp. 2–19). Normal, IL: Philosophy of Education Society.

Fine, M. (1987). Silencing in the public schools. *Language Arts, 64,* 157–174.

Fisher, M. M. J., & Abedi, M. (1990). Qur'anic dialogues: Islamic poetics and politics for Muslims and for us. In T. Maranhão (Ed.), *The interpretation of dialogue* (pp. 120–153). Chicago: University of Chicago Press.

Foucault, M. (1980). *Power/knowledge: Selected interviews and other writings, 1972-1977.* New York: Pantheon Books.

Foucault, M. (1988). On power. In *Politics, philosophy, culture: Selected interviews and other writings, 1977-1984* (pp. 96-109). New York: Routledge.

Fraser, N. (1989). *Unruly practices: Power, discourse, and gender in contemporary social theory.* Minneapolis: University of Minnesota Press.

Freire, P. (1970). *Pedagogy of the oppressed.* New York: Seabury.

Freire, P. (1985a). *The politics of education: Culture, power and liberation.* South Hadley, MA: Bergin & Garvey.

Freire, P. (1985b). Reading the world and reading the word: An interview with Paulo Freire. *Language Arts, 62,* 15-16.

Friedman, S. S. (1985). Authority in the feminist classroom: A contradiction in terms? In M. Culley & C. Portuges (Eds.), *Gendered subjects: The dynamics of feminist teaching* (pp. 203-208). Boston: RKP.

Gadamer, H-G. (1976). *Philosophical hermeneutics.* Berkeley: University of California Press.

Gadamer, H-G. (1980). *Dialogue and dialectic: Eight hermeneutical studies on Plato.* New Haven: Yale University Press.

Gadamer, H-G. (1982). *Truth and method.* New York: Crossroad.

Gall, M. D. (1970). The use of questions in teaching. *Review of Educational Research, 40,* 707-721.

Gall, M. D. (1984). Synthesis of research on teachers' questioning. *Educational Leadership, 42,* 40-47.

Garrison, J. W., & Phelan, A. M. (1990). Toward a feminist poetic of critical thinking. In R. Page (Ed.), *Philosophy of education 1989: Proceedings of the forty-fifth annual meeting of the Philosophy of Education Society* (pp. 304-314). Normal, IL: Philosophy of Education Society.

Giarelli, J. M. (1991). Philosophy, education and public practice. In D. P. Ericson (Ed.), *Philosophy of education 1990: Proceedings of the forty-sixth annual meeting of the Philosophy of Education Society* (pp. 34-44). Normal, IL: Philosophy of Education Society.

Giroux, H. (1985). Introduction. In P. Freire, *The politics of education: Culture, power and liberation* (pp. xi-xxv). South Hadley, MA: Bergin & Garvey.

Giroux, H. (1988). *Teachers as intellectuals: Toward a critical pedagogy of learning.* South Hadley, MA: Bergin & Garvey.

Giroux, H. (Ed.). (1991). *Postmodernism, feminism, and cultural politics: Redrawing educational boundaries.* Albany: State University of New York Press.

Giroux, H., & McLaren, P. (Eds.). (1989). *Critical pedagogy, the state, and cultural struggle.* Albany: State University of New York Press.

Giroux, H., & Simon, R. (Eds.). (1989). *Popular culture, schooling, and everyday life.* South Hadley, MA: Bergin and Garvey.

Gitlin, A. (1990). Understanding teaching dialogically. *Teachers College Record, 91,* 537-563.

Goffman, E. (1967). *Interaction ritual: Essays on face-to-face behavior.* New York: Pantheon.

Goffman, E. (1969). *Strategic interaction.* Philadelphia: University of Pennsylvania Press.

Goffman, E. (1974). The frame analysis of talk. In *Frame analysis: An essay on the organization of experience* (pp. 496–559). New York: Harper & Row.

Goffman, E. (1983). *Forms of talk*. Philadelphia: University of Pennsylvania Press.

Good, T. L., & Brophy, J. E. (1973). *Looking in classrooms*. New York: Harper & Row.

Grice, H. P. (1989). Logic and conversation. In *Studies in the way of words* (pp. 1–143). Cambridge, MA: Harvard University Press.

Guszak, F. J. (1967). Teacher questioning and reading. *Reading Teacher, 21,* 228–234.

Habermas, J. (1971). *Knowledge and human interests*. Boston: Beacon Press.

Habermas, J. (1976). *Communication and the evolution of society*. Boston: Beacon Press.

Habermas, J. (1977). A review of Gadamer's *Truth and method*. In F. Dallmayr & T. McCarthy (Eds.), *Understanding and social inquiry* (pp. 335–363). Notre Dame, IN: University of Notre Dame Press.

Habermas, J. (1984). *Theory of communicative action: Vol. I. Reason and the rationalization of society*. Boston: Beacon Press.

Habermas, J. (1990a). *Moral consciousness and communicative action*. Cambridge, MA: MIT Press.

Habermas, J. (1990b). *The philosophical discourse of modernity: Twelve lectures*. Cambridge, MA: MIT Press.

Hansen, D. T. (1988). Was Socrates a "Socratic teacher"? *Educational Theory, 38,* 213–224.

Haroutunian-Gordon, S. (1987). Evaluating teachers: The case of Socrates. *Teachers College Record, 89,* 117–132.

Haroutunian-Gordon, S. (1988). Teaching in an "ill-structured situation": The case of Socrates. *Educational Theory, 38,* 225–237.

Haroutunian-Gordon, S. (1989). Socrates as teacher. In P. W. Jackson & S. Haroutunian-Gordon (Eds.), *From Socrates to software: The teacher as text and the text as teacher. 88th yearbook of the National Society for the Study of Education* (pp. 5–23). Chicago: University of Chicago Press, 1989.

Haroutunian-Gordon, S. (1990). Statements of method and teaching: The case of Socrates. *Studies in Philosophy and Education, 10,* 139–156.

Haroutunian-Gordon, S. (1991). *Turning the soul: Teaching through conversation in the high school*. Chicago: University of Chicago Press.

Harvey, D. (1989). *The condition of postmodernity: An inquiry into the origins of cultural change*. Cambridge, MA: Basil Blackwell.

Heath, S. B. (1983). *Ways with words: Language, life and work in communities and classrooms*. New York: Cambridge University Press.

Heidegger, M. (1977). *Basic writings*. New York: Harper & Row.

Hintikka, J. (1982). A dialogical model of teaching. *Synthese, 51,* 39–59.

Holquist, M. (1981). Answering as authoring: Mikhail Bakhtin's translinguistics. In G. S. Morson (Ed.), *Bakhtin: Essays and dialogues on his work* (pp. 59–71). Chicago: University of Chicago Press.

Hostetler, K. (1991). Connecting *techne* and *praxis* in teaching. In D. P. Ericson

(Ed.), *Philosophy of education 1990: Proceedings of the forty-sixth annual meeting of the Philosophy of Education Society* (pp. 337–345). Normal, IL: Philosophy of Education Society.

Howe, K. (1985). Two dogmas of educational research. *Educational Researcher, 14*, 10–18.

Howe, K. (1988). Against the quantitative-qualitative incompatibility thesis. *Educational Researcher, 17*, 10–16.

Huizinga, J. (1950). *Homo ludens: A study of the play element in culture*. Boston: Beacon Press.

Hunkins, F. (1972). *Questioning strategies and techniques*. Boston: Allyn & Bacon.

Hyman, R. (1979). *Strategic questioning*. New Jersey: Prentice-Hall.

Jackson, P. W. (1986). *The practice of teaching*. New York: Teachers College Press.

Johnson, R. S. (1959). Isocrates's methods of teaching. *American Journal of Philosophy, 43*, 25–36.

Kean, R. (1967). Education through dialogue: A revolutionary perspective. In R. Kean (Ed.), *Dialogue on education* (pp. 64–81). New York: Bobbs-Merrill.

Keeney, B. P. (1990). Cybernetics of dialogue: A conversational paradigm for systematic therapies. In T. Maranhão (Ed.), *The interpretation of dialogue* (pp. 242–266). Chicago: University of Chicago Press.

Kelly, M. (1990). MacIntyre, Habermas and philosophical ethics. In M. Kelly (Ed.), *Hermeneutics and critical theory in ethics and politics* (pp. 70–93). Cambridge, MA: MIT Press.

King, N. R. (1987). Elementary school play: Theory and research. In J. H. Block & N. R. King (Eds.), *School Play* (pp. 143–165). New York: Garland.

Kuhn, D. (1992). Thinking as argument. *Harvard Educational Review, 62*, 155–178.

Labov, W. (1972). *Language in the inner city*. Philadelphia: University of Pennsylvania Press.

Lewis, M. (1990, April). *Framing, women and silence: Disrupting the hierarchy of discursive practices*. Paper presented at the 1990 Meeting of the American Educational Research Association, Boston.

Macmillan, C. J. B., & Garrison, J. W. (1983). An erotetic concept of teaching. *Educational Theory, 33*, 156–166.

Macmillan, C. J. B., & Garrison, J. W. (1988). *A logical theory of teaching: Erotetics and intentionality*. Boston: Kluwer.

Maher, F. (1985). Classroom pedagogy and the new scholarship on women. In M. Culley & C. Portuges (Eds.), *Gendered subjects: The dynamics of feminist teaching* (pp. 29–48). Boston: RKP.

Manor, R. (1987). Harrah's theory of questions. *Questioning Exchange, 1*, 15–24.

Maranhão, T. (1990). Introduction. In T. Maranhão (Ed.), *The interpretation of dialogue* (pp. 1–22). Chicago: University of Chicago Press.

Marcondes de Souza Filho, D. (1985). Dialogue breakdowns. In M. Dascal (Ed.), *Dialogue: An interdisciplinary approach* (pp. 415–426). Philadelphia: Benjamin's.

McCarthy, T. (1978). *The critical theory of Jurgen Habermas*. Cambridge, MA: MIT Press.

McKeon, R. (1990). Dialogue and controversy in philosophy. In T. Maranhão (Ed.), *The interpretation of dialogue* (pp. 25–46). Chicago: University of Chicago Press.

McLaren, P. (1986). Postmodernity and the death of politics: A Brazilian reprieve. *Educational Theory, 36,* 389–401.

McLaren, P. (1991). Critical pedagogy: Constructing an arch of social dreaming and a doorway to hype. *Journal of Education, 173,* 9–34.

Mecke, J. (1990). Dialogue in narration (the narrative principle). In T. Maranhão (Ed.), *The interpretation of dialogue* (pp. 195–215). Chicago: University of Chicago Press.

Merleau-Ponty, M. (1962). *The phenomenology of perception.* New York: RKP.

Misgeld, D. (1985). Education and cultural invasion: Critical social theory, education as instruction, and the "pedagogy of the oppressed." In J. Forester (Ed.), *Critical theory and public life* (pp. 77–118). Cambridge, MA: MIT Press.

Monk, R. (1991). *Ludwig Wittgenstein: The duty of genius.* New York: Penguin.

Morgan, N., & Saxton, J. (1991). *Teaching questioning and learning.* New York: Routledge.

Morson, G. S. (1981a). Preface. In G. S. Morson (Ed.), *Bakhtin: Essays and dialogues on his work* (pp. vii-xiii). Chicago: University of Chicago Press.

Morson, G. S. (1981b). Who speaks for Bakhtin? In G. S. Morson (Ed.), *Bakhtin: Essays and dialogues on his work* (pp. 1–19). Chicago: University of Chicago Press.

Moulton, J. (1983). A paradigm of philosophy: The adversary method. In S. Harding & M. B. Hintikka (Eds.), *Discovering reality: Feminist perspectives on epistemology, metaphysics, methodology, and philosophy of science* (pp. 149–164). Dordrecht, Holland: Reidel.

Neiman, A. (1991). Irony and method: Reflections on dialogue. In D. P. Ericson (Ed.), *Philosophy of education 1990: Proceedings of the forty-sixth annual meeting of the Philosophy of Education Society* (pp. 132–135). Normal, IL: Philosophy of Education Society.

Noddings, N. (1984). *Caring: A feminine approach to ethics and moral education.* Berkeley: University of California Press.

Noddings, N. (1991). Stories in dialogue: Caring and interpersonal reasoning. In C. Witherell & N. Noddings (Eds.), *Stories lives tell: Narrative and dialogue in education* (pp. 157–170). New York: Teachers College Press.

Oakeshott, M. (1962). *Rationalism in politics.* New York: Basic Books.

O'Neill, J. (1985). Decolonization and the ideal speech community: Some issues in the theory and practice of communicative competence. In J. Forester (Ed.), *Critical theory and public life* (pp. 57–76). Cambridge, MA: MIT Press.

Palincsar, A. S. (1986). The role of dialogue in providing scaffolding instruction. *Educational Psychologist, 21,* 73–98.

Palincsar, A. S., & Brown, A. L. (1984). Reciprocal teaching of comprehension-fostering and comprehension-monitoring strategies. *Cognition and Instruction, 2,* 117–175.

Paul, R. (1987). Dialogical thinking: Critical thought essential to the acquisition of rational knowledge and passions. In J. Baron & R. Sternberg (Eds.), *Teaching thinking skills: Theory and practice* (pp. 127–148). New York: W. H. Freeman.

Pearson, P. D., & Gallagher, M. C. (1983). The instruction of reading comprehension. *Contemporary Educational Psychology, 8,* 317–344.

Pearson, P. D., & Johnson, D. D. (1978). *Teaching reading comprehension.* New York: Holt, Rinehart & Winston.

Petit, J-L. (1985). The making and breaking of dialogue. In M. Dascal (Ed.), *Dialogue: An interdisciplinary approach* (pp. 427–441). Philadelphia: Benjamin's.

Petrie, H. G. (1981). *The dilemma of enquiry and learning.* Chicago: University of Chicago Press.

Pitkin, H., & Shumer, S. (1982). On participation. *Democracy, 2,* 43–54.

Plato (1961a). *Gorgias.* In E. Hamilton & H. Cairns (Eds.), *Collected dialogues of Plato* (pp. 229–307). Princeton, NJ: Princeton University Press.

Plato (1961b). *Meno.* In E. Hamilton & H. Cairns (Eds.), *Collected dialogues of Plato* (pp. 353–384). Princeton, NJ: Princeton University Press.

Plato (1961c). *Republic.* In E. Hamilton & H. Cairns (Eds.), *Collected dialogues of Plato* (pp. 575–844). Princeton, NJ: Princeton University Press.

Plato (1961d). *Theaetetus.* In E. Hamilton & H. Cairns (Eds.), *Collected dialogues of Plato* (pp. 845–919). Princeton, NJ: Princeton University Press.

Potter, D., & Andersen, M. (1963). *Discussion: A guide to effective practice.* Belmont, CA: Wadsworth Publishing Co.

Quantz, R. A., & O'Connor, T. W. (1988). Writing critical ethnography: Dialogue, multivoicedness and carnival in cultural texts. *Educational Theory, 38,* 95–109.

Rice, S., & Burbules, N. C. (1993). Communicative virtues and educational relations. In H. Alexander (Ed.), *Philosophy of education 1992: Proceedings of the forty-eighth annual meeting of the Philosophy of Education Society* (in press). Normal, IL: Philosophy of Education Society.

Rorty, R. (1979). *Philosophy and the mirror of nature.* Princeton, NJ: Princeton University Press).

Rorty, R. (1987). Science as solidarity. In J. S. Nelson, A. Megill, & D. N. McCloskey (Eds.), *The rhetoric of the human sciences* (pp. 38–52). Madison: University of Wisconsin Press.

Rorty, R. (1989). *Contingency, irony, and solidarity.* New York: Cambridge University Press.

Rosenshine, B., & Meister, C. (1991, April). *Reciprocal teaching: A review of nineteen experimental studies.* Paper presented at the annual meeting of the American Educational Research Association, Chicago.

Sanders, N. M. (1966). *Classroom questions: What kinds?* New York: Harper & Row.

Schniedewind, N. (1987). Feminist values: Guidelines for teaching methodology in women's studies. In I. Shor (Ed.), *Freire for the classroom: A sourcebook for liberatory teaching* (pp. 170–179). Portsmouth, NH: Heinemann.

Searle, J. R. (1962). *Speech acts.* New York: Cambridge University Press.

Shor, I. (1980). *Critical teaching and everyday life.* Boston: South End Press.

Shor, I. (Ed.). (1987). *Freire for the classroom: A sourcebook for liberatory teaching.* Portsmouth, NH: Heinemann.

Shor, I., & Freire, P. (1987a). *A pedagogy for liberation: Dialogues on transforming education.* South Hadley, MA: Bergin & Garvey.

Shor, I., & Freire, P. (1987b). What is the "dialogical method" of teaching? *Journal of Education, 169,* 11–31.

Spiro, R. J. (1977). Remembering information from text: The "state of schemata" approach. In R. C. Anderson, R. J. Spiro, & W. E. Montague (Eds.), *Schooling and the acquisition of knowledge* (pp. 137–165). Hillsdale, NJ: Erlbaum.

Swearingen, C. J. (1990). Dialogue and dialectic: The logic of conversation and the interpretation of logic. In T. Maranhão (Ed.), *The interpretation of dialogue* (pp. 47–71). Chicago: University of Chicago Press.

Tannen, D. (1989). *Talking voices: Repetition, dialogue, and imagery in conversational discourse.* New York: Cambridge University Press.

Tannen, D. (1990). *You just don't understand: Women and men in conversation.* New York: William Morrow.

Thomas, L. (1989). *Living morally: A psychology of moral character.* Philadelphia: Temple University Press.

Thompson, J. (1981). *Critical hermeneutics.* New York: Cambridge University Press.

Toulmin, S. (1990). *Cosmopolis: The hidden agenda of modernity.* New York: Free Press.

Trillin, C. (1984, March 26). Harvard law. *The New Yorker,* pp. 53–83.

Urban, G. (1990). Ceremonial dialogues in South America. In T. Maranhão (Ed.), *The interpretation of dialogue* (pp. 99–119). Chicago: University of Chicago Press.

Vygotsky, L. S. (1962). *Thought and language.* Cambridge, MA: MIT Press.

Vygotsky, L. S. (1978). *Mind and society* (M. Cole, V. John-Steiner, S. Scribner, & E. Souberman, Eds.). Cambridge, MA: Harvard University Press.

Wade, S. E., & Armbruster, B. B. (1990). *Learning from text* (Technical report). Champaign, IL: Center for the Study of Reading.

Walton, D. N. (1990). What is reasoning? What is an argument? *Journal of Philosophy, 87,* 399–419.

Walzer, M. (1990). A critique of philosophical conversation. In M. Kelly (Ed.), *Hermeneutics and critical theory in ethics and politics* (pp. 182–196). Cambridge, MA: MIT Press.

Weiler, K. (1988). *Women teaching for change: Gender, class, and power.* South Hadley, MA: Bergin & Garvey.

Weiler, K. (1991). Freire and a feminist pedagogy of difference. *Harvard Educational Review, 61,* 449–474.

Weinsheimer, J. (1985). *Gadamer's hermeneutics: A reading of* Truth and method. New Haven, CT: Yale University Press.

Wellmer, A. (1990). Practical philosophy and the theory of society. In S. Benhabib & F. Dallmayr (Eds.), *The communicative ethics controversy* (pp. 293–329). Cambridge, MA: MIT Press.

Wertsch, J. V. (1980). The significance of dialogue in Vygotsky's account of social, egocentric, and inner speech. *Contemporary Educational Psychology, 3,* 150–162.

Wertsch, J. V. (1991). *Voices of the mind: A sociocultural approach to mediated action.* Cambridge, MA: Harvard University Press.

Whitbeck, C. (1989). A different view of reality: Feminist ontology. In A. Garry & M. Pearsall (Eds.), *Women, knowledge, and reality* (pp. 51–76). Boston: Unwin Hyman.

White, J. J. (1990). Involving different social and cultural groups in discussion. In W. W. Wilen (Ed.), *Teaching and learning through discussion: The theory, research, and practice of the discussion method* (pp. 147–174). Springfield, IL: Charles C. Thomas.

White, P. (1990, September). *Trust and toleration: Some issues for education in a democratic society.* Paper presented at the Morrell Conference on Toleration, Pluralism, and Multiculturalism, York, England.

Wilen, W. W. (1982). *What research says to the teacher: Questioning skills for teachers.* Washington, DC: National Educational Association.

Wilen, W. W. (1984). Implications of research on questioning for the teacher educator. *Journal of Research and Development in Education, 17,* 31–35.

Wilen, W. W. (1990). Forms and phases of discussion. In W. W. Wilen (Ed.), *Teaching and learning through discussion: The theory, research, and practice of the discussion method* (pp. 3–24). Springfield, IL: Charles C. Thomas.

Wittgenstein, L. (1958). *Philosophical investigations* (3rd ed.). New York: Macmillan.

Wittgenstein, L. (1961). *Tractatus logico-philosophicus.* New York: Routledge & Kegan Paul.

Young, I. M. (1990a). The ideal of community and the politics of difference. In L. J. Nicholson (Ed.), *Feminism/postmodernism* (pp. 300–325). New York: Routledge.

Young, I. M. (1990b). *Justice and the politics of difference.* Princeton, NJ: Princeton University Press.

Young, R. (1990). *A critical theory of education.* New York: Teachers College Press.

Young, R. (1992). *Critical theory and classroom talk.* Philadelphia: Multilingual Matters, Ltd.

Index

About the Author

Nicholas C. Burbules is Associate Professor in the Department of Educational Policy Studies at the University of Illinois at Urbana–Champaign. Before that, he was Assistant Professor at the University of Utah in Salt Lake City. He received his Ph.D. in philosophy of education from Stanford University in 1983, and has published articles on educational philosophy and educational policy in *Educational Evaluation and Policy Analysis, Educational Policy, Educational Theory, Harvard Educational Review, Teachers College Record,* and other journals. Currently, he is the editor of *Educational Theory.*